Trust, Ethnicity, and Identity

Economics, Cognition, and Society

This series provides a forum for theoretical and empirical investigations of social phenomena. It promotes works that focus on the interactions among cognitive processes, individual behavior, and social outcomes. It is especially open to interdisciplinary books that are genuinely integrative.

Editor: Timur Kuran

Editorial Board: Ronald Heiner
Sheila Ryan Johansson

Advisory Board: James M. Buchanan
Albert O. Hirschman
Mancur Olson

Titles in the Series

Ulrich Witt, Editor. *Explaining Process and Change: Approaches to Evolutionary Economics*

Young Back Choi. *Paradigms and Conventions: Uncertainty, Decision Making, and Entrepreneurship*

Geoffrey M. Hodgson. *Economics and Evolution: Bringing Life Back into Economics*

Richard W. England, Editor. *Evolutionary Concepts in Contemporary Economics*

W. Brian Arthur. *Increasing Returns and Path Dependence in the Economy*

Janet Tai Landa. *Trust, Ethnicity, and Identity: Beyond the New Institutional Economics of Ethnic Trading Networks, Contract Law, and Gift-Exchange*

Trust, Ethnicity, and Identity

Beyond the New Institutional
Economics of Ethnic Trading Networks,
Contract Law, and Gift-Exchange

Janet Tai Landa

Ann Arbor

THE UNIVERSITY OF MICHIGAN PRESS
1994

1997 1996 1995 1994   4 3 2 1

A CIP catalogue record for this book is available from the British Library.

Library of Congress Cataloging-in-Publication Data

Landa, Janet T.
    Trust, ethnicity, and identity: beyond the new institutional
economics of ethnic trading networks, contract law, and gift-
exchange / Janet Tai Landa.
        p.   cm — (Economics, cognition, and society)
    Includes bibliographical references and index.
    ISBN 0-472-10361-X (alk. paper)
    1. Economic anthropology. 2. Exchange. 3. Contracts.
4. Customary law. 5. Ethnicity—Economic aspects. 6. Ceremonial
exchange. I. Title. II. Series.
GN448.L35 1994
306.3—dc20   94-1727
                                                                CIP

With grateful appreciation to
Elinor Ostrom and Vincent Ostrom

Foreword

In developed Western economies (e.g., the United States, Canada), individuals, firms, and associations engage, one with another, in sometimes highly sophisticated and complex contractual exchanges without concerning themselves directly about the ultimate trustworthiness of those with whom they engage. That is to say, participants proceed "as if" their exchange partners may be trusted to abide by the explicit and implicit rules of the economic game. They are enabled to do this, however, only because there exists a well-functioning legal order that ensures that violators of the rules or norms will be located and punished.

Only since the 1960s have modern economists generally come to recognize and to acknowledge the importance of the legal structure in promoting the overall efficiency of the complex exchange network. The laws and institutions matter, as Adam Smith stated. And the research program in law and economics remains in its infancy.

Almost all the inquiry carried forward under this program involves a concentration on the legal-institutional structure of developed economies. Relatively little attention has been paid to the institutional analogues to the well-functioning and largely impersonal laws and institutions of developed economies that have emerged, or may emerge, to facilitate complex contractual exchanges in non-Western settings. Clearly, the potential gains from trade exist in every setting, and individual participants, faced with the absence of a well-functioning legal order, are motivated to seek out and to establish non-orthodox avenues for ensuring that these gains are, in fact, realized, even if, overall, the institutions may seem grossly inefficient to Western observers.

Janet Landa's research program, which has extended over more than a decade, has been aimed at filling in this gap in economists' understanding. In a series of important papers, included in this book, Landa has demonstrated through a plethora of historical examples how ties of kinship and ethnicity have offered substitutes for the "as if" trust in trading partners that a legal order facilitates. Because the institutions that she examines are unfamiliar to us, her descriptions are, in themselves, both informative and interesting. But because she approaches the material as an economist who seeks to explicate the emergence of complex exchange relationships, Landa's enterprise succeeds in offering an increment to our understanding of how market economies function, even those economies that allow observer-analysts to take for granted the existence of the institutions that participants in developing economies find so difficult to establish.

Lest we become too complacent, it is useful to be reminded that an erosion or breakdown in the functioning of our own legal order, or in the standards of ordinary behavior within the norms of that order, must generate a predictable return to nonlegal means of mutual adjustment. An advanced economy critically depends on institutions that make complex contractual exchanges relatively easy to accomplish. The fragility and vulnerability of these institutions are not sufficiently appreciated by legal scholars, judges, or economists. An analytical-evaluative detour through a few of those settings where the "as if" trust relationship does not exist is surely good for our social health.

James M. Buchanan

Preface

This book of essays is about the economic role of laws and institutions in achieving social order in a decentralized economy. Specifically, it is about the coordinating role of three major nonprice institutions—contract law, ethnic trading networks, and gift-exchange—in economizing on transaction costs, hence facilitating the process of exchange in decentralized economies in different historical contexts.

The idea for this volume first originated in 1985 with Professor James Buchanan, 1986 Nobel Laureate in Economics. Professor Buchanan suggested to me that my published papers on contract law, ethnic trading networks, and gift-exchange—which extended economics to novel or even exotic phenomena ignored by economists—could be collected together in a volume of essays that would be of interest to scholars in the various social science disciplines. The idea of a volume of essays was very appealing to me as I realized that there were several central themes that link various chapters in this book and that I had used the same Property Rights–Public Choice (PR-PC) theory, part of the New Institutional Economics (NIE), to provide a unifying theoretical framework to explicate these exchange institutions.

As the title indicates, this book deals with three major exchange institutions in achieving social order in different historical settings: contract law in developed capitalist economies, ethnic trading networks in developing economies, and gift-exchange in primitive, stateless societies. This book emphasizes the coordinating role of the state, as well as private orderings such as ethnic trading networks and gift-exchange, in protecting contracts. The title is accurate in two senses. First, it points to a second major unifying theme that ties the various chapters together: *identity* matters for traders operating in an environment characterized by contract uncertainty where the legal framework for the enforcement of contracts is not well developed, hence the importance of *trust* embedded in *particularistic* exchange relations such as *kinship* or *ethnicity* in protecting contracts. Second, it goes beyond the NIE paradigm by incorporating some crucial concepts from sociology, anthropology, and sociobiology such as social structure, social norms, culture, reciprocity, and kin-related altruism.

All the chapters collected in this book, except chapters 1 and 3, are reprints of previously published papers. As such, these chapters appear as they did in their original publication, except for (1) stylistic changes in footnotes, references, tables, and figures to make them consistent throughout the manuscript; (2) the deletion of some repetitious material in the various chapters since the papers were originally written with no thought of collecting them together in a volume of essays; and (3) updating of the relevant chapters by the inclusion of a number of useful references that seem worth adding at various places (these additions are indicated by double asterisks in the original texts or footnotes).

Although most of the previously published essays in this book were written in the late 1970s and early 1980s, I am convinced that none of the chapters have been superseded by work that I was unaware of at the time those papers were written or by a recent spate of related work by other scholars in the late 1980s and early 1990s on social institutions and related themes. The work done by other scholars on social institutions, cooperation, trust, and related themes includes sociologist Niklas Luhmann's (1979) important work on trust entitled *Trust and Power,* sociologist Michael Hechter's (1987) *Principles of Group Solidarity,* a volume of essays on *Trust* (Gambetta 1988), economist Robert Frank's (1988) *Passions within Reason,* political scientist Jon Elster's (1989) *The Cement of Society,* political scientist Elinor Ostrom's (1990) *Governing the Commons,* a volume of essays on *Social Institutions* (Hechter, Opp, and Wippler 1990), economic historian Douglass North's (1990) *Institutions, Institutional Change and Economic Performance,* James Coleman's (1990) *Foundations of Social Theory,* and Kenneth Koford and Jeffrey Miller's (1991) *Social Norms and Economic Institutions.* I have, however, taken account of these related works by other scholars in the introductory chapter.

The book is organized in six main sections. In Part 1, the introductory chapter is intended to serve as a metatheoretical framework for the discussion of the problem of social order from the perspective of different social science disciplines. I then show the analytical power of the PR-PC perspective in (1) providing a unifying theoretical framework to explain such diverse exchange institutions as contract law, ethnic trading networks, and gift-exchange treated separately in law, sociology, and anthropology and (2) showing how the apparently quite different parts of the book all fit together (i.e., how the theoretical perspective brings together such different phenomena as the Kula Ring system of gift-exchange and swarming in honeybees).

Part 2 contains three chapters that deal with the role of contract law in developed capitalist economies. Chapter 2 provides a theory of the legally binding contract as an institutional arrangement that achieves social order via its role in economizing on transaction costs of breach of contract. This chapter uses three central concepts—specialization and division of labor, externalities, and transaction costs—to explicate the function of the institution of contract law in capitalist economie§. The central idea is that in a complex exchange economy, characterized by division of labor among traders, breach of contract by one trader leads to a chain of breaches, hence generating public bad externalities. Under conditions of contract uncertainty, traders have an incentive to divert scarce resources from trade to the private protection of contracts; that in turn generates transaction costs. Faced with high transaction costs, traders have an incentive to enter into a social contract to create the state for the enforcement of contracts. The state, through sanctions imposed on those who breach contracts, helps traders to internalize externalities and hence economize on transaction costs. Chapter 3 expands on some of the ideas developed in the previous chapter. In particular, the chapter uses simple graph-theoretic concepts to explicate the differences between the concepts of functional interdependence and negative externalities. Graph-theoretic concepts are also used to show how contract law achieves the efficiency of a complex exchange economy by simultaneously (1) coordinating the expectations and actions of interdependent traders by assigning liability for damages to those who breach contracts and (2) decomposing or decoupling the complex networks into isolated dyads, via the doctrine of privity, so that interdependent actors linked together in complex networks can be insulated from the public bad externalities of a breach of contract. Chapter 4 revisits the much discussed landmark case of *Hadley v. Baxendale* in contract law by examining a much neglected aspect of the famous case—its role in facilitating trade and capital accumulation. The chapter also provides a public choice theory of the conceptual origins of the mitigation doctrine and specific performance remedy in contract law. The emphasis on the complexity of middleman trading networks also sheds light on the so-called middleman exception in the Uniform Commercial Code (UCC). The three chapters on contract law should be of interest to law-and-economics scholars in general and to legal scholars in particular.

Part 3 contains two closely related chapters that deal with the institution of ethnic trading groups or networks in developing economies where the legal framework for contract enforcement is not well developed. Chapter 5, the centerpiece of my work on exchange institutions in this volume of essays, provides a theory of the ethnically homogeneous middleman group (EHMG), with specific reference to the Chinese in Southeast Asia, as a clublike arrangement alternative to contract law in economizing on transaction costs of breach of contract. The central argument is that in less developed economies where the legal framework is not well developed, personalizing exchange relations along kinship or ethnic lines economizes on transaction costs of protecting contracts. The informal code of ethics embedded in the EHMG promotes mutual trust among exchange partners and hence functions as the equivalent to contract law. The economic function of kinship and ethnic status as efficient signaling and screening devices in establishing the identity of potential trading partners, hence economizing on information costs, is also discussed. Chapter 6, coauthored with Jack Carr, generalizes the theory of the EHMG to other homogeneous trading groups or networks, including Jewish merchants in medieval Europe and Jewish diamond merchants in modern-day New York. The chapter also explains seemingly bizarre social customs and religious and dietary rules as low-cost ways members of a group identify each other while imposing high entry costs on outsiders. The two chapters on ethnic trading networks should be of particular interest to sociologists, anthropologists, and economic historians, for example, Curtin (1984) working in the area of ethnic trading networks and trade diasporas in world history and North (1990) developing a theory of informal constraints as part of a theory of institutional change.

Part 4 consists of one chapter (chap. 7) on gift-exchange. The chapter discusses the factual details of the Kula Ring of the Trobriand Islands of Papua New Guinea, a classic gift-exchange system described in anthropological literature. The chapter also provides a theory of the Kula Ring as an institution that establishes social order among the different tribal groups linked together in Kula gift-exchange. The chapter contributes to the anthropological literature on the Kula Ring by solving two new puzzles of the Kula Ring. I explain (1) the ring structure of the Kula trade as an efficient, two-market system that economizes on the costs of a trader acquiring goods from all other markets in the ring and (2) the clockwise and counterclockwise perpetual circulating of the two different Kula gift valuables around the ring as an efficient institutional arrangement in which traders in stateless societies monitor and enforce the rules of the Kula game so as to enable Kula partners to engage in barter exchanges across tribal boundaries. Finally, the chapter discusses the role of the Kula gifts, magical rites, and mortuary rituals as symbols of individual and group identity, hence as efficient signaling and screening devices that help Kula partners identify each other at low cost and at the same time screen out strangers.

Throughout the various chapters (chaps. 2 through 7), the emphasis in this book is on the importance of contract enforcement and hence the importance of trust and the need to establish the identity of trading partners under conditions of contract uncertainty. One important insight that emerges from these chapters is the capacity of human beings to evolve complex and efficient systems for identifying each other. That, in turn, enables human beings to evolve exchange institutions such as contract law, ethnic trading groups, and gift-exchange to facilitate intragroup and intergroup transactions. It is in this context that part 5, dealing with biological societies, is an integral part of the book.

Part 5 contains one chapter (chap. 8), which deals with the organization of biological societies, specifically honeybee societies. The chapter explains why honeybees do not establish complex institutional arrangements such as a primary-satellite nest system because honeybees, unlike human beings, have a quite limited ability to process information or specifically to identify colony members across nests, since they rely primarily on smells in establishing identity. That may explain why honeybees are observed in nature to create new, independent colonies via swarming rather than to establish a primary-satellite nest system. Understanding the limited information-processing ability of bees for the purpose of identifying each other provides us with greater insight into why traders, under conditions of contract uncertainty, use simple indicators such as kinship or ethnicity to identify a potential trading partner and use it as a proxy for the potential partner's trustworthiness in honoring contracts, despite the fact that a more complex indicator combining kinship or ethnicity, ability, and past performance could be a better indicator.

Part 6 contains one chapter (chap. 9), which develops a unified theory of the emergence, evolution, and functions of exchange institutions—such as money, middleman, ethnic trading networks, and gift-exchange—as part of a self-creating social order. This theoretical chapter is an appropriate conclusion to the whole book because not only does the chapter bring together the various exchange institutions analyzed separately in previous chapters, it also brings the book's various ideas into a broad perspective of understanding the conceptual emergence, evolution, and functions of exchange institutions within a unifying PR-PC framework.

The PR-PC framework used throughout the chapters in this volume to analyze several major nonprice exchange institutions makes possible an unorthodox application of economics to various topics outside mainstream economics. The PR-PC approach turns out to be a nomothetic economic paradigm, one that is capable of providing a general, unifying theoretical framework for understanding a wide range of seemingly unrelated, disparate, and even exotic exchange institutions and phenomena for achieving social order analyzed by social scientists across the various disciplines. And because some of the chapters draw on various central concepts in sociology, anthropology, and sociobiology, this volume of essays goes beyond the NIE framework and is truly interdisciplinary in nature. As such, the book should be of interest not only to economists but also to social scientists in the sister disciplines of law, political science, sociology, anthropology, and sociobiology.

Permissions to reprint the papers have been granted by the holders of the copyright in each case and are acknowledged at the beginning of each chapter.

In producing this book, I am grateful to Professors Elinor Ostrom and Vincent Ostrom—codirectors of the Workshop on Political Theory and Policy Analysis at Indiana University in Bloomington—for providing me with a visiting fellowship to carry out the project from September to December

1987. Not only have I enjoyed the warm hospitality extended to me by Professors Elinor Ostrom and Vincent Ostrom while I was living in Bloomington, I have also learned much from their weekly Monday colloquiums and afternoon seminars on institutions. What I have learned at the workshop has greatly improved my understanding of the nature of institutions and the role they play in human society.

Finally, I wish to thank Professors Jack Hirshleifer and Gordon Tullock for their constructive comments for revising the manuscript; two anonymous referees; and Colin Day, whose excellent editorial suggestions helped to shepherd this book to its final stages.

REFERENCES

Coleman, James S. 1990. *Foundations of Social Theory.* Cambridge: The Belknap Press of Harvard University Press.

Curtin, Philip D. 1984. *Cross-Cultural Trade in World History.* Cambridge: Cambridge University Press.

Elster, Jon. 1989. *The Cement of Society: A Study of Social Order.* Cambridge: Cambridge University Press.

Frank, Robert H. 1988. *Passions within Reason: The Strategic Role of the Emotions.* New York: W. W. Norton & Co.

Gambetta, Diego, ed. 1988. *Trust: Making and Breaking Cooperative Relations.* New York: Basil Blackwell Ltd.

Hechter, Michael. 1987. *Principles of Group Solidarity.* Berkeley: University of California Press.

Hechter, Michael, Karl-Dieter Opp, and Reinhard Wippler, eds. 1990. *Social Institutions: Their Emergence, Maintenance and Effects.* New York: Aldine de Gruyter.

Koford, Kenneth J., and Jeffrey B. Miller, eds. 1991. *Social Norms and Economic Institutions.* Ann Arbor: The University of Michigan Press.

Luhmann, Niklas. 1979. *Trust and Power.* New York: John Wiley.

North, Douglass C. 1990. *Institutions, Institutional Change and Economic Performance.* Cambridge: Cambridge University Press.

Ostrom, Elinor. 1990. *Governing the Commons: The Evolution of Institutions for Collective Action.* Cambridge: Cambridge University Press.

Contents

Part 1
Introduction

CHAPTER 1

Exchange and the Problem of Order in the Social Sciences: An Introduction to This Book

There are negotiations to be undertaken, contracts have to be drawn up, inspections have to be made, arrangements have to be made to settle disputes, and so on. These costs have come to be known as transaction costs. Their existence implies that methods of co-ordination alternative to the market, which are themselves costly and in various ways imperfect, may nonetheless be preferable to relying on the pricing mechanism, the only method of co-ordination normally analyzed by economists. (Coase 1991, 5–6)

Future historians of economic thought will reckon the transaction cost paradigm as a revolution to rival neoclassical marginalism. (Cheung 1990, 27)

I agree that there is now much more intersection of interest [between economics and sociology], in part because the exchange–rational choice sociologists have now become more important. I foresee future development as blurring the distinctions between the social sciences generally, and not only between Economics and Sociology. (Buchanan, quoted in Swedberg 1990, 4 n. 1)

. . . it is ultimately impossible to carve off a distinct territory for economics bordering upon but separated from other social disciplines. Economics interpenetrates them all, and is reciprocally penetrated by them. *There is only one social science*. . . . (Hirshleifer 1985, 53)

Economists in general have paid little attention to the role of nonprice institutions in achieving social order and hence facilitating the process of exchange.

I wish to thank Colin Day, Jack Hirshleifer, Gordon Tullock, and two anonymous referees for helpful comments and suggestions for revising this chapter. Thanks are also due to Paula England, George Farkas, Kevan Lang, and Oliver Williamson for helpful comments on an earlier draft of this chapter. Some of the ideas in this chapter are based on Landa (1988).

3

This is because mainstream (neoclassical) theories of exchange implicitly assume a world with zero transaction costs. In such a world, there is no role for exchange institutions such as money, middleman, contract law, EHMGs, and gift-exchange. The study of these exchange institutions has been relegated to subfields within economics such as monetary theory or to sister disciplines of marketing theory, law, sociology, and anthropology. But precisely because these institutions facilitate the process of exchange via their role in coordinating the activities of interdependent traders, and hence promoting order, they should be amenable to economic analysis.

In the last three decades or so, however, economists are increasingly aware of the importance of institutions and have engaged in economic imperialism into the traditional domains of sister social science disciplines such as law and political science, thus creating subfields within economics such as property rights theory or law and economics, and public choice theory.[1] As Hirshleifer (1985, 53), speaking of the expanding domain of economics, puts it,

> *There is only one social science.* . . . While scientific work in anthropology and political science and the like will become increasingly indistinguishable from economics, economists will reciprocally have to become aware of how constraining has been their tunnel vision about the nature of man and social interactions. Ultimately, good economics will also have to be good anthropology and sociology and political science and psychology.

Nowhere is the expanding domain of economics more powerfully manifested than the emergence of several new subfields within economics, which together compose the NIE.[2] With the emergence of the NIE, the study of Adam Smith's laws and institutions by economists is shifted to the forefront of economic analysis.[3] "Institutions matter" because of their coordination function in promoting social order, hence economizing on transaction costs. Meanwhile, some sociologists such as James Coleman (1986, 1987, and 1990) and Michael Hechter (1987 and 1990) have adopted economists' rational choice approach to the study of social institutions. Thus, the 1990s will

---

1. For a discussion of the imperialism of economics science, see Boulding 1969; Brenner 1980; and Tullock 1972.

2. For a discussion of the NIE, see Cheung 1990; Coase 1984; Eggertsson 1990, chap. 1; Langlois 1986, chap. 1; North 1986; and Williamson 1985, chap. 1. The NIE literature is distinguished from the old institutional economics associated with the work of John R. Commons (1924) in one important aspect; the centrality of the notion of transaction costs in the NIE literature.

3. See Elsner's (1989) discussion of Adam Smith's analysis of institutions.

see an increasing blurring of the traditional boundaries that separate the various social science disciplines as social scientists interested in the role of institutions in achieving social order will inevitably converge on the same NIE theoretical frameworks and draw inspiration from each other's work.

The core of this book consists of three essays on three major nonprice exchange institutions ignored by neoclassical economists: (1) contract law (chap. 2), (2) ethnic trading groups and networks (chap. 5), and (3) Kula gift-exchange (chap. 7). All the other chapters are variations on themes dealt with in these three core chapters. Using a PR-PC approach, a subfield within NIE, I show how these three institutions—discussed separately in the disciplines of law, sociology, and anthropology—can be explicated using a common theoretical framework. In analyzing the institutions of ethnic trading networks, and gift-exchange, however, I go beyond the NIE by (1) assigning a central role to the profit-making middleman-entrepreneur in creating the institutional structure of a market economy to facilitate middleman-entrepreneurship and (2) incorporating crucial concepts from sociology and anthropology such as social norms, social structure, culture, identity, the calculus of relations, and reciprocity.

My theory of exchange incorporates the institution of middleman-entrepreneur because the existence of specialized traders (middlemen) implies functional specialization and division of labor among producers, middlemen, and final consumers, with middlemen linking producers and final consumers indirectly together in complex networks of exchange. A complex exchange economy, with networks of interdependent traders linked directly and indirectly, requires institutions or rules of the game, which, by constraining opportunistic traders from breach of contract, help to coordinate the activities of interdependent traders. By incorporating profit-making middlemen in a theory of exchange, important new insights are gained of the role played by these three exchange institutions in economizing on transaction costs.

It is not enough to understand why these three exchange institutions exist to achieve the efficient functioning of markets; their conceptual emergence or origins should also be examined. Thus, my theory of exchange also examines the conceptual emergence and evolution of exchange institutions such as ethnic trading networks, contract law, and gift-exchange, as well as money and middlemen, within a unifying PR-PC rational choice framework. By using the same economic framework to analyze these exchange institutions, neglected by neoclassical economics, I hope to show the unifying power of PR-PC theory to explain a wide diversity of exchange institutions and social phenomena hitherto treated separately in the social science disciplines.

This chapter provides a road map to a large and complex literature dealing with the problem of order in the social sciences and shows how this book of essays fits into this body of literature. In the next section, I discuss how scholars in the various social science disciplines have analyzed exchange and the problem of social order and relate these disciplines to such concepts as reputation, tit-for-tat strategy, and focal point in game theory; the social contract theory of the state or local community in political science; social norms, roles, social structure, organization, norm of reciprocity, and trust in sociology; culture, kinship, ethnic identity, the calculus of relations, and gift-exchange in anthropology; and finally, kin selection, reciprocal altruism, and in-group cooperation in sociobiology and bioeconomics. The frameworks used in that section are metatheoretical because they describe the various key concepts that are used by scholars in the various social sciences about the problem of order rather than presenting one specific theory of social order.[4] In the third section, I discuss important contributors to the study of institutions in the various subfields that make up the NIE literature. In the fourth section, I outline what I think are the main contributions of this book to the literature on the problem of order in terms of four main interrelated and recurrent themes that tie together the various chapters in this book: how exchange institutions like ethnic trading networks, contract law, and gift-exchange enable interdependent traders linked in complex marketing networks to cooperate and coordinate their activities to facilitate efficiency in exchange. In so doing, I hope to show that my theory of exchange, by incorporating crucial concepts from sociology and anthropology, goes beyond the NIE paradigm to establish links with the other social sciences, and hence contributes toward the unification of the social sciences.

Exchange and the Problem of Order in the Social Sciences

Neoclassical Economics

Neoclassical theories of exchange (Edgeworth, Jevons, Walras, Arrow-Debreu) treat exchange as *impersonal* exchange between anonymous trading partners. Jevon's (1871) "Law of Indifference" in particular emphasizes the impersonality of transactions: it is a matter of indifference to the buyer or the seller with whom they do business, provided that they obtain the same (homogeneous) commodity at the same price. The "Law of Indifference," as interpreted by Leijonhufvud (1976, 75, n.17) also has a sociological interpretation, namely,

. . . that transactors interact in markets on the basis of most favorable price and in so doing, ignore relationships of status, kinship, caste, and

---

4. For an excellent example of the use of a metatheoretical framework for analyzing institutional arrangements, see Kiser and Ostrom 1982.

so on. Nepotism is not a significant determinant of transaction-prices in the resulting theory, for example. So sociology is kept out. Clearly here, too, we have an "internalist" (as it were) theory that may work well for certain periods and societies but not for others.

In focusing attention exclusively on the role of price as a coordinating mechanism (Adam Smith's "invisible hand"), neoclassical economists paid no attention to the role of nonprice social institutions, the rules of the game, or the role of trust in coordinating the activities of interacting individuals and hence facilitating exchange. An important exception is the work of Kenneth Arrow (1971) who emphasizes the importance of trust in facilitating exchange.[5] The reason for this neglect, as James Buchanan (1962) pointed out, is because Edgeworth's (1881) neoclassical theory of exchange (as depicted in the Edgeworth box diagram, with its well-defined Pareto region) really presupposes the existence of rules that, by constraining traders from activities such as fraud, subjugation, and murder, produces Pareto optimality. In other words, the reason mainstream (neoclassical) theories of exchange have ignored the role of social institutions in achieving order in a market economy is because these theories have focused on cooperative behavior (voluntary exchange) to the exclusion of noncooperative behavior (coerced exchange), such as stealing, defrauding, breach of contract, and in certain primitive economies, cannibalism, that create interpersonal conflict. These theories have thus assumed away the problem of order—the problem of how to achieve cooperation and coordination of activities among interacting, interdependent individuals. In so doing, these theories assign no role to social institutions for facilitating the process of exchange via their role in economizing on transaction costs. The centrality of the linkage between social institutions and transaction costs is at the heart of the NIE. See the third section below.

Game Theory

Game theory provides a number of key concepts to analyze conditions leading to cooperative behavior. Take the classic Prisoner's Dilemma (PD) one-shot end game in noncooperative game theory. In the one-period PD game, each of the two players will choose the dominant strategy of not cooperating, such as stealing, robbing, or not contributing to a public good, and both will end up worse off than if both had cooperated. On the other hand, the finitely repeated PD game, played under conditions of imperfect information, allows for the possibility of cooperative behavior emerging as an equilibrium outcome via

---

5. Another exception is the work of McKean (1975). For more recent work on trust by economists, not necessarily of the neoclassical persuasion, see Ben-Porath 1980; Brenner 1983, chap. 2; Breton and Wintrobe 1982, chap. 4; Dasgupta 1988; and Frank 1987 and 1988.

"self-enforcing contracts" (Telser 1980). Reputation and tit-for-tat strategy play a role in such self-enforcing cooperative behavior. A will trust B, based on A's observation of B's past reputation for trustworthiness in cooperating, and A will punish B by not cooperating if B damages his reputation by violating A's trust. B, if he knows that A is a tit-for-tat player, will have the incentive to maintain his reputation for trustworthiness because of the benefits of future transactions (Kreps et al. 1982).[6] David Kreps (1990) has identified two situations in which reputational effects will not work, however:

1. A cannot observe whether or not B is trustworthy, for example, whether B is living up to the terms of the contract.
2. If at the time of contracting, both parties face unforeseen contingencies that make explicit and complete contracting impossible, each of the parties may provide private remedies for dealing with unforeseen contingencies, for example, holding cash.

But each of the private remedies are themselves costly; holding cash means foregoing interest. How can the parties economize on such costs? Here, Kreps invokes Thomas Schelling's ([1960] 1980) concept of "focal point." The concept refers to some principle or rule by which individuals "naturally" select a mode of behavior for the coordination of expectations:

> Among the possible sets of rules that might govern a conflict, tradition points to the particular set that everyone can expect everyone else to be conscious of as a conspicuous candidate for adoption. . . . The force of many rules of etiquette and social restraint . . . seem [sic] to depend on their having become "solutions" to a coordination game: everyone expects everyone to expect everyone to expect observance, so that nonobservance carries the pain of conspicuousness. (Schelling [1960] 1980, 91)

Kreps (1990, 125) then makes an interesting analytical link between the concept of focal point and that of "corporate culture":

> Let us consider first the organization as a single decision-making entity or as a sequence of decision-making entities who, when they have decision-making authority, have that authority all to themselves. This entity's problem is to identify a rule that permits relatively efficient transactions to take place and on which a viable reputation can be based

---

6. This result has been called the *folk theorem* because it is attributed to no one specific game theorist but is supposed to be part of the commonsense result known to game theorists. See Kreps, Milgrom, Roberts, and Wilson 1982.

and then to communicate that rule to current and potential future trading partners.

That rule, when communicated to all those within the corporation, gives the organization its identity or reputation regarding how it will react to unforeseen circumstances. Corporate culture thus serves as a coordination device within the organization. When the principle is communicated well to those outside the corporation to potential trading partners, corporate culture can also be used effectively as a screening device to screen out all those who do not conform to the firm's culture (Kreps 1990, 125–26). Corporate culture, then, has an important economic role to play in an efficient organization.

We can further link up the concepts of focal point and corporate culture with the concept of rules of the game since they both serve coordinating functions. Game theorists, with the exception of Edna Ullman-Margalit (1977), have taken rules of the game and social norms as exogenously given. Thus they do not have a theory of the emergence of rules of the game or social norms that generate stable expectations about other people's behavior. In addition, game theorists in general have ignored the problem of the identity of the players. Implicit in game theoretic models of human cooperation is the assumption that players have the ability to recognize and remember who the other player was, so that the identity of the other player is not an issue. But the identity of a potential player cannot be taken for granted. As Robert Axelrod and William Hamilton (1981, 1382) point out,

> The discrimination of others may be among the most important of abilities because it allows one to handle interactions with many individuals without having to treat them all the same, thus making possible the rewarding of cooperation from one individual and the punishment of defection from another.

Amartya Sen (1985, 349) also points to the importance of identity in inducing cooperative behavior:

> If the sense of identity takes the form of partly disconnecting a person's choice of actions from the pursuit of self-goal, then a non-inferior outcome can well emerge even without formal contract and enforcement. One of the ways in which the sense of identity can operate is through making members of a community accept certain rules of conduct as part of obligatory behavior toward others in the community.

These community behavioral norms or rules of conduct, according to Sen, can be analyzed in terms of a sense of identity generated in a community, and the focus on behavioral norms is an alternative to recent attempts at resolving the

PD dilemma by relaxing the assumption of perfect knowledge in finitely repeated games. Elsewhere, Sen (1987, 19) points to Japanese industrial success as evidence of the importance of group loyalty.

> Indeed, we are beginning to see the development of a whole range of alternative theories about economic behaviour to achieve industrial success, based on comparative studies of different societies with different prevalent value systems (Ronald Dore's 1984 pointer to what he calls the "Confucian recipe for industrial success" being one interesting example of such alternative theories).[7]

Finally, Robert Frank (1987 and 1988, chap. 3), in his commitment model of cooperation in PD situations, has written prominently on the importance of the identity of other players and the role of trust in assuring cooperation.

Although game-theoretic models of human interaction have contributed much to the understanding of how human cooperation can be achieved, the structure of formal game theory at present cannot explain many of the laws and institutions in the real world.

Political Science

In contrast to neoclassical economics, the Hobbesian problem of order is central to political science. Thomas Hobbes ([1651] 1962), a seventeenth-century political philosopher, addressed the problem of order in his classic treatise, *Leviathan*. He argued that people, living in a state of nature, would constantly be at war with each other because each person has the "right to all things" (Hobbes [1651] 1962, 113) and to break covenants. The disorder that emerges from people living in a state of nature, where life is "solitary, poor, nasty, brutish and short" ([1651] 1962, 100), would lead them to enter into a social contract to create what Hobbes calls the "commonwealth" ([1651] 1962, 132), the modern nation-state, to resolve conflicts by providing for defense against foreign aggression and prescribing and enforcing laws for the protection of property rights and the enforcement of covenants. This view that the state emerges from a constitutional social contract is in the classic Hobbesian contractarian tradition. The view that the state is the sole source of social order is in the classic Hobbesian "legal centralism" tradition (Ellickson 1987, 81; Galanter 1981; Williamson 1985, 20).

In contrast to the Hobbesian legal centralism tradition, Robert Axelrod

---

7. See also Redding's (1990) book on the importance of Confucian values and ethics accounting for overseas Chinese success.

(1984) has demonstrated that cooperation between rational egoists can emerge even in the absence of government. Individuals will voluntarily cooperate with each other if they are involved in repeated interactions with each other in a game in which the end period is unknown and if they both employ tit-for-tat strategies. The tool that Axelrod uses to analyze the problem of cooperation is that of computer tournaments based on an iterated PD model from game theory (see also above).

Vincent Ostrom (1980 and 1982) and Elinor Ostrom (1986 and 1990) have also studied the problem of order and the relation of order to social institutions or rules, at the level of the local community rather than at the level of the nation-state. Rules, which are considered to be artifacts rather than taken as given, can be changed by the participants themselves through self-conscious choice to change the structure of a Pareto-inferior situation that the participants have found themselves to be in. Vincent Ostrom and Elinor Ostrom's emphasis on participants' contractarian choice of rules at the community level points to their emphasis on the federalist nature of the modern state. Using "multiple levels of analysis" involving a "configuration of rules," Elinor Ostrom (1990) in her important book, *Governing the Commons,* makes a major theoretical and empirical contribution to the understanding of how individuals confronting "tragedy of the commons" (Hardin 1968) situations will themselves engage in collective action to design institutional arrangements to achieve efficient outcomes.[8] She illustrates her theory by drawing on many examples of successful self-governing commons such as communal tenures in high mountain meadows and forests in Törbel, Switzerland; the *huerta* irrigation institutions in Valencia, Murcia, Orihuela, and Alicante; and the *zanjera* irrigation communities in the Philippines. Her emphasis on successful self-governance in common-pool resource (CPR) situations challenges the conventional wisdom that the tragedy of the commons can be solved only through the privatization of CPRs or through state regulation.[9]

In a paper commenting on the contractarian and New Institutionalism approach to the emergence of institutions, Robert Bates (1988) criticizes the approach for its inadequacy in addressing the issue of the supply of institutions. According to the contractarian approach, individuals enter into a social contract to create institutions to overcome the noncooperative outcomes associated with PD situations. But because the creation of an institution for achieving cooperative outcomes is itself creating a public good, the institution will not emerge because of the free-riding behavior of participants. Bates

---

8. The methodological consequence of considering the configuration character of rules is to point out to theorists the need to specify a set of rules, rather than a single rule when attempting to ask what consequences are produced by changes in a particular rule (Ostrom 1986, 21).

9. See, for example, the widely cited article by G. Hardin (1968).

turns to the work of game theorist such as Kreps et al. (1982) for an alternative theory of the origins of institutions. Kreps et al. (1982) have shown that cooperation based on trust can emerge among rational individuals if they engage in infinitely repeated PD games played under uncertainty. For Bates, the answer to the problem of the supply of institutions is to be found in the role of trust and the power of community in which symbols such as

> badges and regalia enable like-minded players to locate others of their kind within the community. In a world in which there are prisoner's dilemmas, cooperative communities will enable rational individuals to transcend collective dilemmas. . . . We thus have an alternative theory of the origins of institutions. Rather than being founded on notions of contracting, coercion, and sanctions, this notion is instead based on concepts such as community, symbolism, and trust. Driven by a concern with institutions, we re-enter the world of the behaviorists. But we do so not in protest against the notion of rational choice, but rather in an effort to understand how rationality on the part of individuals leads to coherence at the level of society. (1988, 398–99)

In a recent important book, *The Cement of Society: A Study of Social Order,* Jon Elster (1989) analyzes the problem of order by exploring the relation between individual and collective rationality and between self-interest and social norms. Of crucial importance in Elster's treatment of the problem of order is his emphasis on spontaneous order mechanisms for coordination and cooperation, i.e., the role of tradition and social norms, "the vehicles of culture" (1989, 248) in providing for the "cement of society." An important condition for human cooperation is the credibility and trustworthiness of transacting parties; both traits may emerge from long-term self-interest or from the existence of social norms.

Sociology

The problem of order is also central to sociologists via their use of the ubiquitous concept of social norms. Social norms, according to James Coleman (1987, 135),

> . . . are expectations about action—one's own action, that of others, or both—which express what action is right or what action is wrong. A norm may prescribe certain actions such as the norm that an athlete on a team should play his best. Or it may proscribe certain actions, such as the norm among observant Jews and Muslims of not eating pork, or the norm once held among observant Catholics of not eating meat on Friday.

Since norms are accompanied by sanctions, such sanction-supported norms imply that individuals in their interactions with each other have expectations about what is appropriate behavior and what others expect that they should do. That leads to the sociologist's concept of "role" defined as "a set of norms and expectations applied to the incumbent of a particular position" (Banton 1965, 28). Individuals in their role relationships with each other are thus linked together in an organized social network or *social structure,* a term sociologists use to describe the pattern of recurrent and regularized interaction among two or more persons, hence implying the existence of norms for regulating behavior (Blau 1975). The existence of social structure, in turn, implies the existence of social organization. Humans, according to sociologists of the functionalist school such as Emile Durkheim ([1893] 1933 and 1912) and Talcott Parsons (1937), are embedded in social structure and social organizations—the family, the clan, the ethnic or tribal group, the religious group, and the nation—and therefore have internalized the norms and values of the groups in which they are embedded. For functionalists, social order exists because individuals are socialized via the internalization of the norms of the group. Wrong (1961) has criticized this functionalist view of humans in sociology as the "over-socialized conception of man."

Beginning in the mid-1980s, there emerged a small but increasing number of rational choice sociologists such as James Coleman (1986, 1987, and 1990) and Michael Hechter (1987 and 1990) who have rejected the Durkheimian-Parsonian functionalist tradition in sociology in favor of the economists' rational choice approach to the analysis of social institutions. According to rational choice sociologists, functionalist theories of social order are flawed because they assume the existence of institutions and have provided no theories of how norms emerge from the rational choice of interacting individuals. Coleman (1987), drawing on the law-and-economics concepts of externalities and transaction costs, has developed a theory of how social norms emerge from the interaction of rational individuals. Social norms arise when an actor's action imposes externalities on others but markets in rights cannot easily be established or transaction costs are high. Coleman further develops his theory of the emergence of social norms in his monumental book *Foundations of Social Theory* (1990, chaps. 10, 11, and 30), which also analyzes the role of trust in facilitating exchange (chaps. 5, 8, and 28). Although Coleman provided numerous examples of the role of trust in facilitating transactions in different scenarios, he did not provide examples of the role of trust in facilitating merchants' transactions in buying and reselling goods in long chains of trading networks.

In adopting the economists' rational choice approach to explain the emergence of social norms, rational choice sociologists are returning to the *exchange theory* tradition in sociology, which flourished especially in the 1960s in the writings of George Homans (1961), Peter Blau (1964), and Richard Emerson (1969). Exchange theory, as a subfield in sociology that emerged as a reaction to the functionalist framework, is characterized by three distinctive features.

First, exchange theorists adopt a rational choice approach to conceptualize social behavior and social interaction as *social exchange* (Cook, O'Brien, and Kollock 1990; Heath 1976). Social exchange differs in several significant ways from economic exchange. The most important distinction, according to Peter Blau (1964), is that social exchange entails *unspecified* obligations to reciprocate at a future date, and the nature of the return benefit cannot be bargained about but must be left to the discretion of the one who receives the benefit. "Thus, if a person gives a dinner party, he expects his guests to reciprocate at some future date. But he can hardly bargain with them about the kind of party to which they should invite him. . . ." (Blau 1964, 93). In addition, social exchange, unlike economic exchange, carries no exact price in terms of a medium of exchange.

Second, exchange theorists such as Peter Blau (1964), Marshall Sahlins (1969), Peter Ekeh (1974), Georg Simmel ([1907] 1978), and Niklas Luhmann (1979) are among the few sociologists who have paid serious attention to the role of trust in facilitating economic and social exchange.[10] Blau (1964) argues that social exchange, unlike economic exchange, generates trust between people involved in social exchange. That is because (1) there is no way to assure an appropriate return for a social exchange, thus requiring trusting others to reciprocate the benefit (Blau 1964, 94) and (2) an internalized "norm of reciprocity" (Gouldner 1960) exists that would "make him feel guilty if he fails to discharge his obligations . . ." (Blau 1964, 97). Sahlins (1969), in his important paper, "On the Sociology of Primitive Exchange," has developed a theory of primitive exchange in which trust between transactors decreases as kinship or social distance increases. He develops a concentric circle model for analyzing exchange and reciprocity in primitive societies. Ego is at the center of a series of ever-expanding concentric circles—the household, the local lineage, the village, the subtribe, the tribe, and other tribes—in which trust and reciprocity is greatest among close kin within the household and decreases as social distance increases, until at the ethnic or tribal boundary, mistrust or even chicanery emerges between transactors of different tribes. Transactions between members of different tribes may be "consummated by force and guile" (Sahlins 1969, 154). Ekeh (1974) argues that networks of generalized exchange in which "no party gives to the party from whom he receives" and where direct reciprocity is not possible create

---

10. As sociologist Luhmann (1988, 94) puts it, "Trust has never been a topic of mainstream sociology."

high levels of trust among those actors involved in exchange. Thus, for Ekeh, the *network structure* or configuration of exchange relationships, rather than dyadic relationships, has important consequences for the development of trust and group solidarity among members. In his work on money, Simmel ([1907] 1978) argues that individuals became disembedded from their social groups with the use of money since they enter into impersonal exchange relationships with each other in a money economy. But even in this impersonal money economy, individuals need a minimum of trust in the money-issuing authority for money to perform its role as a medium of exchange. Luhmann's (1979) important book of trust emphasized the role of trust in helping actors to realize their expectations and hence contribute to the "reduction of complexity" in the social system.[11]

Third, exchange theory is closely linked with *network theory* in sociology, which emphasizes the importance of exchange between connected pairs of partners as *exchange networks*. Karen Cook, Jodi O'Brien, and Peter Kollock (1990) see the linkage between exchange theory and network theory as a significant one in that exchange theory promises to provide a theoretical framework for making the "micro-macro" link in sociology, i.e., the transition from microphenomena such as rational individuals entering into exchange relations to the emergence of macrophenomena such as social structures and exchange networks.

In linking up with the work of modern rational choice sociologists such as Coleman's recent work on social norms and on trust in exchange networks, exchange theorists also provide a useful linkage with economists' work on institutions and organizations.[12] In a very interesting book entitled *Economics and Sociology,* Swedberg (1990) interviewed a number of sociologists and economists whose work crosses disciplinary boundaries on the current debate on the interaction of economics and sociology. He came to the conclusion that considerable useful work is being done connecting sociology and rational choice economic models. (For more on this subject, see the section below on "Property Rights–Public Choice Theory of Exchange Institutions.")

Anthropology

Unlike the economist's concept of the isolated rational "economic man," anthropologists have always emphasized the importance of kinship in influencing an individual's behavior hence creating social order. As Colson (1974, 25) puts it:

---

11. For his recent paper on trust, see Luhmann 1988.

12. See the special issue of the *American Journal of Sociology* on "Organizations and Institutions," edited by Winship and Rosen (1988).

. . . if you know a person's clan, you have a good chance of being able to find out an appropriate kinship term to signal the etiquette to be used between the two of you and to define the moral imperative that ought to govern your relationships.

How is order attained in a group wider than a kinship group? Clifford Geertz (1973) and Frederik Barth (1969) have implicitly discussed the problem of social order via the concepts of culture, ethnic group, and ethnic boundary. Clifford Geertz (1973, 49), for example, argues that people without culture are "unworkable monstrosities" with

few useful instincts, fewer recognizable sentiments, and no intellect: mental basket cases. . . . To supply the additional information necessary to be able to act, we were forced, in turn, to rely more heavily on cultural resources—the accumulated fund of significant symbols. Such symbols are thus not mere expressions, instrumentalities, or correlates of our biological, psychological, and social existence; they are prerequisites of it. Without men, no culture, certainly; but equally, and more significantly, without culture, no men. We are, in sum, incomplete or unfinished animals who complete ourselves through culture—and not through culture in general but through highly particular forms of it: Dobuan and Javanese, Hopi and Italian, upper-class and lower-class, academic and commercial.

The link between humans and specific forms of culture is further clarified by Barth (1969, 9) via the concept of "ethnic units":

Practically all anthropological reasoning rests on the premise that cultural variation is discontinuous: that there are aggregates of people who essentially share a common culture, and interconnected differences that distinguish each such discrete culture from all others. Since culture is nothing but a way to describe human behaviour, it would follow that there are discrete groups of people, i.e. ethnic units, to correspond to each culture.

So important is the link between the concepts of ethnic group and culture that Barth calls an ethnic group a "cultural-bearing unit." Barth divides the cultural contents of an ethnic group into two kinds: the overt signals or symbols of identity—"cultural diacritica" such as language, religion, rituals, dress style, or dietary preferences that members look for and exhibit to show identity—and the underlying values, codes of ethics, or standards of morality shared by group members. Of particular importance to Barth (1969, 15) is the concept of the ethnic *boundary*:

> the ethnic boundary canalizes social life—it entails a frequently quite complex organization of behaviour and social relations. The identification of another person as a fellow member of an ethnic group implies a sharing of criteria for evaluation and judgement. *It thus entails the assumption that the two are fundamentally "playing the same game."* . . . On the other hand, a dichotomization of others as strangers, as members of another ethnic group, implies a recognition of limitations on shared understandings, differences in criteria for judgement of value and performance, and a restriction of interaction to sectors of assumed common understanding and mutual interest. (emphasis added)

Pierre van den Berghe (1981, 25) goes even further to include the sociobiologists' emphasis of kin selection and reciprocal altruism in the nonhuman world by regarding ethnicity as "kin selection" and the ethnic group ("ethny") as representing the outer limits of that

> inbred group of near or distant kinsmen whom one knows as intimates and whom therefore one can trust. One intuitively expects fellow ethnics to behave at least somewhat benevolently toward one because of kin selection, reinforced by reciprocity. The shared genes predispose toward beneficence; the daily interdependence reinforces that kin selection. Fellow ethnics are, in the deepest sense, "our people."

Ethnocentricism, the identification of us, the insiders whom we trust and the discrimination against them, the outsiders, whom we distrust is an inherent feature of all ethnic groups.

But how is order maintained across ethnic or tribal boundaries, especially when the members are embedded in primitive, stateless societies? The answer is provided by Bronislaw Malinowski ([1922] 1961) in his seminal work on the Kula Ring in which he assigned a crucial role to the institution of Kula gift-exchange in creating order between members of different and often hostile tribes and thus facilitating barter trade across tribal boundaries. Of the role of gift giving in creating the preconditions for trade, Marcel Mauss ([1954] 1969, 80) says,

> In order to trade, man must first lay down his spear. When that is done he can succeed in exchanging goods and persons not only between clan and clan but between tribe and tribe and nation and nation, and above all,

between individuals. It is then that people can create, can satisfy their interests mutually and define them without recourse to arms.

And as George Dalton (1978, 160), speaking of the role of Kula gift-exchange in facilitating barter trade between tribes, puts it,

As long as ceremonial exchanges continued to take place assuring that peace prevailed, the linked groups could continue to carry on other mutually advantageous activities, such as trade in ordinary goods. . . .

Sociobiology and Bioeconomics

Kinship theory is not only central to anthropology, but it is also central to sociobiology. Sociobiology as a discipline emerged with the well-known but controversial work of biologist Edward Wilson (1975), *Sociobiology: The New Synthesis*. The central theoretical question of sociobiology, which seeks to reconcile the widespread phenomenon of cooperation among animals with the Darwinian theory of evolution, according to Wilson (1975, 3) is "how can altruism, which by definition reduces personal fitness, possibly evolve by natural selection." His book addresses this central problem by developing further work that had been done by others before him.

Sociobiologists have used the model of group selection in which kin selection is one variant to explain cooperation among animals. In William Hamilton's (1964) article on "kin-selection theory," he argues that the *degree of kin relatedness* determines the degree of altruism, hence cooperation, among animals. Altruism toward one's kin, in turn, increases the survival of the group; hence, altruistic acts toward one's genetic kin is one of the most important traits of animal behavior. Hamilton's kinship theory implies that animals have the ability to recognize categories of kinship, in effect, to measure degree of relatedness. In Hamilton's more recent work with political scientist Robert Axelrod (Axelrod and Hamilton 1981, see also Axelrod 1984, chap. 5), Hamilton appears to have abandoned the idea that kin-related altruism is the key to cooperation. In their paper, Hamilton and Axelrod place great emphasis on the importance of the *identity* of the two interacting parties in assuring cooperation (see also the section on "Game Theory" above). Robert Trivers (1971) argues that another way that individuals can achieve cooperation is through "reciprocal altruism," in which unrelated individuals exchange altruistic acts.[13]

Wilson (1978), in his other well-known but also controversial book, *On*

---

13. For an excellent review of sociobiological results relating to economics, see Trivers 1985.

Human Nature, as well the book he coauthored with Charles Lumsden, *Genes, Mind, and Culture* (Lumsden and Wilson 1981), has pushed sociobiological research far beyond his 1975 book or the articles by Hamilton (1964) and Trivers (1971). In their book, Lumsden and Wilson (1981) develop a theory of gene-culture coevolution, in which human behavior is determined by the interaction between genetic and cultural environment. Thus there is a convergence in sociobiological research with anthropological literature. The growing convergence has also resulted in a coauthored book entitled *Culture and the Evolutionary Process* by anthropologist Robert Boyd and Peter Richerson (1985). The authors develop their "dual inheritance" theory to show

> that evolution can result in humans whose culturally transmitted behavior is quite different from that predicted by sociobiology or posited by economists. This theory is a simple mechanistic amendment to Darwinian theory and requires no special properties for humans other than a capacity for a cultural system of inheritance. (Boyd and Richerson 1985, 17)

By incorporating culturally transmitted behavior, the authors argue that

> Cultural inheritance models will be useful to economists precisely because they allow a mechanistic explanation of human behaviors that are troubling or paradoxical under the assumption of self-interested rationality. (Boyd and Richerson 1985, 17)

The "dual inheritance" theory of Boyd and Richerson (1985) emphasizes that cooperative behaviors do not require enforcement through sanctions but are learned through cultural transmission of behaviors of individuals embedded in groups. Their theory, which is a theory of how cooperation could survive, however, cannot show how cooperative behavior emerges in newly formed groups.

The sociobiological literature has further been enriched by the work of economists. *Bioeconomics* is the term coined by biologist Michael Ghiselin (1987) for the economic approach to biology. Economists such as Gary Becker, Paul Rubin, Jack Hirshleifer, Gordon Tullock, and myself have all used the bioeconomics approach to explain cooperation in human as well as nonhuman societies. Becker (1976) has developed a bioeconomics model of altruism in which he shows that models of group selection are unnecessary, since altruistic behavior can be selected as a consequence of individual rational behavior. Rubin (1982) argues that evolutionary processes shape the development of human ethics and that hunter-gatherers had genetically wired norms that were adapted to their situation. Hirshleifer (1982), currently the most important practitioner of bioeconomics, uses concepts from economics, game theory, and sociobiology to explain human conflict and cooperation. Of especial importance is Hirshleifer's different use of the economists' concept of efficiency, defined in terms of a group's capacity to outcompete other groups in the struggle for life and resources:

> On all levels of life organisms have found it profitable to come together in patterns of cooperative association. But such cooperation is always secondary and contingent, in at least two respects: (1) in-group coopera-tion is only a means for more effectively and ruthlessly competing against outsiders, and (2) even within the group there will not be perfect parallelism of interests, hence cooperation must generally be supported by sanctions. (1982, 50)

I have developed a theory of why honeybees use the unanimous voting rule when they swarm in search of a new home (Landa 1986) and why honeybees do not organize satellite nests (chap. 8).

Tullock (1971) uses an economic model to depict the coal tit as a careful shopper. In his yet unpublished manuscript, Tullock (1992) uses economic tools to analyze the social organization of ants, termites, honeybees, naked mole rats, sponges, and slime molds. From such an analysis, Tullock develops a theory of cooperation in nonhuman societies using the central concept of environmental coordination, in which each of the members of society carries out its own pattern of behavior and adjusts and responds to environmental changes.

Sociobiology, as it currently stands, has established considerable useful links with economics and with anthropology.

New Institutional Economics: Social Institutions, Externalities, and Transaction Costs

Unlike members of nonhuman societies in which the coordination of work effort is achieved via "environmental coordination" (Tullock 1992), humans achieve the coordination of effort in their societies via price and nonprice social institutions. The study of social institutions is at the heart of the NIE, as noted earlier. But first, what is a *social institution*?

James Buchanan (1975, 6) sees institutions—Adam Smith's "laws and institutions"—simply as "rules." But what precisely are *rules*? According to political scientist Elinor Ostrom (1986, 5),

> Rules . . . refer to prescriptions commonly known and used by a set of participants to order repetitive, interdependent relationships. Prescrip-

tions refer to which actions (or states of the world) are *required, prohibited, or permitted.* Rules are the result of implicit or explicit efforts by a set of individuals to achieve order and predictability within defined situations by: (1) creating positions (e.g., member, convener, agent, etc); (2) stating how participants enter or leave positions; (3) stating which actions participants in these positions are required, permitted, or forbidden to take; and (4) stating which outcome participants are required, permitted, or forbidden to affect.

Take, for example, the institution of contract law. A party to a contract is permitted to breach a contract for a fungible good provided that party pays damages to the victim if the latter sues the former in court. Thus, parties to a contractual relationship are subject to a legal norm enforced by the courts. Note the following in the above definition of institutions as rules:

1. Rules may emerge via an invisible hand process—the spontaneous order approach to rules—or may emerge explicitly via a public choice process. But since some rules are external to the set of individuals (i.e., imposed on a group of individuals), we need to include not only rules that emerge endogenously, implicitly or explicitly, but also rules that are exogenous to the group.
2. What Elinor Ostrom calls "positions" is related to what sociologists call "roles" (see the section on "Sociology" above).
3. That rules have prescriptive force means that violations of the rules will lead to sanctions being imposed on the offending parties.

The NIE includes several subdisciplines within economics such as (1) Property Rights theory or Law and Economics, (2) Public Choice theory, (3) the Austrian theory of institutions and entrepreneurship; (4) the governance approach associated with the work of Oliver Williamson, and (5) the New Economic History associated with the work of Douglass North.

Property Rights Theory or Law and Economics

Coase's (1937) seminal paper, "The Nature of the Firm," introduced the new subdiscipline of transaction cost economics, thereby establishing the foundations of the NIE. The important contribution of this paper is the explicit introduction of the concept of transaction costs into economic analysis. Coase argues that the institution of the firm emerges in a specialized exchange economy to economize on certain kinds of transaction costs, especially contract negotiation costs. If the price mechanism is used, input owners would be required to enter into a number of contracts with other factors with whom they cooperate. By organizing a firm, however, the costs of contract negotiation are reduced because, in place of several separate contracts, one employer-employee contract is substituted. The essence of the employer-employee contract is that the employees agree to obey the direction or order of the entrepreneur within certain limits; and within these limits, the entrepreneur-coordinator directs and coordinates economic activities within the firm. To Coase, then, the distinguishing characteristic of the firm is the supersession of the price mechanism because of the transaction costs of using the latter.

Coase's (1960) other seminal paper, "The Problem of Social Cost," extends the analysis of the institution of the firm to the analysis of legal rules for the protection of property rights, hence laying the foundations of Property Rights theory, also known as the Chicago school of law and economics.[14] Coase argues that, in a world with zero transaction costs, parties involved in an externality relationship will have an incentive to negotiate or bargain among themselves and exchange rights, to internalize the externality. In such a world of zero transaction costs, there is no role for government (the Pigouvian solution) in internalizing negative externalities. A negative externality is defined as the social costs that one individual, through his or her actions (for example, polluting a river) impose on another individual without the latter's consent.[15] Coase put forth what has since been called the Coase Theorem: Regardless of the specific initial assignment of property rights, the final outcome of bargaining to internalize an externality will be efficient, provided that the initial legal assignment is well defined and the costs of bargaining or transacting are zero.[16] Coase argues that in a hypothetical world with zero transaction costs, there is no need for government to intervene to internalize the externality; the bargaining-contracting process—the market solution—will lead the parties to an efficient outcome, i.e., when all opportunities for mutually beneficial gains from trade have been exhausted. But the real contribution of Coase's (1960) paper is not the study of a world with zero transaction costs in which government has no role to play in internalizing externalities but the study of the real world with positive transaction costs in which the law, by assigning property rights, has a vital role to play in internalizing externalities or economizing on transaction costs.[17]

The notion of transaction costs is a key concept underlying Property

---

14. For a review and discussion of Property Rights theory or law and economics, see De Alessi 1983; Barreto, Husted, and Witte 1984; and Furubotn and Pejovich 1972.

15. Note that Coase (1960) never once uses the concept of externality; instead, throughout his article he uses the concept of "social cost."

16. The term "Coase Theorem" was coined by Stigler (1966, 111).

17. Coase (1988, 13–16) lamented that economists have placed too much emphasis on the Coase Theorem, whereas it is the world of positive transaction costs that is of crucial importance in understanding the role institutions play in the economy.

Rights theory. Transaction costs, unlike costs of production, are defined as those costs that are incurred in the process of exchange, such as costs of search for price or trading partners, costs of contract negotiation and enforcement, and costs of breach.[18] The role of institutions is to economize on transaction costs. Inspired by Coase's (1960) article, several economists in the late 1960s and early 1970s have made significant contributions to the development of modern Property Rights literature. Harold Demsetz (1967) develops a theory of the emergence of private property rights in internalizing externalities and hence reducing transaction costs associated with the use of common property.[19] Armen Alchian and Harold Demsetz (1972) develop a theory of the firm as an institution that economizes on the costs of monitoring employees' behavior, to reduce shirking. Steven Cheung (1969) interprets the choice of share contracts in terms of the concept of "risk aversion," which is used to emphasize the existence of enforcement costs. Finally, Richard Posner ([1973] 1992 and 1980), a prominent legal scholar, almost single-handedly spearheaded the law-and-economics movement through his prolific writings on a great diversity of law-and-economics topics published in various journals and also in a widely used textbook on the economic analysis of law. In an article on stateless societies, Posner (1980) emphasizes the importance of kinship ties, kinship groups, and gift-exchange as central institutional arrangements in these societies for providing members with insurance against uncertainties of food shortage, defense, and opportunities for barter trade across kinship and tribal boundaries.

Property Rights–Public Choice Theory (Virginia School of Law and Economics)

James Buchanan carried the Chicago law-and-economics approach to institutions one step further by incorporating public choice theory (the economics of politics).[20] He extended the analysis of institutions to the study of their origins or emergence via a public choice or contractarian process, hence creating the Virginia PR-PC approach to the analysis of institutions. For example,

---

18. For a discussion of the concept of transaction costs, see note 1 above, especially Williamson 1985, chap. 1.

19. The institution of private property emerged, according to Demsetz (1967), to solve what Garrett Hardin (1968) calls the "tragedy of the commons" problem. Demsetz's paper is interesting in that he combines a law-and-economics approach with an Austrian "spontaneous order" or "invisible hand" approach to the emergence of property rights. More than a decade before the appearance of Hardin's much cited paper and Demsetz's paper, Scott Gordon (1954) already had, in his classic paper, developed a theory of the fishery as a commons.

20. For an excellent discussion of a great variety of topics in public choice theory, see Mueller's (1989) excellent book. For a review article on public choice theory, see McLean 1989.

Buchanan (1975, chap. 4), recasts the Hobbesian social contract argument in terms of the PD paradigm to explain the conceptual emergence or origin of law as a result of public choice. In the PD paradigm, two individuals are confronted with two binary choices, e.g., "respect rights" by keeping agreements or "respect no rights" by not keeping contracts, with the payoffs structured so that both are worse off if they do not cooperate by choosing the strategy of "respect rights" by keeping agreements. To get out of this PD situation, both individuals have an incentive to enter into a constitutional social contract to establish a state for the purpose of creating and enforcing the rules of the game so that contracts will be kept. In the Virginia PR-PC school, the law or legal norms, a public good, thus emerge endogenously via a public choice or contractarian process. In this PR-PC paradigm, the rational economic person is also the same person who operates in the political arena choosing the rules for governing his or her and other's behavior, including the constitutional choice of decision-making rules for making collective choices (Buchanan and Tullock 1962). In their seminal book, *The Calculus of Consent,* Buchanan and Tullock (1962) argue that a rational individual, faced with zero decision-making costs, will choose the unanimous voting rule for making collective choices. But in a world with positive decision-making costs, a rational individual will choose a less-than-unanimous voting rule.[21]

Mancur Olson's (1965) seminal contribution to the theory of collective action is to point out that the size of the group is a major determinant of the likelihood of voluntary collective action in providing for a public good. Thus, if the size of the group is large, a public good is not likely to be forthcoming unless "selective incentives" are offered to provide incentives to members not to free ride on the benefits but to contribute to the provision of the public good.[22]

Austrian Theory of Institutions and Entrepreneurship

In contrast to the Virginia school's PR-PC approach to the emergence of social institutions, the Austrian approach associated with the work of Ludwig von Mises, Friedrich A. Hayek, Carl Menger, and others provides a "spontaneous

---

21. Since the 1980s, the aspect of public choice theory that concentrates on the choice of rules at the constitutional level has been called constitutional economics or constitutional political economy. See the book by Brennan and Buchanan (1985). For his seminal contributions to public choice theory and constitutional political economy, James Buchanan was awarded the Nobel Prize in Economics in 1986. For a post-Nobel analysis of the role laws as well as ethical constraints play in internalizing externalities, and hence coordinating actors' actions, see Buchanan 1991, chap. 15. Thus, in more recent years, Buchanan has also emphasized the importance of private orderings such as ethics.

22. Sandler (1992), in his book, has synthesized the voluminous research that has been done on the logic of collective action since Olson's (1965) seminal work.

order" (Hayek 1973) or invisible-hand explanation for the emergence of social institutions.[23] In this spontaneous order approach, institutions evolve as a result of market processes and other forms of spontaneous individual action. In other words, institutions emerge in an invisible-hand manner without any conscious will or design directed toward their creation by the individuals concerned. Menger's (1950) theory of the emergence of money is a good example of the Austrian spontaneous order approach to the analysis of institutions.[24] Of the contributors to the Austrian school, Kirzner (1973) especially emphasizes the central role of the middleman-entrepreneur, ignored in mainstream neoclassical theories of exchange, in achieving an equilibrium in which expectations of interacting individuals are fulfilled. The Kirznerian entrepreneur seeks out opportunities for profit making arising from the existence of price differentials for the same good in different markets: the entrepreneur buys goods at a lower price in one market and resells them at a higher price in another market. It is the ability of the entrepreneur to subjectively perceive and exploit opportunities for arbitrage, based on information not available to everyone else in the economy, that generates the entrepreneur's profits. However, because the Kirznerian entrepreneur is assumed to appropriate these profits "costlessly" in a frictionless market with zero transaction costs, Kirzner's theory of entrepreneurship is incomplete in that his theory provides no insight into the role of institutions such as property rights, contracts, and money in the efficient functioning of an exchange economy.[25]

Transaction Costs and the Governance Approach to Institutions

Oliver Williamson's (1975 and 1985) transaction costs or governance approach to the analysis of the institutions of capitalism explicitly combines the disciplines of law, economics, and organization. Unlike the Chicago school of law and economics, which deemphasizes the importance of opportunistic behavior such as breach of contract, Williamson emphasizes the importance of ex post facto monitoring of contracts (i.e., how contracts are to be protected from opportunism, "self-seeking with guile"). He argues that vertical integration and long-term relational contracts can be viewed as alternative governance structures to protect parties from opportunism. In addition, unlike the Chicago and Virginia schools of law-and-economics scholars who follow the Hobbesian legal centralism tradition, which emphasizes the importance of

---

23. See Hayek's (1973) "spontaneous order" approach to the evolution of institutions. See also Schotter's (1986) discussion of the Austrian approach to the evolution of institutions.

24. For a discussion of Menger's theory of money, see Moss 1978.

25. Lavoie (1991), while praising Kirzner's theory of entrepreneurship, also criticizes his theory for failure to take account of the cultural context in which the entrepreneur operates. See also Landa's (1991) criticism of Kirzner's theory.

the state in achieving social order via its role in protecting property rights and enforcing contracts, Williamson's approach emphasizes the importance of different forms of "private ordering," of which vertical integration and relational contracting are prime examples. Asset specificity in recurrent or relational contracts transforms the contractual relationship into one in which the identity of partners matters because specific assets become hard to deploy elsewhere. Furthermore, Williamson rejects the traditional monopoly explanation of vertical integration; instead, vertical integration is explained in terms of its capacity to economize on transaction costs.

The New Economic History

Douglass North (1981) has rewritten traditional economic history by incorporating a transaction cost approach to economic history. Hence the work associated with North has been called the New Economic History. North argues that traditional economic history has been preoccupied with the development of technology or the development of markets and has neglected the analysis of transaction cost considerations for the emergence of the structure of property rights that facilitate exchange and the development of markets. North (1986) lists four key elements in developing a transaction costs approach to economic history:

1. The cost of measuring the attributes of what is being exchanged and the costs of measuring the agent's performance
2. "The degree to which exchange is personalized exchange or is impersonal exchange. In the former the costs of contracting are embedded within repeat dealings and personal knowledge of the performers; and as a consequence, the costs of contracting and enforcement are lower than in impersonal exchange, when one must specify as precisely as possible the nature of the exchange and the enforcement procedures." (p. 560)
3. The cost of enforcing contracts by the parties themselves or by a third party—the state
4. "The degree to which social and ethical behavioral norms influence the costs of contracting. All contracting is embedded in a setting of social and ethical behavioral norms that modify the degree to which the participants maximize at certain margins. To the degree that standards of honesty, integrity, and good performance are values to the parties engaged in contracting, the costs of specification and enforcement are clearly lower." (p. 560)

Applying the transaction cost approach to economic history, North shows that the four kinds of transaction costs associated with exchange have changed dramatically in the modern Western world. In North's (1990) latest book, he develops a transaction cost analytical framework for analyzing the nature of institutions, the role of institutions in economic performance, and the differential performance of economies through time; the historical material is illustrative and is designed to show the usefulness of the transaction costs approach to economic history.

Recurrent Themes in this Volume and Their Contributions to the Literature on Order in the Social Sciences

Major Interrelated and Recurrent Themes

In this volume of essays on contract law, ethnic trading networks, and gift-exchange, my major contributions to the literature on social order can be stated in terms of the main interrelated and recurrent themes of the economics of middleman-entrepreneurship, trust, ethnicity, and identity that tie together the various essays:

1. The middleman-entrepreneur, who plays a central role in my theory of exchange, has no place in neoclassical exchange theory: he or she is like the postal carrier in G. K. Chesterton's Father Brown story, "The Invisible Man"—ignored.[26] Once the middleman-entrepreneur is included in a theory of exchange, however, a fundamentally different way of conceptualizing the exchange relations in a middleman economy—as complex exchange networks—is required. In these complex trading networks, formal or informal rules of the game, such as contract law or informal norms or codes of conduct embedded in ethnic trading networks, have crucial roles to play in establishing the stability of exchange relations. This stability is accomplished by the role of contract law and by informal social norms via simultaneously *coordinating* the profit expectations of traders linked in complex networks while at the same time *decomposing* or *decoupling* the connected pairs of traders into isolated dyads thus insulating the dyads from the chain effects (externalities) of a breach (see pages 36–37 for the notions of coordinating and decomposing or decoupling).

---

26. This comparison is inspired by Coase's (1990, 1) comment that mainstream economics has ignored obvious features of the economic system (e.g., the institutional structure of production) and that this neglect is akin to the neglect of the postal carrier in G. K. Chesterton's Father Brown tale of "The Invisible Man." While neoclassical economics has no place for the role of the middleman or merchant in the market economy, Hicks (1969) assigns a central role to the specialized trader in the emergence of the market.

The middleman-entrepreneur as a rational profit-maximizer economizes on transaction costs of exchange, including the costs of breach, and in so doing creates the very institutional structure of the exchange economy within which he or she operates: contract law, ethnic trading networks, or gift-exchange, as well as money and credit. These exchange institutions created by middlemen-entrepreneurship, in turn, facilitate the process of capital accumulation by merchants. The middleman is not just an "economic man," the passive maximizing robot of traditional microtheory. In my theory of middleman-entrepreneurship, he or she goes "beyond economic man" (Leibenstein 1976); he or she is also the "contractarian man," the "political man," the "mediator," as well as the Schumpeterian entrepreneur.[27] In neglecting the middleman, the innovator of many of the exchange institutions of a market economy, the question of the missing chapter in economic theory, "Exchange Theory: The Missing Chapter," (Hirshleifer 1973) should be rephrased to "A Theory of Middleman-Entrepreneurship and Exchange Institutions: The Missing Chapter in Exchange Theory."

2. From a comparative institutional perspective, contract law, ethnic trading networks, and gift-exchange can be viewed as alternative governance structures or economic organizations in different historical contexts that function to constrain traders from acting opportunistically by breach of contract. The existence of exchange externalities arising from breach and the transaction costs involved in internalizing the externalities are crucial for the emergence of constraints—formal legal norms or informal social norms—against opportunism. By deterring traders from breach, these exchange institutions internalize externalities and in so doing economize on transaction costs of trading with partners within ethnic or religious groups and across group boundaries. In contrast to contract law, ethnic trading networks and gift-exchange are institutions of private ordering.

3. Under conditions of contract uncertainty, where the legal framework for the enforcement of contracts is not well developed, the identity of potential trading partners matters. Human societies, unlike biological societies such as honeybee colonies, have evolved complex and efficient systems for recognizing, identifying, and hence cooperating

---

27. James Buchanan (1975, 229) has argued that "economics comes closer to being a 'science of contract' than a 'science of choice' . . . [therefore] the maximizer must be replaced by the arbitrator, the outsider who tries to work out compromises among conflicting claims." My theory of middleman-entrepreneurship takes an "economics as a science of contract" approach but supplements the approach with a Schumpeterian entrepreneurial approach that sees the middleman as the innovator and creator of many of the exchange institutions of a market economy.

with each other. Kinship, ethnic, and religious status as well as other symbols of identity (such as the use of the *chai* as a symbol of Jewish identity) serve as low-cost signaling and screening devices that allow a trader to choose to trade with only those traders who are perceived to be trustworthy or reliable in honoring contracts. In addition to symbols of identity, many social rituals and customary practices of specific ethnic or tribal groups, such as Jewish dietary laws, Chinese ancestor worship, and the seemingly bizarre and irrational practice of the Kula gift-exchange, in which two different ceremonial gifts circulate, in opposite directions, perpetually around the Kula islands, can all be viewed as ways individuals in different societies establish individual and group identity for the purpose of coordinating the activities of interdependent individuals. The importance of the institutional arrangement of the EHMG or ethnic trading networks, as an alternative to contract law, is due to the existence of informal social norms or codes of behavior, embedded in particularistic exchange relations, which function as the equivalent to contract law in deterring traders from breach. Contract law and ethnic trading networks may be viewed as alternative economic organizations involving impersonal versus personalistic exchanges in different historical-institutional contexts. In developed capitalist economies, contract law, with its legal norms and sanctions against breach, facilitates the process of impersonal trade with strangers. In contrast, in developing economies characterized by contract uncertainty, the need to protect contracts from breach results in the emergence of informal social norms embedded in ethnic or personalistic trading networks. I consider my PR-PC theory of the EHMG or ethnic trading networks (chap. 5) to be the most important chapter in this volume of essays, and my most important contribution to the literature on the problem of social order in the social sciences. It is here that some of the central concepts from sociology and anthropology such as social norms or codes of ethics, social distance, social structure, and the calculus of relations are explicitly incorporated and integrated into the PR-PC rational choice framework.

The PR-PC approach to the analysis of the emergence and evolution of some of the exchange institutions analyzed in this book of essays may be by an invisible hand process, like in the case of the emergence of the EHMG, or via a public choice process, like in the case of the emergence of contract law. My theory of the emergence and function of contract law is consistent with the Hobbesian-Buchanan contractarian legalist centralism paradigm. My theory of the emergence of EHMG or ethnic trading networks is consistent with the Austrian invisible hand–spontaneous order approach to the emergence of institutions but explicitly incorporates transaction costs. It is also congruent with Williamson's "markets, hierarchies, and relational contracting" paradigm, applicable to Western capitalist settings, but extends beyond the Williamson paradigm by explicitly developing a theory of the process of *personalistic relational contracting* in non-Western settings characterized by contract uncertainty. Thus my theory of EHMG identifies a *non-Western* hybrid form of economic organization, which is an alternative to markets or contracts and hierarchies or vertical integration, for coping with opportunism.

My theory of the EHMG is also congruent with the recent work on sociologist James Coleman's rational choice approach to the emergence of norms and of the role of trust in exchange relations, although my theory explicitly deals with the complexity of middleman exchange networks ignored in Coleman's work. And because the ethnic trading network or EHMG is an emerging macro phenomenon, emerging from the rational choices of many interdependent individual traders operating under conditions of contract uncertainty, my theory of the EHMG also provides a theory of the micro-macro transition in sociology.

My theory of EHMG is also consistent with the work of political scientists Vincent Ostrom and Elinor Ostrom, because the EHMG functions at the community level where traders belonging to the same ethnic community create their own rules of the game for coping with the problems of contract uncertainty. Finally, because the historical, institutional, and cultural contexts in which transactions are embedded are different as we move from developed to less developed economies and to stateless societies, the efficient institutional forms that emerge to achieve social order are different. Thus my theory of the emergence, evolution, and function of exchange institutions in different historical contexts (chap. 9) is also congruent with the New Economic History associated with the work of North (1990) but is more abstract and microanalytical and places greater emphasis on private orderings.

In these various ways, my PR-PC theory of exchange institutions not only establishes links with the NIE literature but also extends beyond the NIE to establish links with the other social sciences, particularly with sociology, anthropology, and political science. In so doing, my theory of exchange institutions also makes a contribution to sociology, anthropology, and political science.

Property Rights–Public Choice Theory
of Exchange Institutions: Toward a Unification
of the Social Sciences

In a very interesting book entitled *Economics and Sociology: Redefining Their Boundaries: Conversations with Economists and Sociologists,* Swedberg

(1990) interviewed a number of economists and sociologists who are engaged in work across their own disciplinary borders, on the current debate between the interaction of economics and sociology. Swedberg individually interviewed the scholars for their comments and reactions. As a result, the book is like a minisymposium or round-table discussion in print, as it were, of the connections between economics and sociology and with the other social sciences. Of special interest and relevance to this book is how several of the interviewees commented and reacted to certain questions asked by Swedberg, questions that are central to the major themes in this book of essays.

Gary Becker (1957, 1964, 1976, and 1981), who held a joint appointment at the University of Chicago's sociology department and was the winner of the 1992 Nobel Prize in Economics for his work on the economics of discrimination, the family, education, and human capital, had this to say of the interaction of sociology and economics in his 1990 pre-Nobel interview with Swedberg:

> And then there is a small minority saying "Rational Choice has something to add. After all, we have exchange theory in sociology that is akin to rational choice." (Swedberg 1990, 37)

> . . . I agree with you that if rational choice doesn't pay off within a certain period of time, sociologists will lose interest in it. And I think rightly so. My own feeling is that this is not going to happen and that rational choice will pay off soon in certain additional fields. Some fields where it has already contributed and there it will pay off more in the future are: the family, crime (or deviant behavior), discrimination, industrial sociology, collective choice, and stratification. These are important parts of sociology, although collective choice has been studied more in economics and political science than in sociology. (Swedberg 1990, 42–43).

> . . . I do believe that the rational choice framework is going to be very important in sociology. I think it already *is* very important in sociology, but it is going to be even more so. Rational choice theory will also continue to be very important in political science, so that you are going to get much more of a unified social science than there is now. But obviously it will be far from a complete unification. (Swedberg 1990, 43)

Kenneth Arrow, Nobel laureate in economics, speaking to Swedberg of an area that economics has done badly in, namely, explaining the differential success of various ethnic groups:

I have not really tried to read everything Becker has done. But it seems to me that the attempt to explain all social interaction as economic interaction in a generalized sense of the word "economic," only represents one side of the coin. The other side is that a lot of the environment in which economic transactions take place is social and historical in nature. I don't know exactly how to fit these pieces together, but there are for example accounts of how special groups have played a distinct role in, say, trade. You have Chinese middlemen in Asia; Jews at certain times; Quakers during one period; and so on. And it is clearly their social characteristics that matter. In the case of the Quakers, as I understand it, the general idea was that a Quaker would keep his word, and he was therefore a very useful intermediary. He would deal with other Quakers and trade over long distances, where trust was important.

. . . For there to be trust, there has to be a social structure which is based on motives different from immediate opportunism. Or perhaps based on something for which your social status is a guarantee and which functions as a kind of commitment. How all this works is not explainable in Becker-type terms. (Swedberg 1990, 136–37)

. . . I think there are a number of elements involved, so there cannot just be one kind of connection between economics and sociology. One of the aspects is the fact that the transactions, which are modeled in ordinary economic theory, depend for their validation in several senses on a larger social system. By "social system" I mean a shared set of symbols, a shared set of social norms, and a set of institutions for the enforcement of the norms. (Swedberg 1990, 138–139)

. . . one of the units in the economy is the contract . . . there has to be some kind of commercial morality for the contracts to be executed . . . a theory which depends merely on reputation is not enough because there will always be circumstances when it pays to violate the rule. The workings of the whole system depend on the fact that these contracts indeed will be executed. (Swedberg, 1990, 139)

. . . my point is that you need all three elements of the social system for the economic system to work: the element of communication, such as codes, symbols, and understanding; the element of shared social norms . . . and thirdly, the existing institutions for enforcement . . . (Swedberg, 1990, 140)

. . . So, to conclude, I think that the key thing when it comes to the relationship between economics and sociology is the willingness to look at new kinds of data, like in savings. I think that once you do that, you are automatically going to be forced to consider social elements. Just ask different questions, and I think that you are going to be forced into considering and drawing upon sociology. And you will probably be contributing to sociology as well. (Swedberg 1990, 150)

In response to Swedberg's question whether Amartya Sen considered the social content of rationality important in his work, Sen replied,

. . . I think the content of rationality for human beings living in society—that is, for *all* human beings—has to have an inescapably social component to it. . . . our behavior pattern can be affected by certain motivations, which can be called "commitment" and which do not necessarily relate to the pursuit of self-interest, not even to sympathy for the well-being of those who are close to us. . . .

. . . So in order to pursue what the role of self is in rationality—we have to look into the issue of our identity much more closely. This perpective provides a much richer outlook on the demands of rational action, in my judgement. It also helps to resolve some of the paradoxes of rationality, which people have earlier discussed in the context of games, such as the "prisoners' dilemma," where each individual is worse off if what looks like individual rationality is pursued. The very recognition that this is the case of course influences what we think the appropriate action should be in this context. And this is not unrelated to our identity as members of certain groups.

. . . The social element in rationality is something I am indeed very much involved with just now, since I am trying to write this book on social rationality at this very moment. (Swedberg 1990, 260–61)

. . . I believe that the task of integration of economics and sociology would be much easier if we recognize clearly how large an area of congruence we have. (Swedberg 1990, 266)

The relation between rationality and identity is further brought up in Swedberg's interview with Albert Hirschman, whose important work *Exit, Voice, and Loyalty* (1970), combines concepts from economics and from political science. Swedberg (1990, 160) asked what Hirschman thinks of the notion that "it would be possible to reorganize all the social sciences—including sociology—on the basis of rationality. This way, it is said, one would get rid of some of the artificial boundaries between the various social sciences." Hirschman replied,

> . . . I think that you can get rid of some of these borders but only at the cost of tautology. In other words, you then have to include certain things into the motivation of the rational actor that are normally left outside. In "Against Parsimony," I mention the idea of collective identity, which I take from Alessandro Pizzorno. If you accept that it is rational for an actor to build up identity or to consolidate some collective identity, then participation in collective action and the refusal of any "free ride" become perfectly rational. In my article, I speak about this on purpose as an "investment." I do this just like people say "investment in human capital," which is considered very rational. . . . Now if you accept the concept of "investment in identity" in addition to "investment in human capital," it is clear that the former represents an earlier stage: in order to accumulate capital, you must first have an identity on which this capital so to speak can be heaped. . . . And you behave exactly in the opposite way to what a rational actor à la Olson would do. But you make it look like a rational action—and the whole thing with rational action becomes totally meaningless. (Swedberg 1990, 160)

James Coleman is the leading sociologist who is spearheading the rational choice movement in sociology and the "one person in the current debate on the relationship between economics and sociology who plays a similar role in sociology to that of Gary Becker in economics" (Swedberg 1990, 47). In responding to Swedberg's question whether it is correct to say that the structure of Coleman's theory of social action is influenced by his interest in law, Coleman replied,

> Yes, very much so. In fact, the closest correspondence to law and the closest link to law which I have developed in the chapters of the manuscript for my new book *Foundations of Social Theory* is a chapter you probably haven't seen. It is the new chapter 30 ("Externalities and Norms in a Linear System of Action"). What is interesting about this chapter is that it is a chapter on norms but it shows very closely the connection between norms and law, at least law conceived as the law and economics people do, as leading toward a socially efficient outcome and law. . . . I see that chapter as very central to my book because a lot of things culminate in that chapter. (Swedberg 1990, 54)

> . . . Economists cannot explain all kinds of things. And I think that they are beginning to recognize that now. So I think that economic sociology

is almost virgin territory, which is really a very important direction to pursue. (Swedberg 1990, 58)

Like Coleman, political scientist Jon Elster considers the study of social norms to be very important in understanding sociological problems. Unlike Coleman, however, Elster considers himself not a hard-core rational choice theorist but a methodological individualist, but not whole-heartedly subscribing to rational choice theory. The study of social norms is important to him from a methodological individualism viewpoint, because

> . . . game theoretic and strategic reasoning cannot generate stable expectations about other people's behavior. And where do we get these expecations from? We get them from social norms. (Swedberg 1990, 245)

The role of social norms in coordinating expectations is also crucial in the work of Thomas Schelling, as noted earlier. Speaking to Swedberg (1990, 190), Schelling says that he still thinks that his concept of "the coordination game" is a worthwhile and important concept and that "clues and signals" are needed for the coordination of expectations. Schelling, without saying it to Swedberg, is, of course, referring to his concept of "focal point" (also known as "Schelling point" in honor of the author who coined the concept) to refer to tradition, rules of etiquette, and restraints that provide the clues and signals for the coordination of expectations.

Unlike Coleman, who is skeptical about economists' ability to "explain all kinds of things," Williamson—whose transaction cost approach to the analysis of markets, hierarchies, and relational contracting has contributed not only to the development of the NIE literature but also to the opening up of the dialogue between economics and sociology—is very optimistic of the power of transaction costs economics to explain many new phenomena, including networks, studied by sociologists but currently neglected by economists. In responding to Swedberg's question whether there has been any critique of his work that he has found particularly useful, Williamson replied,

> There are also those who claim that transaction cost economics is too narrow a formulation and that it only works out of dyadic relations. I am sympathetic to that too. . . . Another interesting complaint along these lines is what sociologists refer to as network analysis. I was just at a conference this week in Italy, where some of these new forms of networks were under discussion that Charles Sabel and others are working on. It's my feeling that a rather huge fraction of what is going on in these network enterprises can be interpreted usefully in transaction costs

terms. . . . So I anticipate that networks can probably be incorporated—at least to some degree—into an extended version of transaction cost economics. But that's just a conjecture; I don't really know. (Swedberg 1990, 122)

. . . Political scientists and economic historians have also been applying transaction costs economics arguments to political institutions—both domestic and international. There are also issues having to do with marketing, networks, and contract law. So altogether we observe new theory, new applications, and new empirical work taking place. There is reason to be optimistic about the future of transaction costs economics. (Swedberg 1990, 127)

Sociologist Harrison White (1978), combining economics and sociology in his paper on production markets as social structures, is skeptical of the usefulness of rational choice sociology as well as neoclassical economics in coping with complexities of markets as social structures. He told Swedberg that economists after the 1930s ignored the "essential problem, which is to simultaneously *embed* and *decouple* the economic process" (Swedberg 1990, 87).

In this context, "decoupling" means that in order to achieve a certain production, you simply have to chop off some causal chains. You have to somehow simplify them, to dissolve their impetus through people's perceptions. . . . I am just using the terminology of "decoupling" to emphasize that it is not just a passive phenomenon—it is *an action*. People must deliberately decouple in order to achieve some of their ends. (Swedberg 1990, 88)

Similarly, White argues that people also use deliberate action with respect to embedding economic actions, the notion of embedding used in the sense of Karl Polanyi ([1944] 1957, chap. 4) to mean that an individual's economic transactions are embedded in social or kinship relations. As to the relationship between economics and sociology, White sees the necessity to include political science as well:

I think that what you are seeing today is that you can't just talk about sociology and economics any more: it is a *triad*. I think you have to have sociology, economics, and political science. . . . Perhaps it was unfortunate that the neoclassical revolution separated out the political element from political economy, and maybe it is time for them to come together again. But political economy can't be the solution. *You need the politi-*

cal, the economic, and the sociological: without sociology to provide a kind of theoretical infrastructure, you can't really make politics and economics work together. (Swedberg 1990, 93)

Economist George Akerlof (1970 and 1976) has developed an approach that he calls "psycho-socio-anthropo-economics" (Swedberg 1990, 64), in which he explicitly incorporated psychological, sociological, and anthropological elements into economic theory. The best examples of Akerlof's approach are to be found in two of his most frequently cited papers: "The Market for Lemons" (1970) and "The Economics of Caste and of the Rat Race and Other Woeful Tales" (1976). I am certain that Akerlof would not only heartily agree with White on the necessity of a "triad" in research strategy, but he would also explicitly include the discipline of anthropology.

Economist Mancur Olson, whose seminal work *The Logic of Collective Action* (1965), is even more ambitious in advocating research that will help unify the different social sciences. He tells Swedberg (1990, 175) that in his nearly completed book, *Beyond the Measuring Rod of Money: Toward A Unified Approach to Economics and the Other Social Sciences,* he uses the key notion of "indivisibilities" to provide a unifying conceptual framework to tackle a vast variety of topics in his book of essays.

In terms of my contribution to the Swedberg (1990) debate between the relationship of economics and the other social sciences, I have made a contribution to the economics of

1. *ethnic middlemen success,* with special reference to Chinese middlemen in Southeast Asia, which is at the same time a theory of discrimination and also a theory of stratification, not of the Becker-type analysis but along the lines of Arrow;
2. *trust,* in my theory of the EHMG, in which I showed the close links between my theory of norms embedded in the EHMG and my theory of contract law, just as there are very close links between the study of norms and law in Coleman's (1990) monumental book;
3. *identity*—a topic of central importance in the current research agenda of Amartya Sen, and to a lesser extent of Albert Hirschman—is central to the analysis of ethnic and Kula trading networks;
4. *ethnic trading networks* (chap. 5) and *contract law* (chap. 3), in which I have incorporated concepts of *embedding* and *decoupling* or *decomposing*, which sociologist Harrison White considers to be critical in analyzing the behavior of individuals linked in "causal chains"; and
5. an "extended version of transaction cost economics" (Williamson, quoted in Swedberg 1990, 122) in my theory of ethnic or Kula trading networks. But my extended version of the transaction cost approach to

ethnic and Kula networks, of necessity, has to *extend beyond* the NIE to establish links with sociology, anthropology, and political science as well.

In this volume of essays, I use the PR-PC rational choice framework, with its key concepts of externalities and transaction costs, to analyze three major exchange institutions—contract law, ethnic trading networks, and gift-exchange—treated separately in the disciplines of law, marketing theory, sociology, and anthropology. In so doing, I have made a contribution toward the unification of the social sciences in the area of exchange theory, even though it is obviously far from a complete unification.[28]

In conclusion, I hope that this volume of essays on exchange theory and exchange institutions will convince readers of this book "how large an area of congruence we have" (Sen, quoted in Swedberg 1990, 266) in exchange theory in terms of the task of integrating economics with the other social sciences. I believe that future developments in exchange theory by scholars in the different disciplines will further blur the boundaries separating the specializations. There is therefore reason to be optimistic about the future role of the PR-PC approach to exchange theory in unifying the social sciences. To quote once more from Hirshleifer (1985, 53):

> *There is only one social science.* . . . Ultimately, good economics [read "good *exchange theory*"] will also have to be good anthropology and sociology and political science and psychology.

REFERENCES

Akerlof, George A. 1970. "The Market for Lemons: Quality Uncertainty and the Market Mechanism." *Quarterly Journal of Economics* 84 (August): 488–500.
———. 1976. "The Economics of Caste and of the Rat Race and Other Woeful Tales." *Quarterly Journal of Economics* 90 (November): 599–617.
Alchian, Armen, and Harold Demsetz. 1972. "Production, Information Costs, and Economic Organization." *American Economic Review* 62 (December): 777–95.
Arrow, Kenneth J. 1971. "Political and Economic Evaluation of Social Effects and Externalities." In *Frontiers of Quantitative Economics,* edited by M. Intrilligator, 3–25. Amsterdam: North-Holland.
Axelrod, Robert. 1984. *The Evolution of Cooperation.* New York: Basic Books.
Axelrod, Robert, and William D. Hamilton. 1981. "The Evolution of Cooperation in Biological Systems." *Science* 211:1390–96.

---

28. I am presently in the process of working on a book on exchange theory and institutions with the aim of making further progress in the integration of economics with the other social sciences.

Banton, Michael. 1965. *Roles: An Introduction to the Study of Social Relations.* London: Tavistock Publications Ltd.

———, ed. 1969. *The Relevance of Models for Social Anthropology.* London: Tavistock Publications Ltd.

Barreto, Humberto, Thomas A. Husted, and Ann D. Witte. 1984. "The New Law and Economics: Present and Future." *American Bar Foundation Research Journal* No. 1 (Winter): 253–76.

Barth, Fredrik, ed. 1969. *Ethnic Groups and Boundaries.* Boston: Little, Brown & Co.

Bates, Robert H. 1988. "Contra Contractarianism: Some Reflections on the New Institutionalism. *Politics & Society* 16:387–401.

Becker, Gary S. 1957. *The Economics of Discrimination.* 2d ed. Chicago: The University of Chicago Press. 1971.

———. 1964. *Human Capital.* New York: Columbia University Press.

———. 1976. "Altruism, Egoism, and Genetic Fitness: Economics and Sociobiology." *Journal of Economic Literature* 14 (September): 817–26.

———. 1981. *A Treatise on the Family.* Cambridge: Harvard University Press.

Ben-Porath, Yoram. 1980. "The F-Connection: Families, Friends, and Firms in the Organization of Exchange." *Population and Development Review* 6 (1): 1–30.

Blau, Peter. 1964. *Exchange and Power in Social Life.* New York: Wiley.

———, ed. 1975. *Approaches to the Study of Social Structure.* New York: The Free Press.

Boulding, Kenneth, 1969. "Economics as a Moral Science." *American Economic Review* 59 (1): 1–12.

Boyd, Robert, and Peter J. Richerson. 1985. *Culture and the Evolutionary Process.* Chicago: The University of Chicago Press.

Brennan, Geoffrey, and James M. Buchanan. 1985. *The Reason of Rules: Constitutional Political Economy.* Cambridge: Cambridge University Press.

Brenner, Reuven. 1980. "Economics—An Imperialist Science?" *Journal of Legal Studies* 9:180–84.

———. 1983. *History—The Human Gamble.* Chicago: The University of Chicago Press.

Breton, Albert, and Ronald Wintrobe. 1982. *The Logic of Bureaucratic Conduct.* New York: Cambridge University Press.

Buchanan, James M. 1962. "The Relevance of Pareto Optimality." *Journal of Conflict Resolution* 6 (December): 341–54.

———. 1975. *The Limits of Liberty: Between Anarchy and Leviathan.* Chicago: The University of Chicago Press.

———. 1991. *The Economics and the Ethics of Constitutional Order.* Ann Arbor: The University of Michigan Press.

Buchanan, James M., and Gordon Tullock. [1962] 1965. *The Calculus of Consent.* Ann Arbor: The University of Michigan Press.

Cheung, Steven N. S. 1969. "Transaction Costs, Risk Aversion, and the Choice of Contractual Arrangements." *Journal of Law and Economics* 12 (April): 23–42.

———. 1990. "On the New Institutional Economics." Discussion Paper No. 118, Department of Economics, University of Hong Kong.

Coase, R. H. 1937. "The Nature of the Firm." *Economica* 4 (November): 386–405.

Reprinted in G. J. Stigler and K. E. Boulding, ed., *Readings in Price Theory.* Homewood, Ill.: Richard D. Irwin. 1952.

———. 1960. "The Problem of Social Cost." *Journal of Law and Economics* 3 (October): 1–44.

———. 1984. "The New Institutional Economics." *Journal of Institutional and Theoretical Economics* 140 (March): 229–31.

———. 1988. *The Firm, the Market, and the Law.* Chicago: The University of Chicago Press.

———. 1991. "The Institutional Structure of Production." The Alfred Nobel Memorial Prize Lecture in Economics Sciences.

Coleman, James S. 1986. "Social Structures and the Emergence of Norms among Rational Actors." In *Paradoxical effects of social behavior: Essays in honor of Anatol Rapoport,* edited by A. Diekmann and P. Mitter, 55–83. Vienna: Physica-Verlag.

———. 1987. *"Norms as Social Capital."* In *Economic Imperialism: The Economic Method Applied outside the Field of Economics,* edited by Gerhard Radnitzky and Peter Bernholz. New York: Paragon House Publishers.

———. 1990. *Foundations of Social Theory.* Cambridge: The Belknap Press of Harvard University Press.

Colson, Elizabeth. 1974. *Tradition and Contract: The Problem of Order.* Chicago: Adeline.

Commons, John R. 1924. *The Legal Foundations of Capitalism.* New York: Macmillan.

Cook, Karen, Jodi O'Brien, and Peter Kollock. 1990. "Exchange Theory: A Blueprint for Structure and Process." In *Frontiers of Social Theory: The New Syntheses,* edited by George Ritzer, 158–81. New York: Columbia University Press.

Dalton, George. 1978. "The Impact of Colonization on Aboriginal Economies in Stateless Societies." *Research in Economic Anthropology* 1:131–84.

Dasgupta, Partha. 1988. "Trust as a Commodity." In *Making and Breaking Cooperative Relations,* edited by D. Gambetta, 49–72. Oxford: Basil Blackwell Ltd.

De Alessi, Louis. 1983. "Property Rights, Transaction Costs and X-Efficiency." *American Economic Review* 73 (March): 64–81.

Demsetz, Harold. 1967. "Toward a Theory of Property Rights." *American Economic Review* 57 (May): 347–59.

Durkheim, Emile. [1893] 1933. *The Division of Labor in Society.* New York: Macmillan.

———. 1912. *Elementary Forms of Religious Life.* New York: Macmillan.

Edgeworth, F. Y. 1881. *Mathematical Psychics: An Essay on the Application of Mathematics to Moral Science.* London: C. Kegan Paul.

Eggertsson, Thráinn. 1990. *Economic Behavior and Institutions.* Cambridge: Cambridge University Press.

Ekeh, Peter P. 1974. *Social Exchange Theory: The Two Traditions.* London: Heinemann Educational Books Ltd.

Ellickson, Robert C. 1987. "A Critique of Economic and Sociological Theories of Social Control." *Journal of Legal Studies* 16 (January): 67–99.

Elsner, Wolfram. 1989. "Smith's Model of the Origins of Institutions." *Journal of Economic Issues* 23, no. 1 (March): 189–213.

Elster, Jon. 1989. *The Cement of Society: A Study of Social Order.* Cambridge: Cambridge University Press.

Emerson, Richard M. 1969. "Operant Psychology and Exchange Theory." In *Behavioral Sociology,* edited by R. Burgess and D. Bushell, 379–405. New York: Columbia University Press.

Fortes, Myer. 1969. *Kinship and the Social Order: The Legacy of Lewis Henry Morgan.* Chicago: Aldine.

Frank, Robert H. 1987. "If *Homo Economicus* Could Choose His Own Utility Function, Would He Want One with a Conscience?" *American Economic Review* 77 (September): 593–604.

———. 1988. *Passions within Reason: The Strategic Role of the Emotions.* New York: W. W. Norton & Co.

Furubotn, Eirik G., and Svetozar Pejovich. 1972. "Property Rights and Economic Theory: A Survey of Recent Literature." *Journal of Economic Literature* 10 (December): 1137–62.

Galanter, Marc. 1981. "Justice in Many Rooms: Courts, Private Ordering and Indigenous Law." *Journal of Legal Pluralism* 19:1–47.

Geertz, Clifford. 1973. *The Interpretation of Cultures.* New York: Basic Books.

Ghiselin, Michael T. 1987. "Principles and Prospects for General Economy." In *Economic Imperialism: The Economic Method Applied outside the Field of Economics,* edited by G. Radnitzky and Peter Bernholz, 21–31. New York: Paragon House Publishers.

Gordon, H. Scott. 1954. "The Economic Theory of a Common-Property Resource: The Fishery." *Journal of Political Economy* 62:124–42.

Gouldner, Alvin W. 1960. "The Norm of Reciprocity: A Preliminary Statement." *American Sociological Review* 25:161–178.

Hamilton, William D. 1964. "The evolution of social behavior," *Journal of Theoretical Biology* 7:1–52.

Hardin, Garrett. 1968. "The Tragedy of the Commons." *Science* 162:1243–8.

Hayek, Friedrich A. 1973. *Law, Legislation, and Liberty.* Vol. 1, *Rules and Order.* Chicago: The University of Chicago Press.

———. 1988. *The Fatal Conceit: The Errors of Socialism.* Chicago: The University of Chicago Press.

Heath, Anthony. 1976. *Rational Choice and Social Exchange: A Critique of Exchange Theory.* Cambridge: Cambridge University Press.

Hechter, Michael. 1987. *Principles of Group Solidarity.* Berkeley: University of California Press.

———. 1990. "The Emergence of Cooperative Social Institutions." In *Social Institutions: Their Emergence, Maintenance, and Effects,* edited by Michael Hechter, Karl-Dieter Opp, and Reinhard Wippler, 13–33. New York: Aldine de Gruyter.

Hicks, John. 1969. *A Theory of Economic History.* New York: Oxford University Press.

Hirschman, Albert O. 1970. *Exit, Voice, and Loyality: Responses to Decline in Firms, Organizations, and States.* Cambridge: Harvard University Press.

Hirshleifer, Jack. 1973. "Exchange Theory: The Missing Chapter." *Western Economic Journal* 11 (June): 129–146.

———. 1982. "Evolutionary Models in Economics and Law: Cooperation versus Conflict Strategies." *Research in Law and Economics* 4:1–60.

———. 1985. "The Expanding Domain of Economics." *American Economic Review* 75 (December): 53–68.

Hobbes, Thomas. [1651] 1962. *Leviathan, or the Matter, Forme, and Power of a Commonwealth Ecclesiasticall and Civil.* Paperback ed. Edited by Michael Oakeshott. New York: Collier Books, Macmillan Publishing Co.

Homans, George C. 1961. *Social Behavior: Its Elementary Forms.* New York: Harcourt Brace Jovanovich.

Jevons, William Stanley. [1871] 1957. *Theory of Political Economy.* New York: Kelly and Millman.

Kirzner, Israel M. 1973. *Competition and Entrepreneurship.* Chicago: The University of Chicago Press.

Kiser, Larry L., and Elinor Ostrom. 1982. "The Three Worlds of Action: A Metatheoretical Synthesis of Institutional Approaches." In *Strategies of Political Inquiry,* edited by E. Ostrom, 79–222. Beverly Hills, Calif.: Sage Publications.

Kreps, David M. 1990. "Corporate Culture and Economic Theory." In *Perspectives on Positive Political Economy,* edited by James E. Alt and Kenneth A. Shepsle, 90–143. Cambridge: Cambridge University Press.

Kreps, David M., Paul Milgrom, John Roberts, and Robert Wilson. 1982. "Rational Cooperation in the Finitely Repeated Prisoner's Dilemma." *Journal of Economic Theory* 27 (August): 245–52.

Landa, Janet T. 1986. "The Political Economy of Swarming in Honeybee Colonies: Voting-with-the-Wings, Decision-Making Costs, and the Unanimity Rule." *Public Choice* 51 (October): 25–38.

———. 1988. "A Theory of the Ethnically Homogeneous Middleman Group: Beyond Markets and Hierarchies." The Hoover Institution, Stanford University, Domestic Study Program, Working Papers in Economics E-88-1.

———. 1991. "Culture and Entrepreneurship in Less-Developed Countries: Ethnic Trading Networks as Economic Organizations." In *The Culture of Entrepreneurship,* edited by B. Berger, 53–72, 217–22. San Francisco: Institute for Contemporary Studies Press.

Langlois, Richard D., ed. 1986. *Economics as a Process. Essays in the New Institutional Economics.* Cambridge: Cambridge University Press.

Lavoie, Don. 1991. "The Discovery and Interpretation of Profit Opportunities: Culture and the Kirznerian Entrepreneur." In *The Culture of Entrepreneurship,* edited by B. Berger, 33–51, 213–17. San Francisco: Institute for Contemporary Studies Press.

Leibenstein, Harvey. 1976. *Beyond Economic Man.* Cambridge: Cambridge University Press.

Leijonhufvud, Axel. 1976. "Schools, 'Revolutions', and Research Programmes in

Economic Theory." In *Methods and Appraisal in Economics,* edited by Spiro J. Latsis. Cambridge: Cambridge University Press.

Luhmann, Niklas. 1979. *Trust and Power.* Chichester: Wiley.

———. 1988. "Familiarity, Confidence, Trust: Problems and Alternatives." In *Trust: Making and Breaking Cooperative Relations,* edited by D. Gambetta, 94–107. Oxford: Basil Blackwell Ltd.

Lumsden, Charles J., and Edward O. Wilson. 1981. *Genes, Mind, and Culture: The Coevolutionary Process.* Cambridge: Harvard University Press.

Malinowski, Bronislaw. [1922] 1961. *Argonauts of the Western Pacific.* New York: E. P. Dutton and Co.

Mauss, Marcel. [1954] 1969. *The Gift: Forms and Functions of Exchange in Archaic Societies.* London: Routledge and Kegan Paul.

McKean, Roland N. 1975. "Economics of Trust, Altruism, and Corporate Responsibility." In *Altruism, Morality, and Economic Theory,* edited by Edmund S. Phelps. New York: Russell Sage Foundation.

McLean, Iain. 1989. "Review Article: Some Recent Work in Public Choice." *British Journal of Political Science* 16:377–94.

Menger, Carl. 1950. *Principles of Economics,* trans. James Dingwell and Bert F. Hoselitz. Glencoe, Ill.: Free Press.

Morgan, Lewis Henry. 1970. "Systems of Consanguinity and Affinity of the Human Family." *Smithsonian Contributions to Knowledge* 17:4–602.

Moss, Laurence. 1978. "Carl Menger's Theory of Exchange." *Atlantic Economic Journal* 6 (3):17–30.

Mueller, Dennis C. 1989. *Public Choice II. A Revised Edition of Public Choice.* Cambridge: Cambridge University Press.

North, Douglass C. 1981. *Structure and Change in Economic History.* New York: Norton.

———. 1985. "Transaction Costs in History." *The Journal of European Economic History* 14, no. 3 (Winter): 557–76.

———. 1986. "The New Institutional Economics." *Journal of Institutional & Theoretical Economics* 142, no. 1 (March): 230–37.

———. 1990. *Institutions, Institutional Change and Economic Performance.* Cambridge: Cambridge University Press.

Olson, Mancur. 1965. *The Logic of Collective Action: Public Goods and the Theory of Groups.* Cambridge: Cambridge University Press.

———, ed. 1982. *Strategies of Political Inquiry.* Beverly Hills, Calif.: Sage Publications.

Ostrom, Elinor. 1986. "An Agenda for the Study of Institutions." *Public Choice* 48:3–25.

———. 1990. *Governing the Commons: The Evolution of Institutions for Collective Action.* Cambridge: Cambridge University Press.

Ostrom, Vincent. 1980. "Artisanship and Artifact." *Public Administration Review* 40 (4): 309–17.

———. 1982. "A Forgotten Tradition: The Constitutional Level of Analysis." In *Missing Elements in Political Inquiry: Logic and Levels of Analysis,* edited by

J. A. Gillespie and D. A. Zinnes, 237–52. Beverly Hills, Calif.: Sage Publications.

Parsons, Talcott. 1937. *The Structure of Social Action.* New York: McGraw-Hill.

Polyani, Karl. [1944] 1957. *The Great Transformation: The Political and Economic Origins of Our Time.* Boston: Beacon Press.

Posner, Richard A. [1973] 1992. *Economic Analysis of Law.* 4th ed. Boston: Little, Brown.

———. 1980. "A Theory of Primitive Society, with Special Reference to Law." *Journal of Law and Economics* 23 (April): 1–53.

Redding, S. Gordon. 1990. *The Spirit of Chinese Capitalism.* New York: Walter de Gruyter.

Rubin, Paul. 1982. "Evolved Ethics and Efficient Ethics." *Journal of Economic Behavior and Organization* 3:161–74.

Sahlins, Marshall D. [1965] 1969. "On the Sociology of Primitive Exchange." In *The Relevance of Models for Social Anthropology,* edited by Michael Banton, 139–236. London: Tavistock Publications.

Sandler, Todd. 1992. *Collective Action: Theory and Applications.* Ann Arbor: The University of Michigan Press.

Schelling, Thomas. [1960] 1980. *The Strategy of Conflict.* Cambridge: Harvard University Press.

Schotter, Andrew. 1986. "The Evolution of Rules." In *Economics as a Process: Essays in the New Institutional Economics,* edited by R. N. Langlois, 117–33. Cambridge: Cambridge University Press.

Sen, Amartya. 1985. "Goals, Commitment, and Identity." *Journal of Law, Economics and Organization* 2 (Fall): 341–55.

———. 1987. *On Ethics and Economics.* Oxford: Basil Blackwell.

Simmel, Georg. [1907] 1978. *The Philosophy of Money.* Translated by Tom Bottomore and David Frisby. London: Routledge & Kegan Paul.

Stigler, George. 1966. *Theory of Price.* London: Macmillan.

Swedberg, Richard. 1990. *Economics and Sociology: Redefining Their Boundaries: Conversations with Economists and Sociologists.* Princeton, N.J.: Princeton University Press.

Telser, Lester G. 1980. "A Theory of Self-Enforcing Agreements." *Journal of Business* 53:27–44.

Trivers, Robert L. 1971. "The Evolution of Reciprocal Altruism." *Quarterly Review of Biology* 46 (4): 35–57.

———. 1985. *Social Evolution.* Menlo Park, Calif.: The Benjamin/Cummings Publishing Co., Inc.

Tullock, Gordon. 1971. "The Coal Tit as a Careful Shopper." *American Naturalist* (January/February): 77–80.

———. 1972. "Economic Imperialism." In *Theory of Public Choice,* edited by James M. Buchanan and Robert D. Tollison, 317–29. Ann Arbor: The University of Michigan Press.

———. 1992. *Coordination without Command: A General Theory of Society.* Department of Economics, University of Arizona. Unpublished manuscript.

Ullman-Margalit, Edna. 1977. *The Emergence of Norms.* Oxford: Clarendon Press.

van den Berghe, Pierre. 1981. *The Ethnic Phenomenon.* New York: Elsevier Science Publishing Co., Inc.

Williamson, Oliver E. 1975. *Markets and Hierarchies: Analysis of Antitrust Implications.* New York: The Free Press.

————. 1985. *The Economic Institutions of Capitalism: Firms, Markets, Relational Contracting.* New York: The Free Press.

Wilson, Edward O. 1975. *Sociobiology: The New Synthesis.* Cambridge: Harvard University Press.

————. 1978. *On Human Nature.* Cambridge: Harvard University Press.

Winship, Christopher, and Sherwin Rosen, eds. 1988. "Introduction: Sociological and Economic Approaches to the Analysis of Social Structure." *American Journal of Sociology* 94 (Supplement), S1–S16.

White, Harrison C. 1978. "Markets as Social Structures." Paper presented at the American Sociological Association annual meeting, Boston.

Wrong, Dennis H. 1961. "The Oversocialized Conception of Man in Modern Sociology." *American Sociological Review* 26:183–93.

Part 2
Contract Law

CHAPTER 2

An Exchange Economy with Legally Binding Contract

It is implicitly assumed in the standard (Edgeworth and Walrasian) theories of exchange that there are no costs in the making of transactions. In such a world of zero transaction costs, institutions such as money, middlemen, and the legally binding contract would be redundant. Recent contributions by monetary theorists to the Walrasian theory of exchange lie precisely in their emphasis on the costliness of the barter exchange process and the positive role played by money and middlemen in reducing transaction costs.[1]

In view of these recent developments to reintroduce institutions into the standard theories of exchange, it is worthwhile to examine the role of the legally binding contract in the functioning of a complex exchange economy with money and middlemen. My theory of exchange incorporates the middleman as an important trader in an exchange economy for the following reasons. First, the middleman exists; historically, the middleman has played a central role in the rise of the market.[2] Second, the middleman is one type of entrepreneur who engages in ongoing transactions involving the exchange of promises to perform some action in the future. The binding contract assumes a role of importance in any economy where transactions involve a time dimension; historically, the law of contract evolved out of the Law Merchant. An emphasis on middleman entrepreneurship offers insights into the important role of the legally binding contract in facilitating entrepreneurship. Third, the appearance of middlemen transforms a simple barter economy into a complex one based on the division of labor between producers, consumers, and the specialized trader. Any complex economy, based on mutual interdependence

This chapter is reprinted from the *Journal of Economic Issues* 10, no. 4 (December 1976): 905–922 by special permission of the copyright holder, the Association for Evolutionary Economics. An early version entitled, "Exchange Externalities, Transaction Costs, Market Failure and the Legally-binding Contract," was presented at the Public Choice Society Annual Meeting in Chicago, April 3–5, 1975. I thank J. Backhaus, T. Borcherding, J. Buchanan, H. Demsetz, V. Goldberg, T. Ireland, M. Olson, W. Samuels, C. Southey, G. Tullock, J. Vanderkamp, and E. West for helpful comments and encouragement.

1. See, for example, Brunner and Meltzer 1971, Niehans 1969, and Ostroy 1973.
2. See Hicks 1969.

between many economic agents, is vulnerable to the deviant behavior of even one individual who withholds his or her cooperation. There must be rules of the game to ensure the attainment of mutually compatible plans. A study of an exchange economy with middlemen, the simplest form of complex economy, aids in understanding the central role of the legally binding contract in achieving social order, a prerequisite for attaining a viable and efficient exchange economy.

It is not enough to understand why the law of contract is necessary in a complex exchange economy. The conceptual emergence of the law of contract must also be examined. My theory of exchange extends the traders' choice to the public choice of the norms of contractual behavior; the legally binding contract itself becomes an endogenous variable subject to traders' rational choice. The theory relies heavily on the economics of property rights[3] and James Buchanan and Gordon Tullock's (1962) cost approach to collective action. In developing this theory of the legally binding contract, the following assumptions, which will greatly simplify the analysis, are made:

1. There is only one kind of trader deviant behavior in the exchange economy, namely, deliberate (bad faith) breach of contract. This assumption allows one to concentrate on the role of the law of contract in attaining social order.[4]
2. There is only one kind of contract uncertainty, supply contract uncertainty, involving a trader's bad faith breach of a promise to deliver goods. I therefore ignore quality contract uncertainty[5] and loan contract uncertainty.[6] I also ignore contract uncertainty arising from exogenous factors,[7] which allows me to concentrate on one specific type of contract uncertainty that is endogenous to the exchange economy.[8]

---

3. The term "economics of property rights" here refers to the writings of contemporary economists who contribute to the modern theory of externalities, transaction costs, and public goods. For a survey of this body of literature, see Furubotn and Pejovich 1972. I also include the old property rights literature, in particular, the writings of the American institutional economist, John R. Commons (1924).

4. The social order or core of the economy that is attained by the legally binding contract is narrowly interpreted here, since social order is attained by a host of laws and institutions, including the law of property. For a discussion of the role of the institution of private property in achieving social order, see Demsetz 1967. See also the contributions in Tullock 1972, which deal with the conceptual emergence of property rights and government out of anarchy. See also Buchanan 1975.

5. For a discussion of quality contract uncertainty, see Akerlof 1970.

6. See Smith 1971 for a discussion of loan contract uncertainty.

7. For a model of the exchange economy characterized by contract uncertainty that arises out of exogenous factors, see the Arrow-Debreu model as discussed by Debreu (1959, chap. 7).

8. Just as Clower (1967) distinguishes between a money and a barter economy based on the

Two fundamental differences between a barter economy and an exchange economy with middlemen will be examined in the next section. These differences are significant for a reformulation of traders' contractual behavior in a complex economy. The role of the legally binding contract in facilitating middleman entrepreneurship will then be discussed in the third section, followed in the fourth section by an examination of how a complex economy might be vulnerable to the deviant behavior of even one trader who, by breach of contract, can impose transaction costs directly and indirectly on many traders and, in the extreme case, may even cause markets to disappear. Finally, in the last section various solutions for coping with contract uncertainty will be presented, and the conditions under which the institution of the legally binding contract will be chosen by traders as the best solution will be specified.

Smithian Division of Labor, Middleman Exchange, and Profit-Seeking Traders

An exchange economy with middlemen, that is, a *middleman economy,* differs in two fundamental ways from a barter economy. These differences require significant modifications to the standard theories of barter exchange in terms of understanding traders' contractual behavior. The first lies in the pattern of trade.[9] An economy with four traders best describes this qualitative (structural) difference. In a barter economy, trade occurs as direct exchanges between producers and consumers. When there are two producers and two consumers, the entire trading settlement can be decomposed into two lone pairs of traders; a barter economy, in the strict sense, is not a market *system* at all. In a middleman economy, in contrast, the producer and the consumer must be indirectly connected via two middlemen (or at least by one where there are only three traders). The pattern of trade can be described either as a chain link arrangement, with middlemen forming the links, or as networks of exchanges between traders in a sequence of spatially separated markets, with middlemen connecting isolated markets. In either case, the final trading settlement cannot be decomposed into lone pairs of traders because the traders are connected directly and indirectly in networks of exchanges to form a system. The presence of middlemen thus transforms a simple barter economy into a complex economy. The complexity of the middleman economy is due to the

---

presence or absence of money, so I distinguish between a middleman and a barter economy based on the presence or absence of middlemen.

    9. I have benefited from developments in monetary theory that emphasize the fundamental difference in the pattern of trade between a barter and a money economy. See especially Clower 1967 and Brunner and Meltzer 1971.

functional interdependence between traders arising from the specialization and division of labor in society. The specialization and division of labor, in which the middleman is the professional trader (merchant), provide the basis for ongoing exchange relations or relational contracts.[10] In abstracting from the Smithian division of labor between producers, consumers, and merchants, the standard theories of exchange give no hint of the complexity of indirect exchange and the specific way independent traders are functionally interdependent in networks of ongoing transactions. In depicting exchanges as discrete transactions between isolated pairs of traders,[11] it is not surprising that the traditional theories give no explicit role to the legally binding contract. In networks of exchanges between many interdependent traders, price signals alone are not sufficient mechanisms for achieving cooperation and the coordination of the plans and expectations of the many traders; social institutions, the rules of the game, also are essential for the attainment of economic equilibrium.[12] A theory of the legally binding contract thus becomes possible.

A second fundamental difference between a barter and a middleman economy hinges on a trader's motive for participation and the extent of opportunities for mutually beneficial trade. In a barter economy, the producer (the seller) participates because of the profit motive; the buyer participates to consume. In a middleman economy, the middleman participates in trade solely because of the profit motive, for the middleman sees opportunities for profit making in the very structure of the economy. The sequence of markets presents the trader with the opportunity to buy goods at a lower price in one market and resell the same goods, at a higher price, in another where price differentials emerge. Thus, the middleman's profit is the gross profit margin arising from arbitrage. Unlike the final consumer, the middleman is the professional profit-seeking trader. A new class of profit-seeking traders appears wherever the structural conditions for profit making are given. But the structural features of the exchange economy are only necessary rather than sufficient conditions for the middleman's profit. Middleman-entrepreneurship also depends on the institutions of capitalism, namely, private property and the law of contracts, as will be seen.

---

10. Macneil (1974) defines a *relational contract* as a long-term contract between seller and buyer involving ongoing contractual relations. The concept of relational contracts plays a key role in Goldberg's theory of contract. See Goldberg 1976b.

11. Macneil (1974) defines a *discrete transaction* as a once-for-all transaction between seller and buyer.

12. For the nature and meaning of equilibrium in economic theory, see Chipman 1965.

The Legally Binding Contract, Economic Equilibrium, and Income Yielding Assets

The nature of the middleman's profit cannot be fully understood unless one recognizes a fundamental difference in the nature of the trading process in a capitalist economy in contrast to the abstract barter economy discussed in standard theories of exchange. In the latter type, trade consists of actual exchange of goods simultaneously between seller and buyer. In the former, trade consists of the mutual transfers of promises to perform an action or of rights to ownership. This is because a capitalist economy is a predominantly private property economy; the sole power of the trader to participate in trade is derived from the ownership of property, and the only possible transaction is the exchange of promises or transfers of rights to ownership via a *contract*.[13] Every transaction, even the simplest, is a species of contract.

To show how the middleman's profit can arise in the process of trading in a capitalist economy, one must specify the middleman's assets prior to trading, the terms of the contract, the sequence of actions between traders, and the institutions of capitalism that facilitate the middleman's profit-making activities.

One of the assets a trader must possess prior to trading is information about market opportunities, that is, about price differentials and price changes and the location of producers and consumers in spatially separated markets. If the middleman does not have such data prior to trading, he or she must invest in acquiring information. Because the middleman possesses valuable information about the location of producers and consumers, the middleman, who links producers and consumers indirectly, reduces their search costs, thus specializing in what Harvey Leibenstein (1968) calls the "input-completing" function or "N-entrepreneurship."

Assume that a middleman, B, has located a supplier, A, and has negotiated a contract with her. Imagine the following terms of the contract. A promises to transfer to B rights to the ownership of a specified quantity and quality of a specified commodity and promises to deliver the goods to B at a specified future date, $t + 1$. In consideration of A's promise, B promises to transfer to A rights to the ownership of a specified sum of money (say, $100)

---

13. The following requirements define a contract: (1) There must be two or more parties. (2) The parties must have the capacity to contract (be of age, sane, and so forth). (3) Consideration must pass between the parties, or the contract must be under seal. (4) There must be a *consensus ad idem*, a meeting of minds. Thus, contracts involving mistake, duress, fraud, and so forth are unenforceable. (5) The terms of the contract must be certain. (6) The contract must be lawful, for courts will not enforce illegal contracts.

and promises to pay that sum to A at a specified future date, $t + 2$. Once the terms of the contract are mutually agreed on and the contract is made, a legally binding contract emerges;[14] such a contract involves the risk of legal penalties for monetary damages if it is breached. Thus, an economic transaction is also a legal one involving a legal relationship between traders. The importance of the latter manifests itself subsequent to the contract made between A and B.

B is now the owner of a claim to goods (Cg) contract against A. Expecting to receive the goods from A at a specified future date, $t + 1$, B now sells forward his Cg contract to C at a higher price. B promises to deliver goods to C at a specified future date, $t + 1$, in exchange for C's promise to pay a specified sum of money (say, \$110) to B at $t + 2$. As soon as B has made the contract with C, B becomes the profit-seeking trader. As such, B has a set of expectations—to receive goods from A at $t + 1$, deliver goods to C at $t + 1$, receive payment from C at $t + 2$, and pay A at $t + 2$—out of which arises B's expectations of future profits (\$10). If all three traders honor their contracts, all the traders' plans and expectations are fulfilled. The legally binding contract, which facilitates mutual cooperation and hence the achievement of economic equilibrium, thus turns out to be a public good. In an economy where traders honor contracts, middleman B does not even need to own money prior to trading to participate; he can depend on a credit transaction with A to help him bridge the gap between receipts from C and payments to A.

Middleman B, however, does depend on the institutions of private property and the law of contracts to facilitate him in making his profit. The essence of the institution of private property is the exclusive legal right of a person to the use of his or her private property, including the right to transfer it by sale to a third party for the purpose of making profits. This implies the exclusion of others who are not owners of the private property. Since B is the owner of a Cg contract against A, B has the exclusive market opportunity to resell his Cg contract to C. By entering into legally binding relations with A and C regarding the future delivery and payment of the same physical goods, B has created a new commodity out of this legal interrelationship: B's Cg contract has become a marketable commodity because B has sold it to C.[15] Assuming that C, in turn, sells his Cg contract against B to D, then middle-

---

14. Having defined what a contract is (in note 13 above), the use of the term *legally binding contract* is misleading, as it implies that there are contracts that are not legally binding. A contract that is not legally binding is not really a contract at all. I am using the term, however, as an antidote to the Edgeworth (1881) concept of contract whereby traders are free to recontract without facing the risk of paying damages.

15. The legal expression for the creation of a new commodity out of contractual rights is called a *chose in action*. See, for example, Guest (1969, 404).

man C has created another commodity. In a private property as opposed to an abstract barter economy, new commodities are created by traders in the very process of trading; the commodity set itself is an endogenous variable capable of expansion via middleman-entrepreneurship. By combining specialized knowledge, a private good input, with the legally binding contract, a public good input, the middleman produces a new commodity;[16] the middleman is an *entrepreneur*.

Since B's activities of buying and reselling his Cg contract are aimed specifically at profit making, B is not simply creating a new commodity; he is transmuting the commodity into what John R. Commons (1924) calls an "intangible asset" or potential income-yielding asset. The newly created asset can be appropriated by B only if all traders honor contracts, because the value of the potential income-yielding asset depends on B's expectations that contracts will be fulfilled. The lower the probability of contract fulfillment, the smaller the value of the asset. This value approaches zero as the probability of contract fulfillment approaches zero, like in the case of extreme contract uncertainty. A basic role of the state in protecting contracts is the creation of a strong incentive for traders to honor contracts (see the last section), hence its role in facilitating middleman-entrepreneurship. To enlarge our understanding of the state's facilitating role, we will next consider the trading process in a capitalist economy under conditions of contract uncertainty.

Contract Uncertainty, Supply-Breach Externalities, and Market Failure

A fundamental feature of traders' behavior in a capitalist economy, characterized by contract uncertainty (or Hobbesian anarchy),[17] is the incentive of traders to break contracts whenever it is profitable to do so. The possibilities of the nonexistence of equilibrium and the emergence of victims of breach of contract are inherent in the very nature of the buyer-seller interdependence under contract uncertainty. But why are these two possibilities ruled out in the neoclassical theories of exchange?

The Walrasian model depicts *simultaneous* barter exchanges between pairs of traders; since contract uncertainty is ruled out by assumption, the

---

16. The notion that the legally binding contract is a public good input to the middleman-entrepreneur is similar to Goldberg's emphasis on the "protection of the right to be served" as an input to the producer. See Goldberg 1976a.

17. Gunning (1972) has defined anarchy as "social interaction under uncertainty" and has presented a theory of the origin of government arising from the need for reducing uncertainty. His theory of contract is based on a two-person model of exchange.

economy is always in equilibrium. In the Walrasian model of the *tâtonnement* process, it is the auctioneer who, by calling bids and offers of the traders, clears the market. But the process also rules out contract uncertainty because disequilibrium transactions are simply not permitted.[18] In the Edgeworth (1881) recontracting model, a trader can break an unfavorable arrangement by recontracting with another trader, but this process assumes that the abandoned trader immediately strikes back with a more favorable offer to the other traders. The Edgeworth process is characterized by inherent instability of swiftly changing trading coalition structures, but there are no contract uncertainty and no costs of recontracting. In the contemporary game-theoretic versions of the Edgeworth model, the inherent instability disappears with the emergence of the competitive price in a competitive (that is, numerous traders) economy; the core (social stability) of an exchange economy is achieved by the invisible hand of perfect competition.[19] Again, contract uncertainty has been ignored in the modern versions of the Edgeworth recontracting model. As long as theories of exchange neglect contract uncertainty,[20] the possibilities of the nonexistence of equilibrium and the emergence of victims of breach of contract are necessarily ruled out.

The problem of contract uncertainty, however, cannot be neglected if one takes account of the dynamics of trading, the limited foresight of traders, and the absence of rules of contractual behavior. In any contract that requires performance in the future, objective circumstances may have changed so that a contract that initially was mutually advantageous may become unfavorable to one of the parties. Because traders are not omniscient, there is always the possibility that some previous contracts will turn out to be costly mistakes.[21] With no rules to constrain a trader's behavior, it is rational for a trader to minimize the cost of mistakes by breaking a contract.[22] Deliberate breach of contract is thus endogenous to a trading economy characterized by contract uncertainty because it is subject to the trader's maximizing calculus.

Assume that A at time $t + 1$ chooses to break her contract to deliver

---

18. For a recent discussion of why the Walrasian theory of exchange is incomplete, see Shubik 1975.

19. On the theory of the "core of an exchange economy," see, for example, Debreu and Scarf (1963) and Aumann (1964).

20. The Arrow-Debreu (1954) model of exchange under contract uncertainty rules out contract uncertainty that is endogenous to the economy. In their work, bad faith breach of contract is ruled out.

21. As Hahn (1970, 6) has said, "the path of the system at any time will be strewn with remnants of past mistakes."

22. Just as Becker (1968) regards criminal behavior as rational behavior subject to benefit-cost calculations, so we also can regard deliberate breach of contract as rational behavior subject to a trader's choice.

goods to B because, with a lapse in time, A has found an opportunity to make larger profits by selling her goods to X. In addition, assume that B has made no private provisions against A's breach of contract. One consequence of A's breach of contract is that the coordination of the plans and expectations between A and B has failed since B's expectations are disappointed. A's breach of contract is a cause of the nonexistence of equilibrium, and disequilibrium is not costless. A's breach of contract imposes costs on B because B, who is forced to break his promise to deliver goods to C, also loses his right to enforce payment from C. Because of A's breach, B has failed to complete his transaction with C; hence his expectations of future profits have failed to materialize. A has imposed social costs or *supply-breach externalities* on B without the latter's consent. Assuming that middleman C did not make provisions against B's breach of contract, C's profit expectations are also disappointed.

Supply-breach externalities, one type of negative externalities generated under conditions of contract uncertainty,[23] are a species of transaction costs, but they differ from the usual type[24] in that they are the *social opportunity costs of exclusion* and hence are the unnecessary transactions costs incurred by a trader. By expanding the meaning of transaction costs to include the economist's basic concepts of *opportunity costs* and *social costs* (negative externalities), one may explore more deeply the meaning and consequences of a trader's breach of contract in the context of a complex economy.

As long as there is a victim of breach of contract, Edgeworth's concept of recontracting should be expanded to include the idea of breach of contract, for this gives quite a different meaning to the concept of freedom to recontract in a situation of mutual interdependence. A's freedom to recontract, from B's vantage point, is deviant behavior involving a breach of contract: A has the coercive power to deprive B of his freedom to complete his transaction with C unless B incurs transaction costs to protect his contract against A's breach. A's freedom to appropriate B's profits, by recontracting, necessarily infringes on B's freedom to appropriate his profits; A's gain is made at the expense of B, so that B's freedom is "volitional" (Samuels 1971) and not voluntary. Breach of contract is an example of a zero-sum game wherein irreconcilable conflicts of interest exist between two rational traders arising out of incompatible claims to the same physical goods. The game of breach is an example of the failure of

---

23. Smith (1971) has identified an externality under conditions of loan contract uncertainty.

24. The concept of transaction costs is currently passing through a rapid and extensive theoretical development, spearheaded by monetary theory; as such, terminological conventions have not clearly emerged. However, as currently understood, *transaction costs* refer to the necessary or unavoidable out-of-pocket costs that a trader must voluntarily incur because of his or her own participation in trade. See Niehans 1969 for a definition of transaction costs.

the invisible hand to produce Pareto optimality: It is impossible for two traders in such a game, each simultaneously pursuing his or her own self-interest, to generate results benefiting both traders.

When the game of breach is shifted from a two-person to an n-person setting, the economic consequences are much more severe. First, the deviant trader may eventually find himself or herself the victim of breach since the game is symmetric.[25] Second, a complex middleman economy is vulnerable to the deviant behavior of even one trader, for that trader may produce a chain reaction by forcing a series of involuntary breaches of contract among interdependent traders.[26] Thus one deviant may impose externalities directly and indirectly on many others, so that the gains captured by the deviant trader may not cancel out sizable losses incurred by many victims of breach. Third, extreme contract uncertainty can destroy the middleman's profit motive (because the income-yielding asset becomes valueless) and drive middlemen out of wholesale and retail markets, leading to market failure.[27]

As opposed to the presence of middlemen in an exchange economy, their disappearance produces two kinds of inefficiencies:

1. All Pareto-relevant mutually beneficial opportunities for trading have not been exhausted.
2. Producers and consumers must incur information costs to locate each other prior to trading; the direct exchange economy is informationally inefficient.[28] In the context of an n-person game in a middleman economy, supply-breach externalities, even though they are pecuniary externalities, must be internalized to protect the middleman's profit motive, which, in turn, makes possible the existence of the middleman economy.

---

25. That the game of breach of contract is symmetric is a notion developed by Tullock (1971) in his theory of contract in the context of a two-person model.

26. Economists seldom recognize the vulnerability of complex economies to disruption and the threat of disruption from even one individual who withholds his or her cooperation. A notable exception is Buchanan (1976) in his interpretation of the Rawlsian Difference Principle.

27. I am using the term *market failure* in the specific sense defined by Arrow (1970, 17): "Market failure is the particular case where transaction costs are so high that the existence of the market is no longer worthwhile." Arrow has in mind two types of market failure: (1) the absence of many markets for risk-bearing and (2) the absence of many future markets. Arrow's definition, however, is general enough to accommodate the type of market failure I have just described, a type that is more akin to the market failure phenomenon discussed by Akerlof (1970), which occurs under conditions of quality contract uncertainty.

28. Monetary economists have explained why an indirect exchange economy with middlemen is informationally efficient (Ostroy 1973) in contrast to a direct exchange economy.

Traders' Individual and Public Choices for Coping with Contract Uncertainty

To become a viable merchant under conditions of contract uncertainty, middleman B must reduce the risk of A's breach of contract to ensure that B does not break his contract with C, even if B might suffer from A's breach. B must give C a promise to deliver goods that is more secure than the promise he has received from A; B may, for example, include a penalty clause in his contract with C should he fail to keep his promise to C. The middleman must acquire a reputation for reliability in his or her dealings; otherwise, buyers would not trade with the middleman. Reputation is an essential asset for trade. The reliability of the middleman in honoring his or her contract to the buyer reduces the vulnerability of the complex economy to a trader's deviant behavior and hence facilitates the flow of goods from producers to consumers. Under conditions of contract uncertainty, the merchant must combine specialized information with reputation, both private good inputs, to produce a new commodity. Thus the middleman-entrepreneur must also specialize in the risk-bearing function and consequently reaps Knightian profits.

Middleman B must choose one or more of several methods for the internalization of externalities via a reduction of risks of contract uncertainty.

1. B can search for information regarding A's reputation prior to entering into a contract with her. However, B must incur information costs.
2. B can personalize exchange relations by trading only with insiders B can trust (see chaps. 5, 6, and 7).[29] In an ethnically heterogeneous society, B must incur the opportunity costs of excluding outsiders from trade.
3. B can rely on the "discipline of continuous dealings" (Tullock 1972) implicit in the ongoing exchange relations between traders in a middleman economy. This method may be effective in relatively homogeneous trading communities where the dense face-to-face communication network functions to mobilize and disseminate information about the reputation of a trader, thus making it difficult for a deviant trader to obtain future business from the trading community (see chaps. 5, 6, and 7). But B cannot rely solely on this method if the

---

29. Chinese middlemen in Southeast Asia rely mainly on personalized trading relations as the best solution for coping with the problems of contract uncertainty in an environment where the legal framework is not fully developed. See Landa 1976.

trading population is large and ethnically heterogeneous and credit transactions are important.[30]

4. B can extend credit and threaten the withdrawal of credit. However, B must take on the money-lending function and hence face the risk of loan default.

5. B can hold commodity inventories as buffers; but B must incur storage costs.

6. B can hold cash balances. This solution helps to mitigate B's damages by allowing him to adjust quickly to A's breach by buying goods from another supplier, but B must incur search costs in finding another supplier.

7. B can pool and spread risks by buying supplies from many suppliers. Yet in so doing, B must incur larger contract negotiation costs.

8. B can purchase an insurance policy against breach of contract. While this risk is insurable or bondable, this is a costly and cumbersome way of protecting contracts.

9. B can bribe A to honor her promise,[31] but B would incur bargaining costs and the costs of the bribe.

10. B can threaten A with physical violence.[32] This nonmarket solution may be workable if B is physically stronger than A. Otherwise, B must invest in resources for threat making (such as buying a gun)[33] or must call on kin or friends to help him enforce the contract. This solution therefore has costs of its own, including the danger that B may generate social costs of disorder that might keep timid traders out of markets.

11. B can integrate vertically backward to the source of supply.[34] However, B must incur costs of intrafirm coordination. Furthermore, this nonmarket solution may not be a feasible method for B if he is a small trader with limited capital.

---

30. Tullock (1972) pointed out that the "discipline of continuous dealings" cannot be relied on to protect contracts if credit transactions are important.

31. Coase (1960) proposes the bribery solution as a solution to the problem of externalities. The bribery solution is akin to the ancient institution of hostages. For a discussion of hostages as strategy for handling conflict situations, see Schelling 1960.

32. For the role of threats for enforcing promises, see Schelling 1960. See also Gunning 1972.

33. Mumey (1971) pointed out that threat-making activity is not costless since resources must be devoted to the development of credible plans for threat making.

34. Williamson (1971) offers an explanation of vertical integration as a solution to the problem of supply reliability arising from "contractual incompleteness." I am emphasizing vertical integration as a solution to the problem of supply reliability arising from bad faith breach of contract.

As can be seen, each of the private solutions for coping with contract uncertainty has its own costs. Acquiring a reputation is not costless. Transaction costs are higher for the middleman operating under conditions of contract uncertainty. The rational trader, realizing the expense of private solutions to protect contracts, will have an incentive to shift from private to collective action. This portion of my theory of exchange, which extends traders' choice to the public choice of the rules of contractual behavior, relies heavily on the Buchanan-Tullock (1962) cost approach to collective action.

Imaging that trader B voluntarily joins with other traders in the economy to establish a merchant guild, a club, to enforce a norm of contractual behavior chosen by the traders themselves. The emergence of the guild internalizes supply-breach externalities, but the solution is not costless. Each trader, before he or she decides to join the guild, must expect to incur decision-making costs,[35] the costs of his or her time and effort to persuade other traders to reconcile differences and reach a unanimous agreement on a norm of contractual behavior. The decision-making costs are expected to increase as the size of the trading group required to agree increases. As long as the benefits from internalization exceed decision-making costs, the rational trader will have an incentive to join the guild. Assume, however, that these costs exceed the benefits from internalization, providing an incentive for traders to favor less than unanimous collective action in choosing a behavioral norm that would economize on such costs. Imagine that traders, faced with prohibitive decision-making costs, decide to abandon the guild solution and choose to enter into a constitutional social contract to establish legal norms of contractual behavior to be imposed and enforced by the state. The "protective state" (Buchanan 1975), as contract enforcer, then emerges from the trader's optimizing calculus.

The state, by imposing the law of contract on all traders, economizes on decision-making costs. At the same time, the state enforces legal sanctions, that is, by assigning liability for damages to the breaching party. Once the state emerges to make contracts legally binding, the rational trader must weigh the benefits against the expected costs (the payment of monetary damages) of breach. The trader then takes the calculated risk of paying damages to the victim if the trader chooses to break the contract. To be sure, the risk is sometimes worth it, but in general the legally binding contract introduces an element of inertia into the trader's choice calculus: Once the trader has made a contract, he or she has a strong incentive to honor it.[36]

---

35. Decision-making costs play a key role in the Buchanan and Tullock (1962) cost approach to collective action. See also Olson 1965.

36. Thus, the fundamental role of the legally binding contract is to deter traders from bad faith breach of contract. See Tullock 1971.

The emergence of the legally binding contract, which establishes a nexus between the market economy and the polity, transforms the former into the social economy. This latter exhibits a social structure[37] or social order that ensures that economic equilibrium can be achieved; the core of a capitalist exchange economy is an artificial core achieved by the institution of the legally binding contract.

The conceptual emergence of social order from a state of Hobbesian anarchy is Pareto superior for several reasons. The existence of social order (1) reduces unnecessary transaction costs arising from a trader's breach of contract and hence gives the middleman freedom to pursue his or her profits subject to a legal constraint; (2) facilitates the impersonal process of exchange by encouraging the trader to trade with outsiders, thus ensuring all opportunities for trading are exhausted; and (3) gives the trader the opportunity to shift some of the resources tied up in the protection of contracts into trade or capital accumulation, thereby facilitating the dynamic process of the expansion of existing markets and the creation of new ones. Social order thus turns out to be a public good,[38] a prerequisite for a viable and efficient exchange economy. The legally binding contract, in the context of a complex economy, thus turns out to be the best solution for traders for coping with the problems of contract uncertainty.[39]

Perhaps it is precisely because of the efficiency of organized markets with rules of contractual behavior that, historically, markets have not been in a state of Hobbesian anarchy. As Karl Polanyi (1957, 68) has remarked, "regulation and markets, in fact, grew up together." Unlike Hobbes, Kropotkin (1902) emphasized the importance of the mutual aid principle in organizing society. He saw the institution of the medieval merchant guilds as one classic example of mutual aid among merchants who, among many others, perform the function of enforcing contracts, a task later appropriated by the modern state.

In the long run perspective, one may view the evolution of the market economy from guild rules of contractual behavior to the legal norms of behav-

---

37. *Social structure* is a key concept in sociology and is used to describe the pattern of recurrent and regularized interaction among two or more persons.

38. For the notion of law and order as a public good, see Ireland 1968. See also Buchanan 1975.

39. In saying that the legally binding contract is the best solution for coping with the problems of contract uncertainty, I am not saying that it is the only one or that it is always the most important. To quote Macneil (1974, 716), "Command, status, social role, kinship, bureaucratic patterns, religious obligation, habit, and other internalizations all may and do achieve such projections." See also note 29 above and chapters 5 and 7 of this book. Furthermore, to the extent that instituting courts of law to protect contracts itself is not costless, all that is possible to achieve in the real world is a second best solution.

ior as the dynamic adjustment process of traders' public choice of ever more efficient institutions for reducing transaction costs via the establishment of social order. Economists have explained the existence of the firm (Alchian and Demsetz 1972; Coase 1937) and the vertically integrated firm (Williamson 1971) as economic organizations that reduce transaction costs in a market operating within a well-defined legal framework. The theory of the legally binding contract, developed here, suggests that the state is to be regarded as an economic organization that emerges to reduce transaction costs arising from contract uncertainty. The state, through its role in protecting contracts, may be viewed as a supercoordinator of interfirm transactions creating a super vertically integrated firm, which is, in reality, a well-functioning and efficient exchange economy.

REFERENCES

Akerlof, George A. 1970. "The Market for 'Lemons': Quality Uncertainty and the Market Mechanism." *Quarterly Journal of Economics* 84 (August): 488–500.

Alchian, Armen, and Harold Demsetz. 1972. "Production, Information Costs, and Economic Organization." *American Economic Review* 62 (December): 777–95.

Arrow, Kenneth J. 1970. "Political and Economic Evaluation of Social Effects and Externalities." In *The Analysis of Public Output,* edited by Julius Margolis. New York: National Bureau of Economic Research.

Aumann, Robert J. 1964. "Markets with a Continuum of Traders." *Econometrica* 32 (January–April): 39–50.

Becker, Gary S. 1968. "Crime and Punishment: An Economic Approach." *Journal of Political Economy* 76 (March–April): 169–217.

Brunner, Karl, and Allan H. Meltzer. 1971. "The Uses of Money: Money in the Theory of an Exchange Economy." *American Economic Review* 61 (December): 784–805.

Buchanan, James M. 1975. *The Limits of Liberty: Between Anarchy and Leviathan.* Chicago: The University of Chicago Press.

———. 1976. "A Hobbesian Interpretation of the Rawlsian Difference Principle." *Kyklos* 29:5–25.

Buchanan, James M., and Gordon Tullock. [1962] 1965. *The Calculus of Consent.* Ann Arbor: The University of Michigan Press.

Chipman, John S. 1965. "The Nature and Meaning of Equilibrium in Economic Theory." In *Functionalism in the Social Sciences: The Strengths and Limits of Functionalism in Anthropology, Economics, Political Science and Sociology: A Symposium,* edited by Don Albert Martindale, 35–64. Philadelphia: American Academy of Political and Social Science.

Clower, Robert. 1967. "A Reconsideration of the Microfoundations of Monetary Theory." *Western Economic Journal* 5 (December): 1–8.

Coase, Ronald H. 1937. "The Nature of the Firm." *Economica* 4 (November): 386–405.

Commons, John R. 1924. *The Legal Foundations of Capitalism.* New York: Macmillan.

Debreu, Gerard and H. Scarf. 1963. "A limit theorem on the core of an economy." *International Economic Review* 4 (September): 235–246.

Demsetz, Harold. 1967. "Toward a Theory of Property Rights." *American Economic Review* 57 (May): 347–59.

Edgeworth, F. Y. 1881. *Mathematical Psychics: An Essay on the Application of Mathematics to Moral Science.* London: C. Kegan Paul.

Furubotn, Eirik G., and Svetozar Pejovich. 1972. "Property Rights and Economic Theory: A Survey of Recent Literature." *Journal of Economic Literature* 10 (December): 1137–62.

Goldberg, Victor P. 1976a. "Protecting the Right to Be Served by Public Utilities." Working Paper. Blacksburg, Va.: Center for Study of Public Choice, February.

———. 1976b. "Toward an Expanded Economic Theory of Contract." *Journal of Economic Issues* 10 (March): 45–61.

Guest, A. G., ed. 1969. *Anson's Law of Contract.* Oxford: Clarendon Press.

Gunning, J. Patrick. 1972. "Toward a Theory of the Evolution of Government." In *Explorations in the Theory of Anarchy,* edited by Gordon Tullock, 19–26. Blacksburg, Va.: Center for Study of Public Choice.

Hahn, F. H. 1970. "Some Adjustment Problems." *Econometrica* 38 (January): 1–17.

Hicks, John. 1969. *A Theory of Economic History.* New York: Oxford University Press.

Ireland, Thomas R. 1968. "Public Order as a Public Good." Chicago: Loyola University. Typescript.

Kropotkin, Petr. 1902. *Mutual Aid: A Factor of Evolution.* New York: McClure Phillips and Co.

Landa, Janet T. 1976. "An Economic Theory of the Ethnically-Homogeneous Chinese Middleman Group." Paper presented at the Public Choice Society Annual Meetings, Roanoke, Va., April 16.

Leibenstein, Harvey. 1968. "Entrepreneurship and Development." *American Economic Review* 58 (May): 72–83.

Macneil, Ian. 1974. "The Many Futures of Contracts." *Southern California Law Review* 47 (May): 691–816.

Mumey, G. A. 1971. "The 'Coase Theorem': A Reexamination." *Quarterly Journal of Economics* 85 (November): 718–23.

Niehans, Jurg. 1969. "Money in a Static Theory of Optimal Payments Arrangements." *Journal of Money, Credit and Banking* 1 (November): 706–26.

Olson, Mancur. 1965. *The Logic of Collective Action: Public Goods and the Theory of Groups.* Cambridge: Harvard University Press.

Ostroy, Joseph M. 1973. "The Informational Efficiency of Monetary Exchange." *American Economic Review* 63 (September): 597–610.

Polanyi, Karl. [1944] 1957. *The Great Transformation: The Political and Economic Origins of Our Time.* Boston: Beacon.

Posner, Richard A. 1973. *Economic Analysis of Law.* Boston: Little, Brown.

Samuels, Warren J. 1971. "Interrelations between Legal and Economic Processes." *Journal of Law and Economics* 14 (October): 435–50.

Schelling, Thomas C. [1960] 1980. *The Strategy of Conflict.* Cambridge: Harvard University Press.

Shubik, Martin. 1975. "The General Equilibrium Model is Incomplete and Not Adequate for the Reconciliation of Micro and Macroeconomic Theory." *Kyklos* 28: 545–73.

Smith, Vernon L. 1971. "The Borrower-Lender Contract under Uncertainty." *Western Economic Journal* 9 (March): 52–56.

Tullock, Gordon. 1971. *The Logic of the Law.* New York: Basic Books.

———. 1972. "The Edge of the Jungle." In *Explorations in the Theory of Anarchy,* edited by Gordon Tullock, 65–75. Blacksburg, Va.: Center for Study of Public Choice.

Williamson, Oliver E. 1971. "The Vertical Integration of Production: Market Failure Considerations." *American Economic Review* 61 (May): 112–23.

CHAPTER 3

Specialization, Exchange Externalities, and Contract Law: A Graph-Theoretic Approach

A number of writers have provided a rationale for the role of the institution of contract law in an exchange economy.[1] These models deal primarily with two-person direct seller-buyer transactions rather than with the effects of breaches on the functioning of an entire market. As the previous chapter has shown, the institution of the law of contracts is even more necessary to the efficient functioning of a complex exchange economy with chains of intermediaries indirectly linking sellers and ultimate buyers. In a complex economy, characterized by specialization and division of labor among producers, consumers, and middlemen,[2] contract breach by an offending party can have significant third-party effects (i.e., on parties contracting with the victim of breach via chain reaction effects, hence generating public bad externalities. The role of

---

This is a revised and updated version of a paper entitled "Pareto-Relevant Exchange Externalities: The Basis of the Law of Contract," originally presented at the Law and Economics Workshop, Faculty of Law, University of Toronto, February 7, 1979.

1. There is a large literature on the economics of contract law. But a great deal of this literature focuses on analyzing remedies for breach rather than on the rationale of the institution of contract law in an exchange economy. The few writers who deal with the function of contract law in facilitating trade include Goldberg (1976), Muris (1981), Posner ([1977] 1985, chap. 4, 79–81), and Kronman (1985).

2. Economists have paid very little attention to the Smithian notion of division of labor. An important exception is George J. Stigler (1951). The study of the role of contract law in a complex economy must start with the notion of division of labor. Emile Durkheim (1964), the sociologist, recognized this necessity when he analyzed the functional significance of the division of labor for achieving "organic solidarity" among people via the law of contracts. Ian R. Macneil (1974) also emphasized the importance of specialization and division of labor in analyzing the role of contract law. For a plea from a biologist to economists to pay more attention to Adam Smith's notion of division of labor, see Ghiselin 1978. In this connection, it is significant to note ". . . that the problem of enforcing contracts was originally handled by merchants themselves—merchants being, of course, intermediaries of a fairly subtle kind of the sort that characterize all complex exchange economies" (Robert W. Clower, personal communication, July 24, 1979). The Law Merchant, created by merchants for the enforcement of contracts, later evolved into the Law of Contracts enforced by the state. (See also chap. 4.) For a recent study of the merchant guild, see Greif, Milgrom, and Weingast 1990.

contract law in a complex economy is to help internalize public bad externalities, hence economizing on transaction costs.[3]

The purpose of this chapter is to analyze in greater detail aspects of the theory of contract law developed in the previous chapter. In the second section we shall discuss how graph theory can be used as a tool to explicate the fundamental differences between a direct exchange economy and a middleman economy to better understand why the introduction of trading intermediaries leads to a nontrivial modification of traditional theories of exchange. This leads to a discussion in the third section of a class of market games that generate externalities arising out of breaches of contract. The fundamental nature of externalities arising from breach of contract is clarified by developing a more complex taxonomy of market games and a case is made for identifying these as a new class of "non-orthogonal coalition games" (Shubik 1971) that generates exchange externalities. In the fourth section, I discuss exchange externalities in the familiar terminology of pecuniary externalities and transaction costs and argue that they may cause market failure; hence, exchange externalities are Pareto relevant. In the fifth section, I discuss the role of contract law and the doctrine of privity of contract. It is suggested that the state, as contract enforcer, may emerge as an efficient solution for the internalization of Pareto-relevant exchange externalities, hence transforming a nonorthogonal coalition game (non-OCG) with externalities into an orthogonal coalition game (OCG). The sixth section concludes the chapter by working out some of the implications of our theory of contract and showing how this theory differs from the implications of theories of contract developed by previous writers.

Direct Exchange Economy versus Middleman Economy: A Graph-Theoretic Approach

As noted in the previous chapter, a fundamental difference between a Walrasian direct exchange economy and a middleman economy lies in the pattern of trade. An economy with four traders best describes this qualitative (structural) difference: a direct exchange economy can be decomposed into two isolated pairs of trading partners whereas a middleman economy cannot be decomposed. The precise structural differences between the alternative exchange economies, with $n = 4$ traders, can be formally represented by graph theory.[4]

---

3. A truly general theory of the law of contracts need not introduce any intermediaries in the exchange process. All that is necessary is to posit a complex system of interdependencies among economic agents linked by contractual obligations. In this chapter, we introduce the middleman or merchant as an example of the intermediary because the merchant has played a central role in the rise of the market. See Hicks 1969. See also note 2 above.

4. Graph theory, a branch of topology, is concerned with concepts and theorems relating to

A directed graph or digraph D is a finite set of elements, V, called *points,* and a set of elements, X, called *lines.* The points are depicted by dots labelled $v_1, v_2, \ldots, v_p$; the lines are depicted by arcs labelled $x_1, x_2, \ldots, x_q$ (Harary, Norman, and Cartwright 1965, 9). The direction of each line is indicated by an arrowhead. Let the points represent traders and let the two-way arrows represent exchange relations.

The Walrasian economy, in equilibrium, can be represented by a *disconnected digraph* (Harary, Norman, and Cartwright 1965, 71–72) composed of two *subgraphs* (Harary, Norman, and Cartwright 1965, 53–54) representing two sets of lone pairs of traders, $s_1 = (v_1, v_2)$ and $s_2 = (v_3, v_4)$. See figure 1a. The middleman economy in equilibrium can be presented by a *symmetric tree digraph* (Harary, Norman, and Cartwright 1965, 260–61) with a set of four traders, $s_1 = (v_1, v_2, v_3, v_4)$, connected in a transactions chain arrangement. See figure 1b. The structure of exchange relations in an exchange economy can be clearly reflected in two types of Boolean matrices: the *adjacency matrix* $A(D)$[5] and the *reachability matrix* $R(D)$.[6]

The Walrasian economy is *decomposable,*[7] as figure 1a shows that not every point is reachable from every other point. The indirect exchange econ-

---

abstract configurations called *graphs,* which consists of *points* and *lines;* when the direction of the lines are indicated, graphs become *digraphs* (short for directed graphs). The digraph terminology used in this chapter is that defined in Frank Harary, Robert Z. Norman, and Dorwin Cartwright (1965).

5. Given a digraph D, its *adjacency matrix,* $A(D) = (a_{ij})$ is a square matrix with one row and one column for each point of D, in which the entry $a_{ij} = 1$ if line $v_i v_j$ is in D, while $a_{ij} = 0$ if $v_i v_j$ is not in D. See Harary, Norman, and Cartwright 1965, 15.

6. The entries of the *reachability matrix* $R(D)$ are denoted (r_{ij}) and defined as follows: $r_{ij} = 1$ if v_i is reachable from v_j; otherwise $r_{ij} = 0$. That is, if D contains a sequence from v_i to v_j, then $r_{ij} = 1$. In constructing the reachability matrix of a digraph, the fact that each point is reachable from itself means that the entries on the diagonal of $R(D)$ are, therefore, all 1's. See Harary, Norman, and Cartwright 1965, 117. One other matrix, the *connectedness matrix* $C(D)$, reveals the pattern of connectedness of points and gives additional insights into the structure of exchange relations; but this matrix will not be used here.

7. If A is a square matrix and can be partitioned into submatrices such that A_{11} and A_{22} are square and A_{12} and A_{21} consist entirely of zeroes, then A is said to be decomposed by the partition

$$A = \begin{bmatrix} A_{11} & A_{12} \\ A_{21} & A_{22} \end{bmatrix}$$

In other words, a matrix is said to be decomposable only if it can be reducible into its irreducible "block" form:

$$A = \begin{bmatrix} A_1 & 0 \\ 0 & A_2 \end{bmatrix}$$

See Harary, Norman, and Cartwright 1965, 132.

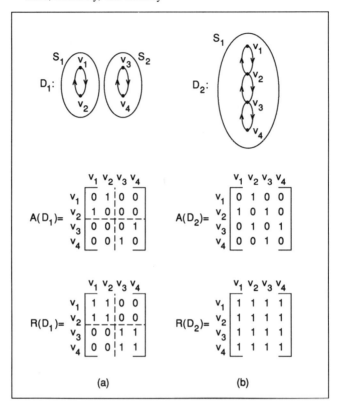

Fig. 1. Adjacency matrices and reachability matrices for two different types of exchange economies showing how the graph of the exchange economy is reflected in the structure of the matrix. *a*) A Walrasian decomposable economy: represented by a disconnected digraph. *b*) A Middleman economy: represented by a symmetric tree digraph.

omy, in contrast, is *nondecomposable*,[8] as is reflected in the corresponding adjacency matrix of the symmetric tree digraph. See figure 1b. Furthermore, the reachability matrix of the disconnected digraph of the Walrasian economy shows that not every point is reachable from every other point; see figure 1a. In contrast, the reachability matrix of the symmetric tree digraph of the middleman economy shows that every trader is reachable from every other trader, specifically by a sequence of length of three or less. See figure 1b.

The appearance of middlemen affects a structural transformation of a

---

8. For a matrix to be nondecomposable, it must have at least one nonzero off diagonal element in each row and column. If there is an $n \times n$ nondecomposable matrix, there are at least $n - 1$ nonzero elements above and below the diagonal.

simple decomposable Walrasian economy into a complex nondecomposable sequence economy. The nondecomposability of the middleman sequence economy is due to the functional interdependence between traders arising from specialization and division of labor in society. The specialization and division of labor, in which the middlemen are the professional traders, provide the basis for an ongoing relationship of continuous dealings or "relational contracts" (Macneil 1974) among many traders resulting in a complex n-person recurrent and sequential market game. The sequential mode of transacting in a middleman economy introduces the dimension of time into the exchange process so that breach of time-binding contracts becomes a possibility. The middleman economy must be seen as a particular kind of spatially-temporally connected sequence economy[9] that is vulnerable to coordination failure arising from breaches of contract. The transformation of the Walrasian economy into the middleman sequence economy has far-reaching implications for the role of institutions such as money and legally binding contract in the efficient functioning of a complex economy.

A Taxonomy of Exchange Externalities, Games of Breach, and Nonorthogonal Coalition Games

Suppose traders operate in a Hobbesian state of nature in which there are no constraints on contractual behavior. In such a setting, any trader has the option of making a binary choice of honoring or behaving "opportunistically" (Williamson 1975, 26) by breaking contracts. Under contract uncertainty, breach is a source of coordination failure because plans of interdependent traders fail to mesh. Hence, opportunities for some traders will not materialize. Take the example of traders A and B discussed in the previous chapter, in which A and B have entered into a bilateral contract.

Imagine that at $t + 1$, A chooses to break her contract to deliver goods to B as a result of recontracting with middleman X who offers better terms than B. As a result of A's *fundamental breach*,[10] B is involuntarily forced to break

---

9. Monetary economists, attempting to explain the role of money in an exchange economy, have been turning to the study of multimarket models or models of a sequence of markets. Ulph and Ulph (1975, 362), in surveying the literature on transaction costs in general equilibrium theory, note that ". . . we can obviously think of a multi-market model as describing a number of spatially different markets. To our knowledge no one has explicitly pursued this interpretation and reinterpreted, say, Hahn's conclusions about the role of money in sequential models to discuss the role of money in linking trade between countries." Also see Hahn 1973. The sequence economy in this chapter describes a number of spatially (and temporally) separated markets linked together by intermediaries; hence the emphasis here is on trading intermediaries, not money, in linking spatially-separated markets.

10. In the literature on the law of contracts, there is the doctrine of the *breach of a*

his contract to deliver goods to C and as a result B is unable to enforce his entitlement to C's promised sum of money. Because of A's breach, B's profit expectations fail to materialize; B becomes the victim of what one may call *seller's abrogation externalities*. B's breach of contract also forces C to break his contract to D, so that there is more than one victim of exchange externalities arising from A's breach of contract (specifically, B, C, and D). Imagine an alternative situation in which B fulfils his contract to deliver goods to C but C refuses to accept the goods. Because of C's breach, B's profit expectations fail to materialize; B becomes the victim of what we shall call *buyer's abrogation externalities*. Imagine a third situation in which A, after taking B's money, refuses to deliver the goods to B. Because of A's breach, B becomes the victim of what we shall call *seller's goods-defraud externalities*. Imagine a fourth situation in which C, after accepting delivery of goods from B, refuses to pay B. In this case, B becomes the victim of what we shall call *buyer's money-defraud externalities*.[11] Imagine a fifth situation in which A fulfills her contract to deliver goods to B but the goods delivered are of an inferior grade. In this case, B becomes the victim of what we shall call *quality externalities*.[12] These different species of externalities arising from breaches of contract fall under the generic term of what we shall call *exchange externalities*.

A game of breach that generates exchange externalities is a new kind of market game not so far identified. What is needed, therefore, is a more complete taxonomy of market games. Martin Shubik's typology may be used here. Shubik (1971) divides market games into two basic categories: (1) OCGs and (2) non-OCGs. An OCG is a game without externalities,[13] while a non-OCG is a game in which the groups can no longer be decentralized in the presence of physical or technological externalities that link the groups together. The presence or absence of technological externalities provides Shubik with the criterion for the separation of market games into two

---

fundamental term or *fundamental breach*. According to this doctrine, in every contract, certain terms are fundamental, the breach of which amount to complete nonperformance of the contract. Thus, in the example here, A's failure to deliver the goods to B as promised constitutes a fundamental breach. For the nature of a fundamental breach, see, for example, Guest 1969, 153–56.

11. The identification of a debt-default externality is somewhat analogous to Vernon Smith's (1971) identification of an externality under loan-contract uncertainty. But, in the example here, B is not a lender of money who suffers from loan default. Rather, B is a trader who delivers goods to C and suffers a debt-default externality when C fails to pay him.

12. For a discussion of the problem of trading under conditions of quality uncertainty, see Akerlof 1970.

13. According to Shubik (1971, 715–16), "If an organization can be described as an orthogonal coalition game, this means that it is possible to decentralize it in such a complete manner that the performance of any sub-division will depend only upon itself."

basic categories. But this taxonomy of market games does not exhaust the possibilities once the game is extended to include a third class of economic agents—the middlemen—and to include a new class of exchange externalities. Thus, once the market game is extended to include n-person complex exchanges via middlemen, pairs of traders can no longer be decentralized or decomposed, as noted. There is a subcategory of non-OCGs: non-OCGs without exchange externalities. In the presence of breach, in which many traders become victims of exchange externalities via chain reaction effects, we have a second subcategory of non-OCGs: non-OCGs with exchange externalities. The range of market games can be extended via a three-by-two matrix illustration where the three alternative forms of market games are shown along the columns and the two possible n-classes of economic agents along the rows. See figure 2. Within each cell, directed graphs are used to represent the various types of market games. Cell I represents Shubik's OCG as a disconnected digraph; the game in a Walrasian economy can be described as an OCG. Cell III represents a non-OCG with technological externalities imposed by v_2 on all other actors (v_1, v_3, v_4). The single arrow represents an externality (i.e., an arrow from v_2 to v_3 indicates that v_2 is imposing an externality on v_3). Cell V depicts the market game in a Pareto-optimal complex economy with intermediaries as a symmetric tree digraph whose adjacency matrix is nondecomposable, as noted. Cell V depicts the market game in a Pareto-optimal middleman economy as a symmetric tree digraph whose adjacency matrix is nondecomposable as noted. Cell VI depicts the market game in a non-Pareto-optimal middleman economy with three victims of exchange externalities as an acyclic tree from a point digraph, whose adjacency matrix, while still nondecomposable, has become upper triangular, i.e., when all of its nonzero entries are on or above the main diagonal.

Attention is directed to the situation depicted in cell VI because the situation depicts the new class of non-OCG with exchange externalities that, as will be shown, prevent the attainment of Pareto efficiency. The specific species of externalities involved in this situation that we shall consider is seller's abrogation externalities arising from the opportunistic behavior of v_1, who by breaking a contract to deliver goods to v_2, imposes externalities directly and indirectly on three other traders (v_2, v_3, and v_4). What is the nature of exchange externalities that cause the market to be nonoptimal? To answer this question, it is first necessary to define the nature of externalities. Buchanan (1965, 4–5) defines externalities as follows:

> When one person acts so as to impose either benefit or damage in a second person, without the consent of the latter, the acting party is said to generate external effects. His behavior, externally or independently affects others than himself. When the effect is beneficial, economists refer

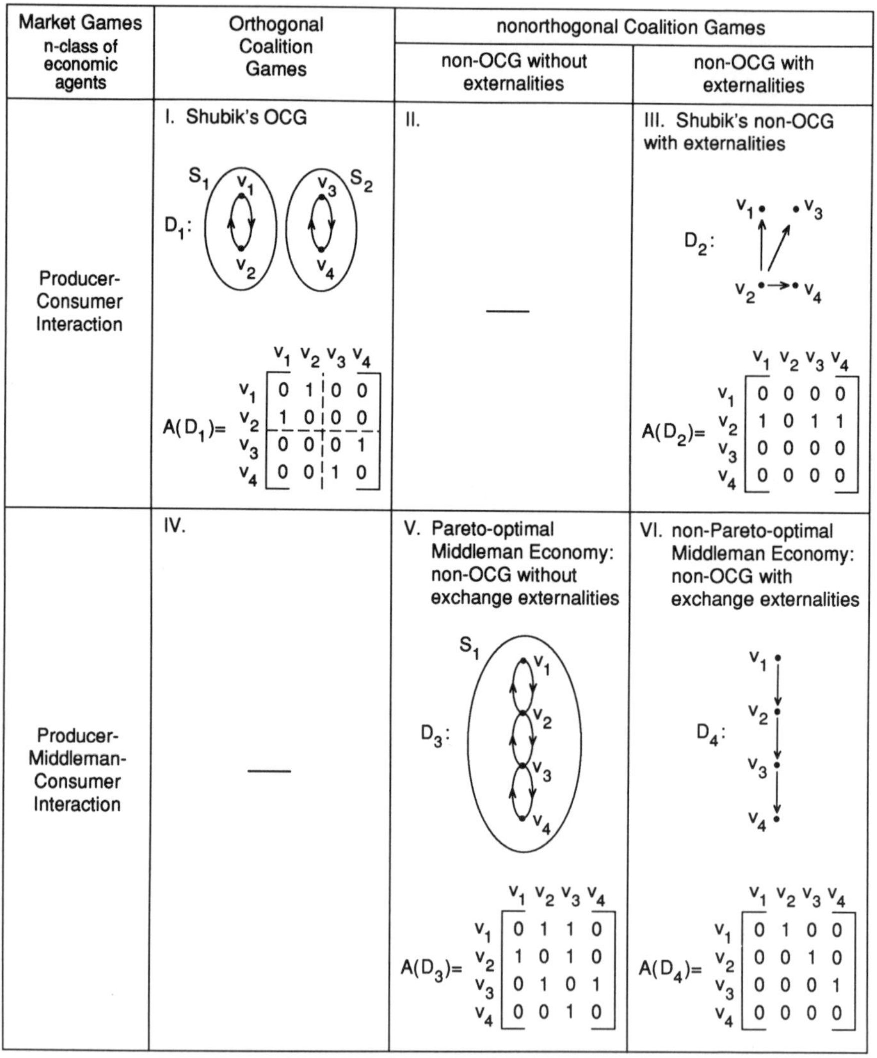

Market Games n-class of economic agents	Orthogonal Coalition Games	nonorthogonal Coalition Games	
		non-OCG without externalities	non-OCG with externalities
Producer-Consumer Interaction	I. Shubik's OCG D_1: (graph with S_1: $v_1 \leftrightarrow v_2$; S_2: $v_3 \leftrightarrow v_4$) $A(D_1)=$ $\begin{array}{c c c c c} & v_1 & v_2 & v_3 & v_4 \\ v_1 & 0 & 1 & 0 & 0 \\ v_2 & 1 & 0 & 0 & 0 \\ v_3 & 0 & 0 & 0 & 1 \\ v_4 & 0 & 0 & 1 & 0 \end{array}$	II. —	III. Shubik's non-OCG with externalities D_2: (graph $v_1\bullet\ \ \bullet v_3$; $v_2 \bullet \rightarrow \bullet v_4$) $A(D_2)=$ $\begin{array}{c c c c c} & v_1 & v_2 & v_3 & v_4 \\ v_1 & 0 & 0 & 0 & 0 \\ v_2 & 1 & 0 & 1 & 1 \\ v_3 & 0 & 0 & 0 & 0 \\ v_4 & 0 & 0 & 0 & 0 \end{array}$
Producer-Middleman-Consumer Interaction	IV. —	V. Pareto-optimal Middleman Economy: non-OCG without exchange externalities D_3: (graph S_1: $v_1 \leftrightarrow v_2 \leftrightarrow v_3 \leftrightarrow v_4$) $A(D_3)=$ $\begin{array}{c c c c c} & v_1 & v_2 & v_3 & v_4 \\ v_1 & 0 & 1 & 1 & 0 \\ v_2 & 1 & 0 & 1 & 0 \\ v_3 & 0 & 1 & 0 & 1 \\ v_4 & 0 & 0 & 1 & 0 \end{array}$	VI. non-Pareto-optimal Middleman Economy: non-OCG with exchange externalities D_4: (graph $v_1 \bullet \downarrow v_2 \bullet \downarrow v_3 \bullet \downarrow v_4 \bullet$) $A(D_4)=$ $\begin{array}{c c c c c} & v_1 & v_2 & v_3 & v_4 \\ v_1 & 0 & 1 & 0 & 0 \\ v_2 & 0 & 0 & 1 & 0 \\ v_3 & 0 & 0 & 0 & 1 \\ v_4 & 0 & 0 & 0 & 0 \end{array}$

Fig. 2. Extension of Shubik's taxonomy of market games: graph-theoretic and Boolean matrix representation

to external economies. When the effect is harmful, one refers to external diseconomies.

Several features in this definition merit special attention. First, Buchanan's definition of externalities implies the existence of interdependence among individuals. But there is no implication that interdependence and externalities are the same phenomenon. Consider the example in which middleman B can carry out his contract to deliver goods to C only if A honors her contract to B. There is interdependence between A and B but no externalities as long as A does not impose costs on B by breaking the contract. If A breaks her contract to B, the situation is characterized by the existence of both interdependence and externalities. The concepts of interdependence and externalities are closely related but different, hence the distinction between non-OCGs without externalities and non-OCGs with externalities.

A second important feature in Buchanan's definition is the unilateral nature of externalities: A imposes costs on B, but B does not, in turn, impose costs on A. This definition implicitly assumes the existence of a legal framework within which decision makers operate and the assignment of rights to one of the interacting parties that thus determines the external effects as unidirectional. Thus, A, who violates B's contractual rights by breaking her contract to B, in the example, is identified as the party who imposes externalities on B. Without the initial specification of a legal framework that allows a definition of whose rights are to be protected, an externality relationship is reciprocal:[14] to avoid costs to B is to impose costs on A. Thus, while an externality relationship is always two-sided, it is not necessarily reciprocal in the sense that it involves mutual coercion in the imposition of costs, once initial property rights have been assigned. Inherent in Buchanan's notion of externalities is the coercive power of one party to impose costs on another party without the latter's consent. The graph-theoretic representation of externalities in terms of a directed line from the offending party to the victim captures the essence of Buchanan's notion of an externality relationship as a coercive relationship in contrast to a mutually voluntary exchange relationship. A third feature is the generality of Buchanan's definition. It is broad enough to include both technological externalities and pecuniary externalities as well as externality-producing activities that are legitimate as well as illegal.[15] It is meaningful to speak of the coercive activity involving breach of contract as an activity that generates negative externalities. Since these externalities exist in the sphere of exchange, it is therefore appropriate to call these exchange externalities, terminologically analogous to production externalities and consumption externalities. The identification of a new class of externalities in the sphere of exchange provides the key to a theory of the law of

---

14. For a discussion of the institutional structure of externality relationships that determine the direction of external effects, see Buchanan 1973. See also Coase 1960 and Samuels 1972.

15. In this respect, Buchanan's definition is broader than Mishan's, which excludes externality-producing activities that are illegal. According to Mishan (1971, 2), "the essential feature of the concept of an external effect is that the effect produced is not a deliberate creation but an *unintended* or *incidental* by-product of some otherwise legitimate activity."

contracts and of ethical codes embedded in ethnic trading networks (see chap. 5). Therefore the nature of exchange externalities must be explored in greater detail and with some attempt to forge links with familiar concepts of pecuniary externalities, transaction costs, and market failure.

Pecuniary Externalities, Transaction Costs, and Market Failure

Exchange externalities may be considered as a species of pecuniary externalities. However, unlike the usual species of pecuniary diseconomies that stem from the phenomenon of rising supply curves, exchange externalities may be considered to be a species of a broader category of pecuniary externalities that taxonomically differ from technological externalities. Technological externalities refer to the costs incurred by a decision maker when there exists direct physical interdependence between units such that the output (for example, smoke) of one unit is an input for the other unit. So long as the effects are external at the margins, it is customary to regard technological externalities as "Pareto-relevant" (Buchanan and Stubblebine 1962). They must be internalized in some fashion to achieve Pareto efficiency. Pecuniary externalities, on the other hand, are regarded as Pareto irrelevant because effective functioning of the market will ensure that the necessary conditions for Pareto efficiency are met.[16] Thus, some economists have suggested that the concept of pecuniary externalities be scrapped because it is not meaningful and that the notion of externalities be restricted to genuine externalities, i.e., technological externalities.[17] If the concept of pecuniary externalities is to be salvaged as a meaningful separate concept, it is necessary to find an instance where the presence of such externalities leads to market failure. That instance may be provided if pecuniary exchange externalities are considered as a source of transaction costs that could, under conditions of extreme contract uncertainty, cause markets to disappear.[18]

As noted in the previous chapter, under conditions of contract uncertainty, each trader has an incentive to make private provisions for the protection of contracts. But private solutions for internalizing exchange externalities generate their own species of transaction costs. Thus, while exchange exter-

16. For a discussion of this, see Shubik 1971.

17. See, for example, Mishan 1971.

18. See Ulph and Ulph 1975 for a survey of the literature on transaction costs in general equilibrium theory. For a discussion of the relationship between transaction costs and externality, see Arrow 1970. See also Dahlman 1979. For a discussion of setup costs as a species of transaction costs, see Heller 1972. For a survey of the literature on transaction costs in the NIE, see Williamson 1985, chap. 1. For a recent discussion of activities generating transaction costs, see Eggertsson 1990, 13–16.

nalities by themselves are not considered to be a species of transaction costs, they are a source of transaction costs that may cause middlemen to exit from markets, hence causing market failure.

Contract Law, Privity of Contract, and Orthogonal Coalition Games

Faced with the high transaction costs of private protection of contracts, traders will have an incentive to get together to choose a norm of behavior for constraining traders' contractual behavior. To economize on collective decision-making costs, traders will have an incentive to enter into a constitutional social contract to create the state for the protection of contracts. The state economizes on decision-making costs because the state imposes a legal norm of contractual behavior, embodied in the law of contracts, binding on all traders in the economy. By imposing liabilities for monetary damages on the offending party,[19] the effect of the law of contracts is to introduce costs into the private calculus of traders when making a binary choice to keep or break a contract. A primary function of the institution of the law of contracts is to alter incentives for breach of contract to achieve a greater internalization of exchange externalities. Once two traders sign a legally binding contract, both have an incentive to honor the contract. In this way, a non-OCG with externalities is transformed into a non-OCG without externalities as soon as pairs of traders enter into legally binding contracts. The institutional setting shifts from that depicted in cell VI of figure 2 to that depicted in cell V.

Contract law, on the other hand, does not deter "efficient breach" (Goetz and Scott 1977).[20] Thus, if A finds that, in breaking her contract with B, she can compensate B and still make herself better off by recontracting with X, then A is engaging in efficient breach. Efficient breach is facilitated by the doctrine of privity of contract in contract law. In the context of an A-B-C trading network, A knows that she can avoid liability to C by using the privity doctrine in the event of a breach that causes a chain-reaction involving B and C as victims of breach. C cannot sue A because C was not in privity with the A-B contract and because A was not in privity with the B-C contract. By the

---

19. Property rights can be protected either by a property rule or a liability rule. For a discussion of the distinction between property rules and liability rules, see Calabresi and Melamed 1972. As is well known, the law of contracts protects most contractual rights via a liability rule rather than a property rule (via compelling specific performance of a contract). Specific performance is restricted to a class of contracts involving goods or services that are considered to be unique. For a discussion of the economic rationale underlying the uniqueness test for invoking specific performance of a contract, see Kronman 1978.

20. For a recent law-and-economics contribution to a theory of efficient breach, see Craswell 1988.

doctrine of privity of contract, only B can sue A, and C can sue only B.[21] Once two traders have signed a contract, in the context of an interdependent trading network, each pair of traders can behave as if they are completely decentralized. Thus, contract law, via the privity doctrine, transforms a non-OCG without externalities into an OCG by decomposing four functionally interconnected pairs of traders into two isolated pairs of traders, to achieve a Shubik-like equilibrium. The institutional setting shifts from that depicted in cell VI to that depicted in cell I.

In transforming a non-OCG into a OCG, the law of contracts helps to achieve Pareto efficiency in several ways. First, profit-seeking traders are able to appropriate profit expectations as intangible assets with a high degree of certainty because they expect that contracts will be honored; the law of contracts thereby facilitates entrepreneurship. Second, public protection of contracts enables traders to reduce transaction costs of private protection of contracts. Third, by supplying contracting parties with a set of normal terms that, in the absence of the law, the parties would have to negotiate themselves, the law of contracts reduces negotiation costs. This function of contract law, as Richard Posner (1977, 69) pointed out, is similar to that performed by a standard or form contract. By supplying potential contracting parties with information concerning the many unforeseen contingencies that may frustrate an exchange, contract law also further helps to reduce transaction costs by encouraging parties to be aware of the obstacles in the process of exchange and hence to carefully plan their transactions. The law of contracts turns out to be a fundamental part of the laws and institutions of a decentralized market economy: it is a public good. To the extent that the provision of this public goods is itself not costless, we may predict that the optimal solution is a mix of private and public solutions to cope with the problem of contract uncertainty.

One reason why standard theories of exchange implicitly assume abstract markets always to be in a state of equilibrium and hence Pareto efficient is precisely because they ignore Pareto-relevant exchange externalities. Thus, these theories assign no essential role to laws or rules of the game that constrain traders' behavior to produce such Pareto-optimal results.[22]

---

21. From the viewpoint of A, privity of contract facilitates efficient breach. From the viewpoint of the A-B-C trading network as a system, however, the privity doctrine imposes unnecessary contract enforcement costs since two lawsuits are involved in the event of A's breach. This may explain why the doctrine of privity of contract has come under attack in product liability law in the United States. In a product liability case, C can sue A for a defective product under strict liability in tort, which is free from problems, including privity of contract, that have plagued product liability cases in the past. For a discussion of the fall of the "citadel of privity," see Prosser 1960. See also Landa and Grofman 1981.

22. Economists in general and exchange theorists in particular, have paid too little attention to the role of the rules of the game in achieving Pareto-optimal results. One significant exception

It thus appears that the notion of pecuniary externalities can be rescued as a meaningful concept when exchange externalities are identified as pecuniary externalities. One reason economists have ignored Pareto-relevant pecuniary externalities as the basis for the law of contracts may be that when externality concepts came on the scene, the legal infrastructure for the internalization of such externalities already existed in well-developed market economies.[23]

Conclusions and Some Implications of the Theory

Contract law achieves Pareto optimality in a market economy, as noted. However, as Posner (1977, 66) suggests, ". . . one doubts that without a law of contracts the system of voluntary exchange would break down completely." In economies where the legal framework is not well developed, traders have created institutional arrangements, alternative to contract law, for the coordination of plans of many traders connected in networks of exchange. They have devised mechanisms to facilitate the ability of parties to rely on the strength of previous trading linkages, such as particularizing exchange relations (see chaps. 5 and 6) and relying on gift-exchange (see chap. 7). The codes of ethics[24] embedded in personalistic relations provides the sanctions against breach that, in turn, generate mutual trust among members of the homogeneous trading group. These homogeneous trading groups may be regarded as low-cost clublike arrangements, alternative to contract law and to vertically integrated firms, for the protection of contracts (see chaps. 5 and 6).

---

is James Buchanan (1962), who emphasized that the Edgeworth box, with its well-defined Pareto region, really presupposes the existence of rules, which, by constraining traders from activities such as fraud, robbery, subjugation, and murder, produces Pareto optimality. See also Stubblebine 1972 and Demsetz 1967. For a more recent study of the reason of rules, see Brennan and Buchanan 1985.

23. Coase 1937, in a classic paper, provided a rationale for the emergence of the institution of the firm in a specialized exchange economy. Coase argues that if the price mechanism is used, input owners would be required to enter into a number of contracts with other factors with whom they cooperate. By organizing a firm, however, the costs of contract negotiation are reduced because, in place of several separate contracts, one employer-employee contract is substituted. We may regard our theory of the state as an institution that emerges in a specialized economy to economize on transaction costs associated with breach of contract via its role in coordinating interfirm transactions. Just as it is costly for owners of firms to negotiate and conclude a separate contract for each transaction, so it is also costly for traders to agree unanimously on a common norm of behavior binding on all traders. By organizing a legal order, however, (a) decision-making costs are reduced because, instead of achieving unanimous consent, which requires numerous bilateral agreements, *one* social contract is substituted; and (b) Pareto-relevant exchange externalities are internalized because of the penalties for breach of contract.

24. Codes of ethics are the noncontractual elements that Macauley (1963) emphasized. But for such noncontractual elements to be a substitute for contracts, not only on-going exchange relations are required, but some shared mutual understandings and mutual trust among the contractual parties must exist.

A theory of contract based on two-person exchange models cannot explain the phenomenon of homogeneous trading groups because the notion of the inclusion of insiders and the exclusion of outsiders from trade is basic to such a theory. The exclusion of outsiders from trade implies that all profitable opportunities for trade have not been exhausted. In an attempt to reduce the opportunity costs of the exclusion of outsiders from trade, Chinese middlemen in Southeast Asia, for example, have resorted to cash transactions in their dealings across ethnic boundaries (see chap. 5). The institution of money sublimates the need for trust in situations where trust is problematic since money is simultaneously exchanged with goods.

Another mechanism for coordinating the plans of many traders linked together in complex exchange networks is through the institution of gift-exchange. For example, the Kula Ring, found in the Trobriand and surrounding islands of Papua New Guinea, is a gift-exchange system involving a chain of trading intermediaries connected together in a ring. The Kula gift-exchange system greatly facilitates intertribal commercial trade. Prior to the emergence of the Kula Ring, members of different tribes often practiced warfare, raiding, and even cannibalism, all of which inhibited intertribal commercial exchange. Kula traders who violate the rules of Kula gift-exchange face the potential threat of being bypassed by the network of Kula traders. The rules of the Kula game may be interpreted as club law, alternative to contract law, for the enforcement of contracts in stateless, primitive societies. (See chap. 7.)

While institutional devices such as money and gift-exchange help to bridge the distinction between insiders and outsiders, they do not erase them. The emergence of contract law constitutes a Pareto-superior move because it helps to eliminate the mistrust element in interactions between strangers. That is because contract law, via its liability for damages, helps to standardize contractual behavior, making it possible for traders to enter into impersonal, legally binding relations across kinship, ethnic, and tribal boundaries. By helping to extend traders' "moral-ethical limits" (Buchanan 1978) beyond tribal boundaries to the boundaries of the nation-state, numerous new options to trade with other impersonal or anonymous traders are opened up.[25] Existing markets are expanded and new ones are created by the existence of a legal framework for the protection of contracts. Contract law thus turns out to be a fundamental part of the institutional infrastructure of a society. We may interpret the emergence of contract law as attempts by society to achieve Pareto optimality under contract uncertainty via contract law's role in internalizing externalities and to expand the size of markets by extending the size of the moral community.

---

25. According to Anatol Rapoport (personal communication, December 1979), "degree of civilization is measured by the extent to which distinction between 'us' and 'them' is erased."

REFERENCES

Akerlof, George A. 1970. "The Market for 'Lemons': Quality Uncertainty and the Market Mechanism." *Quarterly Journal of Economics* 84 (August): 488–500.

Arrow, Kenneth J. 1970. "Political and Economic Evaluation of Social and Economic Effects and Externalities." In *The Analysis of Public Output*, edited by J. Margolis. New York: National Bureau of Economic Research, 1970.

———. 1974. "Limited Knowledge and Economic Analysis." *American Economic Review* 63 (March): 1–10.

Aumann, Robert J. 1964. "Markets with a Continuum of Traders." *Econometrica* 32 (January–April): 39–50.

Brennan, Geoffrey, and James M. Buchanan, 1985. *The Reason of Rules: Constitutional Political Economy*. Cambridge: Cambridge University Press.

Buchanan, James M. 1962. "The Relevance of Pareto Optimality." *Journal of Conflict Resolution* 6 (December): 341–54.

———. 1965. "The Economic Context for Ethical Action." Unpublished manuscript.

———. 1973. "The Institutional Structure of Externality." *Public Choice* 14 (Spring): 69–82.

———. 1978. "Markets, States, and the Extent of Morals." *American Economic Review* 68 (May): 364–68.

Buchanan, James M. and Wm. Craig Stubblebine. 1962. "Externality." *Economica* 29 (November): 371–84.

Calabresi, Guido, and A. Douglas Melamed. 1972. "Property Rules, Liability Rules, and Inalienability: One View of the Cathedral." *Harvard Law Review* 85 (April): 1089–1128.

Coase, Ronald J. 1937. "The Nature of the Firm." *Economica* 4 (November): 382–405. Reprinted in *Readings in Price Theory*, edited by G. J. Stigler and K. Boulding, 331–51. Homewood, Ill.: Richard D. Irwin. 1952.

———. 1960. "The Problem of Social Cost." *Journal of Law and Economics* 3 (October): 1–44.

Crasswell, Richard. 1988. "Contract Remedies, Renegotiation, and the Theory of Efficient Breach." *Southern California Law Review* 61:629–70.

Dahlman, Carl J. 1979. "The Problem of Externality." *Journal of Law and Economics* 22:141–62.

Demsetz, Harold. 1967. "Toward a Theory of Property Rights." *American Economic Review,* 57 (May): 347–59.

Durkheim, Emile. 1964. *The Division of Labor in Society.* Translated by G. Simpson. New York: The Free Press.

Eggertsson, Thráinn. 1990. *Economic Behavior and Institutions*. Cambridge: Cambridge University Press.

Ghiselin, Michael T. 1978. "The Economy of the Body." *American Economic Review* 68 (May): 233–37.

Goetz, Charles J., and Robert E. Scott. 1977. "Liquidated Damages, Penalties and the Just Compensation Principle: Some Notes on an Enforcement Model and a Theory of Efficient Breach." *Columbia Law Review* 77:554–94.

———. 1980. "Enforcing Promises: An Examination of the Basis of Contract." *Yale Law Journal* 89: 1261–1322.

Goldberg, Victor P. 1976. "Toward an Expanded Economic Theory of Contract." *Journal of Economic Issues* 10 (March): 45–61.

Greif, Avner, Paul Milgrom, and Barry Weingast. 1990. "The Merchant Gild as a Nexus of Contracts." Hoover Institution, Stanford University, Domestic Studies Program, Working Paper Series, E-90-23-10.

Guest, A. G. 1969. *Anson's Law of Contract.* 23d ed. Oxford: Oxford University Press.

Hahn, Frank. 1973. "On Transaction Costs, Inessential Sequence Economies and Money." *Review of Economic Studies* 40 (October): 449–61.

Harary, Frank, Robert Z. Norman, and Dorwin Cartwright. 1965. *Structural Models: An Introduction to the Theory of Directed Graphs.* New York: John Wiley and Sons.

Heller, Walter P. 1972. "Transactions with Set-Up Costs." *Journal of Economic Theory* 4 (June): 465–78.

Hicks, John. 1969. *A Theory of Economic History.* New York: Oxford University Press.

Kronman, Anthony T. 1978. "Specific Performance." *University of Chicago Law Review* 45:351–75.

———. 1985. "Contract Law and the State of Nature." *Journal of Law, Economics and Organizations* 1 (Spring): 5–32.

Landa, Janet, and Bernard Grofman. 1981. "Games of Breach and the Role of Contract Law in Protecting the Expectation Interest." *Research in Law and Economics* 3:67–90.

Macauley, Stewart. 1963. "Non-Contractual Relations in Business: A Preliminary Study." *American Sociological Review* 28:55–70.

Macneil, Ian R. 1974. "The Many Futures of Contracts." *Southern California Law Review* 47 (May): 691–816.

Mishan, E. J. 1971. "The Postwar Literature on Externalities: An Interpretative Essay." *Journal of Economic Literature* 9 (March): 1–28.

Muris, Timothy J. 1981. "Opportunistic Behaviour and the Law of Contracts." *Minnesota Law Review* 65:521–90.

Posner, Richard A. [1977] 1985. *Economic Analysis of Law.* Boston: Little, Brown.

Prosser, W. L. 1960. "The Assault upon the Citadel (Strict Liability to the Consumer)." *Yale Law Journal* 69:1099–1148.

Samuels, Warren J. 1972. "Welfare Economics, Power, and Property." In *Perspective of Property,* edited by G. Wunderlich and W. L. Gibson, Jr., 61–148. University Park, Pa.: Institute for Research on Land and Water Resource, Pennsylvania State University.

Shubik, Martin. 1971. "Pecuniary Externalities: A Game Theoretic Analysis." *American Economic Review* 61 (September): 713–18.

———. 1973. "Commodity Money, Oligopoly, Credit and Bankruptcy in a General Equilibrium Model." *Western Economic Journal* 10 (March): 24–38.

Smith, Vernon L. 1971. "The Borrower-Lender Contract under Uncertainty." *Western Economic Journal* 9 (March): 52–56.

Stigler, George. 1951. "The Division of Labor is Limited by the Extent of the Market." *Journal of Political Economy* 59 (June): 185–93.

Stubblebine, Wm. Craig. 1972. "On Property Rights and Institutions." In *Explorations in the Theory of Anarchy,* edited by G. Tullock, 39–50. Blacksburg, Va.: Center for the Study of Public Choice, Virginia Polytechnic and State University.

Ulph, A. M., and D. T. Ulph. 1975. "Transaction Costs in General Equilibrium Theory—A Survey." *Economica* 42 (November): 355–72.

Williamson, Oliver E. 1971. "The Vertical Integration of Production: Market Failure Considerations." *American Economic Review* 61 (May): 112–23.

———. 1975. *Markets and Hierarchies: Analysis and Antitrust Implications.* New York: The Free Press.

———. 1985. *The Economic Institutions of Capitalism: Firms, Markets, Relational Contracting.* New York: The Free Press.

CHAPTER 4

Hadley v. Baxendale and the Expansion of the Middleman Economy

In this chapter, I turn my attention to the famous *Hadley* foreseeability rule in contract law. I focus on some neglected aspects of the much discussed *Hadley* rule by examining the operation of the rule in one particular historical context which was of increasing importance during the formative years of the *Hadley* rule—the middleman economy of nineteenth-century England. The framework adopted here is that of PR-PC perspective that has proved increasingly useful in a wide range of contexts. Using the PR-PC approach, I am able to explain: (a) the "middleman exception" in the Uniform Commercial Code; and (b) the conceptual emergence of the mitigation doctrine and specific performance remedy in contract law.

The chapter is organized as follows: The second section discusses the foreseeability rule in contract law. The third section examines the way in which the *Hadley* rule could protect the plaintiff's expectation interest in the middleman economy. The fourth section then carries the analysis over to the conceptual emergence of the mitigation doctrine and the specific performance remedy. The fifth section discusses the relationship between contract law, intangible property rights, and merchant capital. The sixth section concludes the chapter.

The Foreseeability Rule in Contract Law

The famous 1854 English contract case, *Hadley v. Baxendale*,[1] has long been recognized as a landmark decision in the history of English contract law.

This chapter was originally published in the *Journal of Legal Studies* 16, no. 2 (June 1987): 455–70. I gratefully acknowledge the permission of the journal's publisher, The University of Chicago Press, to republish the paper. © 1987 by The University of Chicago. All rights reserved.

The author is a National Fellow at Hoover Institution, Stanford University and Associate Professor of Economics, York University. I have benefited from comments on earlier drafts of this paper from Professors James M. Buchanan, Robert D. Cooter, Lawrence M. Friedman, Victor P. Goldberg, Jeffrey MacIntosh, Anthony I. Ogus, T. Nicolaus Tideman, Michael Trebilcock, Kenneth Vogel, Barry Weingast, Donald Wittman, Richard O. Zerbe, and participants at the Law and Economics Workshop, Center for Economic Analysis of Property Rights, University of Western Ontario, and at the Law and Economics Seminar, Stanford Law School.

1. 9 Exch. 341, 156 Eng. Rep. 145 (1854). The case involved a mill owner—the

Before that decision was handed down, the law of contract damages was in its infant state, so that the jury was given wide discretion in the choice of damage level. Contract damages were better described as matters of fact rather than as matters of law, so that the operation of the contract system as a whole was covered with a shield of uncertainty that made any evaluation of its operation difficult to achieve. With *Hadley*, a general principle, often loosely described as one of foreseeability was crystallized.

The foreseeability rule was subsequently refined and restated by Lord Asquith and came to be known as the "two rules" of *Hadley v. Baxendale:*

> In cases of breach of contract the aggrieved party is only entitled to recover such part of the loss actually resulting as was at the time of the contract reasonably foreseeable as liable to result from the breach . . .
>
> What was at the time reasonably so foreseeable depends on the knowledge then possessed by the parties, or, at all events, by the party who later commits the breach. . . .
>
> For this purpose, knowledge "possessed" is of two kinds—one imputed, the other actual.[2]

If a person, as a "reasonable man," can foresee from the imputed knowledge that he possesses of the general nature and character of the business of his contracting partner that damages will flow naturally from his breach, then the "first rule" of *Hadley v. Baxendale* would make such losses recoverable by the plaintiff. If knowledge is actually communicated by the plaintiff to the defendant at the time the contract is being negotiated of the special circumstances in which damages would flow from a breach, then the "second rule" of *Hadley v. Baxendale* would make additional or "consequential" damages also recoverable by the plaintiff. The two *Hadley v. Baxendale* rules actually constitute a single foreseeability rule with two tests of foreseeability.

Is the foreseeability rule of *Hadley v. Baxendale* efficient? Barton (1972, 296) concluded that the rule is efficient "in its reliance upon notice and information" and thus transmits information with respect to the magnitude of the risk to be transferred. Posner (1977, chap. 4) also concluded that the rule is efficient because it increases the chances of the potential contract-breaking

---

plaintiff—who entered into a contract with a common carrier, the defendant, to transport a broken crankshaft to engineers in Greenwich as a pattern for a new shaft. The defendant breached the contract by delaying the transportation of the crankshaft, and as a result the mill could not operate for several days. The plaintiff claimed £300 damages for lost profits due to the breach. The court, in a landmark ruling, held that the plaintiff's lost profits were not recoverable, as they were not foreseeable by the defendant. In other words, the defendant is liable only for the foreseeable consequences of a breach.

2. *Victoria Laundry (Windsor) Ltd. v. Newman Indus. Ltd.* 2 K.B. 528, 529 (1949).

party undertaking appropriate precautions to protect himself. Bishop (1983) in turn has noted the importance of the rule in insuring that the contract parties communicate to each other any special losses that they might suffer consequent upon breach. Danzig (1975, 259) analyzed the efficiency implications of the rule set in the specific institutional-historical setting of mid-nineteenth-century England: "Arising squarely in the middle of the 'industrial revolution' and directly in the midst of the 'Great Boom' of 1842–1874, *Hadley v. Baxendale* was a product of these times." From a historical point of view, the rule emerged in response to the increased complexity of the economy of mid-nineteenth-century England, which was undergoing rapid industrialization and capital accumulation.[3] Danzig (1975, 282) also came to the same conclusion regarding the societal gain from the rule, i.e., the rule improved "the seller's calculation about whether to breach in this situation." In short, the rule permits potential contract-breakers to engage in efficient breach. On the other hand, Perloff came to a very different conclusion from that of Barton. Perloff (1981, 39) argued that "in a risk-neutral world, virtually any rule, including foreseeability, will be efficient, whereas none of the [four] rules considered here guarantees efficiency in a world of risk-averse people."

In one sense the desirability of the *Hadley* rule is difficult to assess given that it is a default provision that applies presumably to the full range of contractual situations.** But assessing the desirability of the *Hadley* rule in protecting traders' expectation interest in the context of a middleman economy is much simpler, as will be shown below.**

Contract Law and the Protection of the "Expectation Interest": Special Features of the Middleman Economy

Markets with middlemen or merchants are different from other markets in three essential aspects. First, the presence of middlemen in an exchange economy radically transforms the structure of exchange relations. Instead of a single market composed of producers and ultimate consumers, there exist two interrelated markets: one consisting of producers and middlemen, the other of middlemen and final consumers. The middleman economy cannot be decomposed into lone pairs of traders. The contractual relations between traders in middlemen markets are relational contracts because of the recurrent process of profit making by merchants.

Second, markets with middlemen are characterized by informational asymmetry in the producer-middleman market and the middleman–final con-

---

3. There may be some difficulty in relating the *Hadley v. Baxendale* rule specifically to mid-nineteenth-century industrial developments since French law had adopted a similar rule in the Napoleonic Code (1804).

sumer market: producer-sellers know only of the prices in their own market and not of the prices in the resale (second) market, while final consumers know of prices in the second market and not of prices in the first market. Only the middleman possesses information on prices in both markets because, in his role or identity as the middleman, he is both a buyer (in the first market) and a seller (in the second market). Price information flowing between the two markets is the result of entrepreneurial activities of middlemen.

Third, the middleman must engage in a sequence of two bilateral transactions in order to realize his profits; he must first buy goods from the producer located in the first market before he can resell the same goods to ultimate consumers located in the second market. The need to engage in a sequence of transactions necessarily introduces a temporal dimension into the exchange process in a middleman economy. Breach of contract becomes a possibility in an exchange economy in which traders engage in executory contracts rather than spot contracts. Controlling the potential loss of profit expectations makes it important for traders to establish "rules of the game" via a public choice process.

Public Choice of Pareto-Optimal "Rules of the Game"

Which Pareto-optimal rules of the game will be predicted to emerge from public choice by traders in the middleman economy? The choice of rules will depend on whether the goods contracted for are fungible goods that have a ready market or whether they are "unique" goods. Let us use the A-B-C marketing network developed in earlier chapters, where B is the profit-making middleman.

Fungible Goods: The Mitigation Doctrine

The two traders, A and B, can enter into a constitutional social contract to choose between a rule that protects the reliance interest or the expectation interest.[4]

A Rule That Protects the Plaintiff's Reliance Interest

Under this rule, B will be compensated for the reliance costs, which will restore him to his initial no-trade position vis-à-vis trader C. However, under this rule, B has wasted his time in engaging in entrepreneurship since his lost profits are not compensated. A rule that protects plaintiff's reliance interest

---

4. **There are three interests that contract law can protect: (1) the restitution interest, (2) the reliance interest, and (3) the expectation interest. In this chapter, we assume no restitution interest is involved because B did not pay for A's goods at the time of contracting. For a discussion of the three interests that contract law can protect, see Fuller and Perdue 1936.

and not his expectation interest compensates a plaintiff for his out-of-pocket transaction costs but not for the costs of foregone profits. These are very different kinds of costs and have very different implications for entrepreneurship, as noted in chapter 2. Under a rule that protects only plaintiff's reliance interests, but not expectation interests, the high transaction costs involved in private protection of traders' profit expectations may so squeeze profit margins that it is no longer profitable for middlemen to stay in markets, thus causing market failure.

A Rule That Protects Plaintiff's Expectation Interest

Under this rule, B recovers not only his investment expenditures on searching for the final consumer (that is, not only reliance costs), but also his profit expectations.[5] This will restore B to a position as if A has honored her contract to B. From the point of view of B, this rule is efficient because A is providing insurance to B, insuring B against risks of breach since his net profit expectations will be protected whether or not A chooses to breach her contract. Therefore, from the point of view of B, a rule that protects the plaintiff's expectation interest internalizes exchange externalities and hence facilitates entrepreneurship.

But such a rule will only emerge if there is mutuality of interest. From the point of A, however, a rule that protects the plaintiff's expectation interest may be inefficient because it might prevent A from engaging in efficient breach (that is, A can compensate B for his lost profits and still can make herself better off by recontracting with X). For A to engage in an efficient breach, A must be able to foresee, at the time X comes along to offer her a higher price, for example, $110 for the goods which A sold to B for $100: (1) that if she breaches the contract with B, the lost profits suffered by B are caused solely by her breach and (2) the magnitude of B's lost profits. Because of the recurrent nature of the transactions between A and B, and because A knows the identity of B as the profit-seeking middleman who buys in order to resell for profit, A can perfectly foresee that her breach will cause B to lose profits. Hence the first rule of *Hadley v. Baxendale* is embedded in the contractual relations between traders in a middleman economy. My theory of contract law can thus throw light on the so-called middleman exception to the foreseeability rule of *Hadley v. Baxendale*, which is found in comment 6 of the UCC section 2-715 (1976):

> In the case of sale of wares to one in the business of reselling them, resale is one of the requirements of which the seller has reason to know within the meaning of subsection 2(a). Subsection 2(a) of section 2-715

---

5. For a fuller discussion of the measure of money damages for buyers and sellers damages, see Farnsworth 1982, 863–64. See also Farnsworth 1970.

reads: Consequential damages resulting from the seller's breach includes any loss resulting from general or particular requirements and needs of which the seller at the time of contracting had reason to know and which could not reasonably be prevented by cover or otherwise.

That is to say, under the UCC, a middleman who is the victim of a seller's breach is entitled to recover lost profits damages without proof of foreseeability beyond his identity as middleman. A good example is the case of *Jennings v. Lamb*, 201 Tenn. 1, 296 S.W.2d 828 (1956). Plaintiff (a lumber middleman) entered into a contract with defendant for the purchase of timber for resale. Before plaintiff sold the lumber, which had not yet been delivered by defendant, defendant breached the contract by selling the lumber to someone else. Plaintiff was unable to cover by going into the market to replace the lumber because of a scarcity of supply. The court, satisfied that the plaintiff could have sold all the lumber purchased from the seller, awarded plaintiff lost profits on the basis of the difference between the contract price of lumber and the price at which plaintiff could have resold them. Plaintiff did not have to prove foreseeability in order to recover lost profits since the seller knew the identity of the plaintiff as a lumber-dealer who bought in order to resell for profits.[6]

However, A cannot foresee the exact magnitude of B's profit losses and hence she cannot engage in efficient breach. This is due to the information asymmetry that is a characteristic of the producer-middleman markets discussed earlier: unlike middleman B, A knows only of prices in her own market and not of prices of the goods in the resale market. Hence A has no way of estimating the size of B's lost profits.

If A insists that B, in order to obtain insurance from A, must choose a rule that protects the plaintiff's expectation interest, subject to the second rule of *Hadley v. Baxendale* (that is, B must communicate to A the size of his lost profits at the time they negotiate the contract), B is not likely to agree on such a rule. This is because such a rule, which requires B to disclose information on the size of his profit losses, is likely to create both a free-rider problem and an incentive problem that together will almost certainly discourage middleman-entrepreneurship.

An essential element of middleman-entrepreneurship is the possession of information of price differentials in different markets, as noted earlier. Such price information may be deliberately acquired because of superior ability of middlemen to perceive profitable opportunities for arbitrage.[7] The middleman-

---

6. For a discussion of the so-called middleman exception to the foreseeability doctrine, see Dunn 1978, chapter 2, 48–52.

7. Kronman (1980) emphasizes the importance of deliberate search for information, whereas Kirzner (1973) emphasizes entrepreneurial ability to perceive profitable opportunities.

entrepreneur, by buying goods at a lower price in one market and reselling the same goods at a higher price in another market, has according to Kirzner's (1973) theory of entrepreneurship, thereby created a new value (profit opportunity) that had not hitherto been discovered. Thus, the entrepreneur is entitled to appropriate this new value for himself according to the "finders-keepers ethic" (Kirzner 1979, 212–13). Only by assigning to B—the trader with superior access to information on price differentials—a property right in information and also a property right in the newly created value (profit opportunity) will B have the incentive to engage in profit-seeking activities. Imposing the second rule of *Hadley v. Baxendale,* as an adjunct to the rule that protects the plaintiff's expectation interest, is tantamount to a requirement that the private benefit of information on price differentials be shared with A at zero cost to A. If B is to provide information as a public good to A, the free-rider problem associated with supplying of public goods arises. Middleman B will have no incentive to invest in information that is essential for entrepreneurship. In addition, if A is able to appropriate B's information on price differentials costlessly, this possibility may give rise to an incentive problem. Producer A, realizing the magnitude of profits to be made from reselling her goods, may have the incentive not to enter into a contract with B. Producer A may instead decide to integrate forward into marketing, bypassing the middleman and selling her goods directly to final consumers if she perceives that the profits from doing so outweigh the costs of searching for final consumers and other marketing costs that are borne by middlemen.[8] Because of the free-rider problem and the incentive problem there is therefore no incentive for B to communicate to A the size of his future possible lost profits at the time that A and B are negotiating their contract. Therefore, a rule that protects the plaintiff's expectation interest, subject to the second rule of *Hadley v. Baxendale,* will not emerge by public choice.

A Rule That Protects the Plaintiff's Expectation Interest
Subject to the Mitigation Doctrine

Fortunately, a damage rule does exist that protects the plaintiff's expectation interest but does not require the plaintiff to disclose information regarding the amounts of the profits or losses. Such a rule requires B to mitigate damages. Under this rule, B must (1) take all reasonable actions to reduce damages (to mitigate) and (2) refrain from taking action to increase damages (to avoid harm). The mitigation doctrine in fact consists of two doctrines: the mitigation doctrine and the avoidable-harm doctrine. The effect of the mitigation doctrine is to allow the defendant, A, to quantify objectively the magni-

---

8. There are, of course, advantages from specialization, such that producers may prefer to leave the marketing of goods to merchants even if producers know of the size of profits middlemen earn from taking over the marketing function of producers.

tude of B's lost profits, while eliminating the free-rider problem and the incentive problem. For goods that are fungible (that is, easily replaceable) and hence have a ready market, the plaintiff (B) must take reasonable steps to mitigate his losses by going into the (first) market to "cover"[9] (that is, to buy an equivalent quantity and quality of goods to replace the goods not delivered). By buying from another producer at the time of A's breach, and delivering the goods to C, B is not made worse off by A's breach if the market price remains unchanged from the contract price.[10] If the spot price for the goods rises to $107, A must compensate B by the difference in contract price and the market price (that is, $7), to make B whole. The use of the contract price-market price damage rule for fungible goods performs three useful functions. The rule (1) restores the plaintiff to a position as if A has honored the contract; (2) protects the plaintiff's private property in information on price differentials;[11] and (3) allows the potential contract-breacher to engage in efficient breach. At the time that X appears on the scene to offer A a higher price of $110 for her goods, A can foresee that this breach of contract with B will cause B to incur lost profits. Producer A can also perfectly foresee, by the use of the contract price-market price formula, the magnitude of the lost profits since she has information on prices in her own market at the time of her breach. Thus A can breach her contract with B, compensate B for $7 in lost profits and still make herself better off by $3 in recontracting with X. The value of the contract price-market price damage rule to the potential contract breaker is that he has the right to breach contracts, provided he pays compensation to the victim for the difference between the contract price and the market price of the goods at the time of breach. The right to breach is a valuable right because A can choose between honoring or breaking contracts in response to benefit-costs calculations. In this sense, A can be viewed as buying an option.[12] If A delivers the goods, A receives the contract price of $100 from B. If A breaches, then she pays $7, the price of the breach option.[13]

---

9. To "cover" means to make a substitute transaction in the market in which the offending party breaches the contract. The word "cover" first appears in the UCC 2-712(1).

10. I am assuming that there are no "incidental damages" (that is, the additional cost spent to cover). When incidental damages are positive, the court allows plaintiff to recover incidental damages. See UCC 2-715(1).

11. It may be noted that constraining the free rider is not an unmixed blessing. It could be argued that, with market information being protected, individuals will have an incentive to oversearch for special information. I owe this insight to Victor P. Goldberg (personal communication).

12. I owe this idea to Stuart Turnbull (personal communication). See also Goldberg 1984.

13. Thus far the analysis has focused on the incentive effects on the breaching promisor. However, there is also a problem concerning the incentive effects for reliance by the promisee. Specifically, if greater reliance by the promisee increases the damages that he will receive in the

Unique Goods: Specific Performance

Suppose that the executory contract entered between A and B is the same as the earlier example, with the exception that the good involved is a unique good (for example, a rare work of art) for which there are no close substitutes. Suppose that B possesses superior entrepreneurial ability to perceive profitable opportunities for resale of the unique good. This entrepreneurial ability enables B to sell forward the good, purchased for $100, to a final consumer who is willing to pay $300 for the good upon delivery. Assume that the reliance cost in this example is $10. If A breaches the contract to deliver the good, B's gross profit expectation of $200 is disappointed. Because of the potential for a dealer in unique goods to suffer large losses due to the seller's breach, which Pareto-optimal rule would A and B agree on at the time of contract formation that would protect their respective expectation interests?

Middlemen B would be interested in a rule that entitled him to lost profits, that is, a rule that would award him money damages based on the difference between the contract price and the price obtained from a resale. As in the fungible-good case, A will not agree to such a rule unless B is willing to disclose information on the size of the lost profits, since A does not possess information on the resale price of the unique good. Because of the lucrative gain arising from B's superior entrepreneurial ability, B, who is entitled to appropriate the gain for himself according to the finders-keepers ethic, has even less incentive than a dealer in fungible goods to reveal such information to A since the free-rider problem and the incentive problem are exacerbated in the case of unique goods.[14] Hence B would have little incentive to agree to include a liquidated damage clause that stipulates a fixed amount of damages payable if A breaches.[15]

Without B disclosing information on the size of lost profits, A cannot

---

event of breach, then he will tend to over-rely. One way to prevent over-reliance is to impose a duty to mitigate. Another way is to make damages invariant with respect to reliance. Since the *Hadley v. Baxendale* doctrine makes damages invariant with respect to reliance, its effect is to reduce the incentive to over-rely. I owe this insight to Robert Cooter (personal communication). Cooter (1985) analyzes the reliance problem at length in his paper.

14. Had A known that the unique good could be sold to someone else at a much higher price, she would not have sold it to B at a much lower price.

15. There is some empirical evidence for this insight. Yorio (1982) interviewed seven lawyers who together have represented more than twenty rare art dealers in New York City. One lawyer recounted a case in which the seller asked for a liquidated-damage clause to guard against a breach by the buyer. The buyer also wanted such a clause. Both agreed to liquidated-damage clauses in lieu of any other remedies, including specific performance. Yorio said that the case was unique.

Note that courts are generally suspicious of liquidated-damage clauses. For discussions as to why, see Clarkson, Miller, and Muris 1978.

engage in an efficient breach ex ante even if such breaches are possible. If A breaches, A may well find herself engaging in an inefficient breach. That is, A may find herself worse off by breaching the contract with B and recontracting with X: A must subtract her gain of $10 from the $200 that A must pay to B to compensate for B's lost profits and reliance costs.

For unique goods it may well be the case that breach of contract is rarely efficient in a situation where A has access to a fairly competitive market of resellers who possess superior information in seizing profit opportunities for themselves. Under these circumstances, A may either honor the contract or choose specific performance remedy to protect traders' expectation interests. Thus a shift from a liability rule to a property rule (in this case, a specific performance remedy) would be Pareto optimal for both traders in the case of unique goods. Thus the conceptual emergence of the specific performance remedy may be seen as a response to the free-rider problem from the point of view of B and as a response to the problem of inefficient breach from the point of view of A.

To this point, I have analyzed the constitutional choice of the Pareto-optimal contract rule in terms of a three-trader economy. In such a three-person exchange economy, the decision-making costs of getting together to agree on the Pareto-optimal rule would be low; the rule would be predicted to emerge by unanimous consent. In markets with many middlemen, an n-person economy, the decision-making costs would increase as the size of the group that is necessary to secure unanimous agreement increases. The high decision-making costs of securing unanimous consent among numerous traders, however, are counterbalanced by the homogeneity of shared interest and expectations of members of the middleman group. In addition, if middlemen belong to the same ethnic group (for example, Jews in medieval Europe, Chinese middlemen in Southeast Asia), the ethics of mutual aid embedded in the ethnically homogeneous middleman group will further reduce decision-making costs. Thus in a close-knit, homogeneous middleman group, the Pareto-efficient contract rule would be predicted to emerge among merchants by unanimous or close-to-unanimous agreement. In the self-government of the merchant group, the emergence of the rules of the game provides the constitutional framework for regulating the contractual relations among merchants. Historically, the set of rules merchants created to regulate the relations among merchants both within and across national boundaries was embodied in the Law Merchant. By late eighteenth century in England, Lord Mansfield declared that the traders' law was not a special or unusual customary law but would be applied by all of His Majesty's judges: "The Law Merchant is the law of the land" (Tigar and Levy 1977, 50). Thus, by the late eighteenth century, the Law Merchant had begun to evolve into a modern law of contract.

This process of "double institutionalization of norms" (Bohanan 1968) may be interpreted as a method of economizing on decision-making costs of establishing legal norms of contractual behavior.

Contract Law, Intangible Property Rights, and Merchant Capital

The emergence of the Law Merchant/contract law in an exchange economy constitutes a Pareto-superior move in three ways. First, by legally protecting traders' profit expectations, all potentially Pareto-relevant exchange externalities are internalized. The internalization of negative externalities transmutes traders' reasonable expectations of future profits into intangible assets that traders can appropriate for themselves as realized profits, as noted in chapter 2. As Fuller and Perdue (1936, 20–21) state it:

> The essence of a credit economy lies in the fact that it tends to eliminate the distinction between present and future (promised) goods. Expectations of future values become, for purposes of trade, present values. In a society in which credit has become a significant and pervasive institution, it is inevitable that the expectancy created by an enforceable promise should be regarded as a kind of property, and breach of the promise as an injury to that property. In such a society, the breach of a promise works an "actual" diminution of the promisee's assets.

Or, as Atiyah (1979, 429) puts it:

> The "loss" of an expectation, which is only a loss in an extended sense of the term, came to be seen as a real loss, a present loss. A plaintiff with an egg was, in short, entitled to be treated as though he had a chicken.

In the context of the mercantile economy in which merchants are engaged in the recurrent process of buying and reselling for profit, the "chicken" at the end of the cycle is, in fact, merchant-capital. Second, legal protection of traders' expectation interest make it possible for some of the scarce resources used for private protection of contracts to be channeled into trade. Third, contract law, by imposing liability for damage on the contract breaker, standardizes contractual behavior, thus making it possible for new markets to appear, as strangers enter into impersonal legally binding relations across kinship, ethnic, or tribal boundaries regardless of the status of contracting parties. The progress of society, Sir Henry Maine (1861) wrote, is "from Status to Contract."

Conclusions

The chapter revisits *Hadley v. Baxendale,* set in the institutional context of an expanding middleman economy, from a PR-PC perspective and arrives at new insights regarding the "middleman exception" in the UCC, and the conceptual origins of the mitigation doctrine and the specific performance remedy in contract law. With respect to the conceptual emergence of the mitigation doctrine, the central argument of the chapter is that contract law is designed in such a way that the middleman-entrepreneur is awarded expectation damages without being forced to divulge to his suppliers the price at which he can resell. This fact creates tension with the doctrine that the supplier's liability for breach is limited by foreseeability. We argue that the tension can be resolved by the mitigation doctrine for fungible goods and by the specific performance remedy for unique goods.

REFERENCES

Atiyah, P. S. 1979. *The Rise and Fall of Freedom of Contract.* Oxford: Clarendon Press.
Barton, John H. 1972. "The Economic Basis of Damages for Breach of Contract." *Journal of Legal Studies* 1:277–304.
Bishop, William. 1983. "The Contract-Tort Boundary and the Economics of Insurance." *Journal of Legal Studies* 12:241–66.
Bohanan, Paul. 1968. "Law and Legal Institutions." *International Encyclopedia of the Social Sciences* 9:73–78.
Clarkson, Kenneth, Leroy Miller, and Timothy Muris. 1978. "Liquidated Damages v. Penalties: Sense or Nonsense?" *Wisconsin Law Review*: 351–90.
Cooter, Robert D. 1985. "Unity in Tort, Contract, and Property: The Model of Precaution." *California Law Review* 73:1–51.
Danzig, Richard. 1975. "Hadley V. Baxendale: A Study of Industrialization of the Law." *Journal of Legal Studies* 4:249–84.
Dunn, Robert L. 1978. *Recovery of Damages for Lost Profits.* Tiburon, Calif.: Law Press Corp.
Farnsworth, E. Allan. 1970. "Legal Remedies for Breach of Contract." *Columbia Law Review* 70:1145–1216.
———. 1982. *Contracts.* Boston: Little, Brown & Company.
Fuller, Lon L., and William R. Perdue. 1936. "The Reliance Interest in Contract Damages." *Yale Law Journal* 46:52–98.
Goldberg, Victor P. 1984. "An Economic Analysis of the Lost-Volume Retail Seller." *Southern California Law Review* 57:283–97.
Kirzner, Israel M. 1973. *Competition and Entrepreneurship.* Chicago: The University of Chicago Press.

————. 1979. *Perception, Opportunity, and Profit: Studies in the Theory of Entrepreneurship.* Chicago: The University of Chicago Press.

Kronman, Anthony. 1980. "Contract Law and Distributive Justice." *Yale Law Journal* 89:472–511.

Maine, Henry. 1861. *Ancient Law.* London: J. Murray.

Perloff, Jeffrey M. 1981. "Breach of Contract and the Foreseeability Doctrine of Hadley v. Baxendale." *Journal of Legal Studies* 10:39–61.

Posner, Richard H. [1977] 1985. *Economic Analysis of Law.* Boston: Little, Brown.

Tigar, Michael E., and Madeleine R. Levy. 1977. *Law and the Rise of Capitalism.* New York: Monthly Review Press.

Yorio, Edward. 1982. "In Defense of Money Damages for Breach of Contract." *Columbia Law Review* 82:1365–1424.

Part 3
Ethnic Trading Networks

CHAPTER 5

A Theory of the Ethnically Homogeneous Middleman Group: An Institutional Alternative to Contract Law

This chapter addresses the theoretical question: How do traders cope with the problem of contract uncertainty in an environment where the legal framework is nonexistent or poorly developed? The work by anthropologists such as Alice Dewey (1962), in reference to Chinese traders in Java, and Cyril Belshaw (1965), in reference to traders in "traditional" markets suggests that traders *personalize* or *particularize* exchange relations as a way of coping with contract uncertainty.

Questionnaire surveys of and interviews with Chinese middlemen engaged in the marketing of smallholders' rubber in Singapore and West Malaysia in 1969 revealed that (a) the marketing of smallholders' rubber—through the various levels of the vertical marketing structure—was dominated by a middleman group with a tightly knit kinship structure from the Hokkien-Chinese ethnic group; (b) that mutual trust and mutual aid formed the basis for the particularization of exchange relations among Chinese middlemen; and (c) that within the Chinese economy transactions among middlemen were based on credit, while Chinese middlemen used cash transactions with indigenous smallholders to reduce contract uncertainty.

The fieldwork, the subsequent analysis of data, and the findings thus revealed that Chinese middlemen were not just a random collection of Chinese traders. Rather, they were linked together in complex networks of particularistic exchange relations to form an EHMG. But the real significance of the visible, surface structure of the EHMG lies in its underlying deep structure: the invisible codes of ethics, embedded in the personalized exchange relations among the members of the EHMG, which function as constraints against

This article was originally published in the *Journal of Legal Studies* 10, no. 2 (June, 1981): 349–62. I wish to thank the journal's publisher, The University of Chicago Press, for permission to reprint the article. © 1981 by The University of Chicago. All rights reserved.

This is a revised, shorter version of the Institute of Policy Analysis Working Paper No. 7924, Oct. 1979. I am indebted to Alan Abouchar, Albert Breton, Thomas E. Borcherding, James M. Buchanan, Jack Carr, John Dales, Louis De Alessi, and Allan Hynes for helpful comments on a previous draft. I also wish to thank Robert McKay and Francis X. Tannian for their comments on an early version presented at the Public Choice Society meetings, April 15–17, 1976, Roanoke, Virginia. Finally, thanks are due to Richard A. Posner and an anonymous referee for suggestions for improving this chapter.

breach of contract and hence facilitate exchange among Chinese middlemen. The EHMG thus reveals itself to be a low cost clublike institutional arrangement, serving as an alternative to contract law and the vertically integrated firm, which emerged to economize on contract enforcement and information costs in an environment where the legal infrastructure was not well developed.

Two studies confirm my findings. Clifford Geertz (1978) rationalizes the institutional peculiarities of the bazaar economy (e.g., "clientalization," the pairing off of buyers and sellers in recurrent transactions) in terms of the bazaar's function in reducing information costs under contract uncertainty. Richard Posner (1980, 26), in his insightful paper on institutions of primitive societies, discusses alternative responses for coping with the costliness of contract uncertainty:

> Another response to market transaction costs is the transformation of an arms-length contract relationship into an intimate status relationship. In some primitive societies if you trade repeatedly with the same man he becomes your blood brother and you owe him the same duty of generous and fair dealing that you would owe a kinsman. This "barter friendship" resembles the pairing of buyers and sellers in bazaars that Geertz noted. It is a way of bringing reciprocity into the exchange process and thereby increasing the likelihood that promises will be honored despite the absence of a public enforcement authority.

Independent of the work of Geertz and Posner, this chapter develops a theory of the EHMG, using a PR-PC approach and drawing on the economics of signaling. The second section of the paper develops a theory of the emergence of the EHMG as a result of individual choices, on the part of many interdependent traders, to join a network of personalistic exchange relationships. The third section develops a theory of codes of ethics, embedded in kinship/ethnic relations, as a functional equivalent to the law of contracts. The fourth section develops a theory of the EHMG as an efficient institutional arrangement for economizing on information costs in an environment characterized by imperfect information. The concluding section will suggest some implications of our theory for further research.

A Theory of the Formation of the Ethically Homogenous Middleman Group: An Analysis of Particularistic Exchange under Contract Uncertainty

Standard theories of exchange (Edgeworth and Walrasian models) depict competitive trade as an impersonal process of exchange. This is because these theories refer to a zero transaction costs economy with no contract uncertainty. In such an economy, there is no need to identify trading partners nor any reason for the institution of contract law since trading partners can be regarded as homogeneous with respect to contract behavior. Thus, impersonal market forces alone determine the pairing of buyers and sellers. Under conditions of contract uncertainty with positive transactions costs, on the other hand, a rational trader will not indiscriminately enter into impersonal exchange relations with anonymous traders. At any particular point in time, an individual is embedded in a "social structure"[1] with rules of the game that serve to constrain his behavior. Hence, a rational trader will enter into particularistic exchange relations with traders bound by institutional constraints whom he knows to be trustworthy and reliable in honoring contracts.

In order to choose a particularistic network of trading partners that will minimize the out-of-pocket costs of protection of contracts, a rational trader will equip himself with a "calculus of relations." Such a calculus allows the trader to rank all traders in a market according to a small number of categories corresponding to different "grades" of traders, in descending order of trustworthiness.[2] Consider the system of discriminatory rankings established by a typical Hokkien trader (call him "Ego") as shown in table 1.

The system of discriminatory rankings of traders can be represented by the use of a von Thünen series of concentric circles to depict differences in grades of trading partners, with the best grade located at the center. Assume smooth differences in the grades of trading partners up to the first ethnic boundary separating Hokkiens from non-Hokkiens; thereafter assume a significant change in the grade of partners after crossing the Hokkien-Chinese boundary and an abrupt change as the major ethnic boundary is crossed. See figure 3. Assume that Ego, equipped with this subjective calculus of relations, begins his choice of a least-cost network of trading partners. The cost implications of five homogeneous trading networks of size *N*, each composed of a different grade of traders, are illustrated in figure 4. Note that each transactions costs curve rises as the size of the trading network increases. The rising transaction cost curve is due to the presence of two kinds of costs:

1. Coordination costs of interdependent traders rise as the network increases in size, because the coordination costs of two isolated pairs of traders are lower than the coordination costs of two pairs of traders connected in a network. If we start from two traders at point *a*, the

---

1. "Social structure" is a key concept used by sociologists to describe the pattern of recurrent and regularized interaction among two or more persons, hence implying the existence of norms for regulating behavior. See, for example, Blau 1975.

2. For a theory of clubs that explicitly incorporates discrimination in the choice of consumption-sharing partners, see Tollison (1972). Tollison's theory is an extension of Buchanan's (1965) theory of clubs.

TABLE 1.   Ranking of Traders

Categories of Social Relations	Grades/Ranking
Insiders	
Near kinsmen from family	1
Distant kinsmen from extended family	2
Clansmen	3
Fellow-villagers from China	4
Fellow-Hokkiens	5
Outsiders	
Non-Hokkiens (Teochews, Cantonese, etc.)	6
Non-Chinese (Malays, Europeans, etc.)	7

movement will not be from a to b on the horizontal-transaction cost curve T_1 as the size of the network increases from two to four traders. Rather, the movement is from a to b' on the rising transaction cost curve T_1'.

2. Costs of contract enforcement rise as the number of interdependent

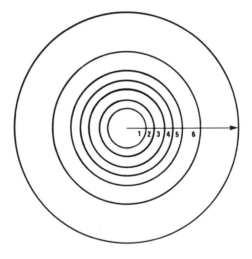

1. **Near kinsmen from family**
2. **Distant kinsmen from extended family**
3. **Clansmen**
4. **Fellow-villagers**
5. **Fellow-Hokkiens**
6. **non-Hokkiens**
7. **non- Chinese**

Fig. 3.   Von Thünen concentric circles to depict seven grades of trading partners.

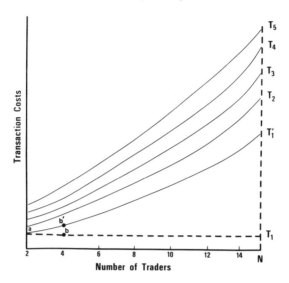

T'_1 - Trading network composed of near kinsmen
T_2 - Trading network composed of distant kinsmen
T_3 - Trading network composed of clansmen
T_4 - Trading network composed of fellow-villagers
T_5 - Trading network composed of Hokkiens

Fig. 4.   Cost implications of five homogeneous trading networks composed of different grades of traders

traders in the trading network increases. As a trading network increases in size, it is increasingly vulnerable to the antisocial behavior of even one trader who, in breaking his contract, may cause "chain reaction" effects of a breach, as noted in chapter 3.

Faced with five trading networks of size N, a rational trader will choose the least-cost trading network, $T_1(n)$ since $T_5(n) > T_4(n)$ . . . $T_1(n)$. With a larger network of trading partners, with fixed group size K, Ego will choose all his trading partners from category 1 before moving outward to the next category. As Ego moves outward from the center, members of his trading network or "club" will be chosen from ever-widening circles with the result that "club" members become increasingly more heterogeneous as more than one grade of trading partners are included. The transaction-cost implications of two trading networks, T_1 and T_2, for a fixed group size K, each with a different "mix" of trading partners, are illustrated in figure 5. T_1 is drawn with a discontinuity at Y to denote that beyond Y, costs rise abruptly as trading partners are chosen from a different ethnic group (outsiders). Such a discon-

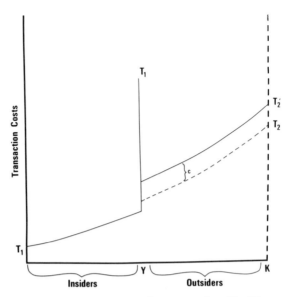

Fig. 5. Cost implications of two trading networks with differences in the "mix" of trading partners

tinuity manifests itself by Ego's choice of a well-defined EHMG, with membership size Y. The relevant transaction-costs curve for the homogeneous network is T_1, which has a sharp kink at the group boundary. For transactions outside the ethnic boundary, Ego resorts to the use of cash to reduce contract-enforcement costs to zero. Were there no opportunity costs in using cash, the relevant transaction-cost curve for the heterogeneous trading network with membership size K would be T_2. But since there are opportunity costs associated with the use of cash transactions, the relevant transaction curve is T_2' which exhibits a discontinuity at Y. The vertical distance, C, measures the opportunity costs incurred by Ego in using cash transactions with outsiders. For some traders, T_2' is the relevant transaction-cost curve associated with a heterogeneous trading network. This would involve a situation where the Chinese middleman, in his role as village dealer, has to enter into exchange relations with a large number of smallholders belonging to a different ethnic group. If the Chinese middleman refuses to trade with "outsiders," he must incur the opportunity costs of exclusion, the costs of foregone profits. So long as the opportunity costs of excluding outsiders from trade exceed transaction costs, a trader has an incentive to cross ethnic boundaries to incorporate outsiders into his trading network. The importance of Ego's *subjective* calculus of relations in determining the *objective* optimal "mix" of trading partners therefore depends upon the number of members in the constituent concentric circles, the degree of heterogeneity of the population, and a balancing off, at the margin, between transaction costs of including outsiders and the opportunity costs of exclusion of outsiders. The outcome of Ego's discriminatory choice of trading partners is the formation of a particularistic trading network comprised of members who share the same (Confucian) code of ethics. Given a nondecomposable middleman economy, the structural effect of many individual Chinese middlemen's discriminatory choice is the formation of an EHMG.[3]

Code of Ethics as the Functional Equivalent of the Law Merchant or Law of Contracts

Under conditions of contract uncertainty, kinship/ethnic status embodying the Confucian ethics is a valuable intangible asset for a potential trading partner because of the "priority rights" Ego confers upon his trading partner; kinship/ethnic status is an essential input in the middleman's transaction technology. But the costs of obtaining his valuable input is zero for the trading partner possessing a kinship/ethnic status. Kinship or ethnic status is not a "right" that can be purchased by those who do not possess the requisite status.[4] Status is acquired by virtue of a person being born into a particular kinship/ethnic group. Kinship/ethnic rights may therefore be regarded as a species of "status rights" (Dales 1972), the set of rights lying between the subset of private property and common property rights. These rights are equivalent to rights of citizenship, including preferential access to job opportunities, but are accessible only to subsets of the total population.

Since status rights, as an essential input, are nontransferable and nonmarketable by nature—it is a human capital (*in personam*) assignment—the opportunity sets of traders are *not* the same in markets dominated by a particular kinship/ethnic group. Only those "insiders" who can marshal all the essential inputs, including kinship/ethnic status, can become middleman. The "outsiders," being de facto without status rights, are excluded from middleman roles because they cannot obtain an essential nonmarketable input necessary for middleman-entrepreneurship under conditions of contract uncertainty. If industry conditions are favorable for expansion of middlemen activities, the value of status rights as an entry ticket into personalistic markets rises. Thus under conditions of contract uncertainty, "insiders" have a differential advantage vis-à-vis outsiders in appropriating new middleman roles for themselves.

---

3. Ego (v_1) chooses his trading partners, v_2 and v_3, on a kinship or ethnic basis; v_2 and v_3, in turn, choose their trading partners on the same particularistic basis; then the result is the emergence of an EHMG.

4. But some of these rights may be acquired by marriage or conversion.

To neutralize somewhat the unequal access to trading opportunities, outsiders may substitute reputation for kinship/ethnic status. But, acquisition of reputation is not costless, as noted in chapter 2. The transaction costs of an outsider, in the role of middleman, are higher than his counterpart who is an insider. The higher transaction costs of outsiders constitute an entry barrier into personalistic markets. Because of the low costs of entry into one's own trading community in contrast to the high costs of entry into another ethnic trading community, a partner has a strong incentive to remain loyal to his own trading partner and the kinship/ethnic group of which he is a member. Furthermore, the economic sanctions facing a trader who violates group norms take the following forms: (a) withdrawal of credit so that the trader has to deal on a cash basis; (b) exclusion from future dealings; and (c) "expulsion" from the group via bankruptcy proceedings. The code of ethics, embedded in kinship/ethnic networks, functions to deter Ego's trading partner from breach of contract and hence may be seen as the functional equivalent of the Law Merchant or modern law of contracts.

Once the code of ethics emerges in a Chinese middleman economy, all externalities are internalized.[5] The existence of an ethical code of conduct helps to achieve efficiency in several ways. First, Chinese middlemen are able to appropriate profit expectations as intangible assets with a high degree of certainty, thereby facilitating middleman-entrepreneurship. Second, Chinese middlemen are able to reduce out-of-pocket costs of private protection of contracts; this shifts the total transaction-cost curve of a middleman firm downward. Third, middlemen are able to economize on the holding of commodity inventories and money by the creation of an efficient forward market in goods and money within the boundaries of the Chinese middleman economy. The result is the creation of "dual markets": the existence of forward markets and credit transactions within the Chinese middleman economy side by side with spot markets and cash transactions within the indigenous economy.

The "Calculus of Relations," Informal Social Networks, and Mutual Aid Associations: Efficient Information Screening and Mobilizing Devices

To this point, we had proceeded on the implicit assumption that Ego possessed the requisite nonprice information about the trustworthiness of a potential trading partner. This assumption must now be relaxed to include Ego's search

---

5. The types of exchange externalities associated with breach of contract, in the context of smallholder rubber are: (a) supply-breach externalities (failure to deliver); (b) quality-externalities (delivering an inferior grade of smallholder rubber, smallholder rubber being divided into five grades); and (c) debt-default externalities.

for nonprice information and the strategies Ego invents for economizing on information costs. An ingenious strategy Ego can use is to equip himself with the "calculus of relations" (Fortes 1969). The calculus of relations, as will be shown, is an informationally efficient screening device because it enables Ego to pick up nonprice market signals directly from social characteristics of the potential trading partner (such as kinship distance, ethnic identity, etc.), and hence predict the contractual behavior of his potential trading partner with a high degree of accuracy.

To equip himself with an informationally efficient calculus of relations, Ego must be able: (a) to establish a system of discriminatory rankings of all traders in a market into a small number of categories corresponding to "grades" of traders, in descending order of reliability; and (b) to identify his potential trading partner at low cost. It may be inferred from a typical Hokkien trader's system of discriminatory rankings that Ego uses four basic structural principles to classify all traders into seven categories of traders: kinship, clanship, territory, and ethnicity; the general classifactory principle being based on the degree of "social distance" (Sahlins 1965) between Ego and his potential trading partner. Ego's discriminatory system of ranking of trading partners reflects the *content* and the *limits* of the Confucian code of ethics.[6]

Confucian ethics, in overseas Chinese society, prescribes differences in the patterns of mutual aid obligations between people with varying degrees of social distance within a well-defined social structure—near kinsmen, distant kinsmen, clansmen, fellow villagers, and fellow Hokkiens. Kinship relations, in which social distance is at a minimum, are strong ties that involve the severest degree of constraint in dealings among kinsmen. Kinship relations are the irreducible jural and moral relations, and kinsmen are thus the most reliable people with whom to trade. Because of differences in the degree of behavioral constraint, each of the five categories of members occupies a special place within the overall social structure of the Hokkien ethnic community. This implies that different behavioral patterns can be predicted for each category of members corresponding to their location in the social structure. The most orderly or reliable pattern of contractual behavior is predicted for close kinsmen and the least reliable or most disorderly behavior is predicted for fellow Hokkiens. This, then, forms the basis for Ego's internal differentiation of Hokkien traders into five different categories of traders.

The limits of Confucian ethics form the basis for Ego's classification of all traders into two categories: (a) the "insiders" (the Hokkien traders) who, by virtue of their shared code of ethics, form a "moral community" of reliable traders; and (b) the "outsiders," not constrained by the Confucian ethics, who are perceived by Ego to be unreliable. Since non-Hokkien Chinese traders are

---

6. For a discussion of the limits of morality, see Buchanan 1978.

socially closer than non-Chinese traders, the former are perceived to be more reliable than non-Chinese traders and hence non-Hokkien traders are assigned to category six. Between Ego and a non-Chinese trader, social distance is at a maximum. Ego perceives cooperation with a non-Chinese to be difficult since an outsider may withhold cooperation or may even exhibit behavior of the "negative reciprocity" type.[7] Thus, non-Chinese traders are assigned to category seven.

In a society in which members adhere strictly to the code of conduct of the group and have a clear idea of who is an "insider" and who is an "outsider": (a) consistency in subjective discriminatory rankings of trading partners is to be expected of members of the group;[8] and (b) consistency in behavior is expected of different categories. This being the case, Ego is able to establish a small number of categories of social relations for the discriminatory ranking of all traders in a market.

Having established his system of ranking of traders, it remains for Ego to identify a potential trading partner in order to place him in the proper category. To do this efficiently, Ego looks for certain relational attributes of his potential trading partner. The ethnic attribute of a non-Chinese trader is highly visible and distinguishable to a Chinese trader. This means that Ego, when encountering a non-Chinese trader, needs to acquire only one piece of information by a mere glance to completely remove uncertainty regarding the identity of the non-Chinese trader and hence assign him to the proper category (i.e., category seven). To correctly identify a Chinese trader and hence assign him to his proper category, Ego needs to acquire at most only four pieces of information—what dialect he speaks, his place of origin, his surname, and his relationship to Ego. Ego can acquire information necessary to identify all his potential trading partners at a very low or virtually zero cost. Kinship/ethnic attributes are thus nonprice market signals that convey valuable information to Ego about the reliability of his potential trading partner at low cost.[9] The trader's calculus of relations may be regarded as a *low-cost screening device.* Once a trading partner is identified, he is assigned to his proper category and hence "graded." Ego then proceeds to use the calculus of relations as a tool of action for the actual choice of his trading partners in the manner discussed in the second section.

There are additional reasons why Ego prefers to choose potential trading partners from his own ethnic community. First, the existence of dense person-

---

7. This is a term used by Sahlins (1965, 144).

8. For a discussion of this, see White 1963.

9. For the economics of signaling and screening in the context of a job market paradigm, see Spence 1974 and Akerlof 1976. For an anthropological discussion of classificatory kinship systems as signaling devices for the creation and maintenance of social order in primitive societies, see Morgan 1970, Fortes 1969, and Colson 1974.

to-person informal communication networks within Ego's ethnic community make it possible for Ego to pool information regarding the contractual behavior of a potential partner. The exchange of nonprice information among members without charge economizes on information costs. This contrasts with the higher information costs Ego may expect to incur when he searches for information regarding an "outsider" across ethnic boundaries where the withholding of information is always a possibility. Second, members of Ego's own ethnic community, being "insiders" with strong ties to Ego, are perceived to be more trustworthy than "outsiders."[10] Information acquired from insiders is therefore considered by Ego to be more *reliable;* hence he can economize on the quantity of information he collects. Third, by knowing the background of the potential trading partner—his clan, his place of origin in China—Ego can acquire information from the networks of mutual aid associations within his own community or from the community leaders who maintain extensive networks of contacts throughout the community.

Confining choice of a potential trading partner within Ego's own community therefore greatly economizes on information costs. Conceptually, however, Ego's problem does not end with searching for information regarding his potential partners. In a vertical market structure, where traders are linked directly and indirectly together by long chains of mutual interdependence, Ego needs to acquire information not only about his own set of potential trading partners but also his partner's partners. Information costs would be prohibitive. This, however, implicitly assumes impersonal networks of traders. In personalistic middleman markets, where traders are linked together by kinship or ethnic ties, if $v_1 T v_2$ (read: v_1 trusts v_2) and $v_2 T v_3$, then $v_1 T v_3$. Mutual trust, via "transitive trust," becomes *collective trust,* a public good because it enables Ego to decompose the complex network of traders into his own subset of traders and confines search to this subset.

Finally, by choosing trading partners from one's own ethnic community, Ego minimizes the presence of "semantic noise" between senders and recipients of price information thereby creating an efficient communication channel for the acquisition and transmission of fast and reliable price information.[11] This contrasts with an alternative setting in which Ego does not speak the language of the "outsiders" and must make an initial investment in learning to speak the language if he chooses a network of "outsiders" as trading partners.[12] Because of the high degree of dependence of Chinese traders on the spoken word for information, and because of the mutual unintelligibility

---

10. For a discussion of the role of strong and weak ties in transmission of job information, see Boorman 1975.

11. For a discussion of the importance of creating an efficient communication channel, see Marschak 1968.

12. For a discussion of the difficulties of communication across nations, see Arrow 1963.

of the different Chinese dialects, traders who speak the same dialects are thus drawn together into networks of exchange relations to form an EHMG.

Conclusions

In this chapter, we have developed a theory of the EHMG in the context of an exchange economy characterized by contract uncertainty. We have argued that the EHMG may be viewed as a clublike structural arrangement, an alternative to contract law and to the vertically integrated firm, which emerged to economize on contract enforcement and information costs.[13] The theory has broad applications and lends itself readily to extensions for further research, only two of which will be noted here:

1. A general theory of homogeneous entrepreneurial groups engaged in either illegal or legal activities. We may develop a theory of the ethnically homogeneous (Italian) Mafia group as a low cost club for the enforcement of contracts since Mafia-entrepreneurs, by the very nature of their illegal activities, operate outside the legal framework.[14] Similarly, the theory may explain why successful trading groups operating in other underdeveloped economies characterized by contract uncertainty are *socially homogeneous groups:* the East Indians in East Africa, the Syrians in West Africa, the Lebanese in North Africa,[15] the Jews in medieval Europe[16], and the Medici merchant-bankers in fifteenth-century Florence. This general theory of homogeneous trading groups would examine: (a) the assignment of property rights, the structural principles—kinship, clanship, caste, ethnicity, religion—for the delineation of the *boundaries* of groups (see chap. 6), and the institutions for facilitating exchange among members and between members and outsiders (see chap. 7); as well as (b) the dynamics within the homogeneous trading group as the group responds to the development of the economy. The function of the

---

13. Our theory of the EHMG may be regarded as an extension of the Alchian-Demsetz (1972) theory of the firm. The Alchian-Demsetz theory is an extension of Coase's (1937) classic paper on the nature of the firm.

14. This linkage was suggested to the writer by Francis X. Tannian, commenting on an early version of the paper presented at the Public Choice Society meetings, April 15–17, 1976, Roanoke, Va.

15. The major exception to our theory is the absorption of Lebanese traders into the dualistic economy of Brazil.

16. **Greif (1989) has developed a theory of how Jewish traders, Maghribi traders, in medieval Europe protect contracts by the formation of a "coalition" of traders who share the same identity, a theory very similar to my theory of the EHMG developed in this chapter.

homogeneous trading group as a low cost arrangement for contract enforcement may become increasingly redundant as the economy evolves a more developed legal infrastructure. Consequently, the particularistic exchange networks based on mutual trust will gradually be replaced by impersonal exchange networks based on contract.

2. The economic theory of optimal jurisdictions. Our theory of the EHMG may be extended to include the spatial dimension in which ethnic boundaries coincide with political boundaries.[17] It may be used to explain, for example, why standard marketing areas in traditional China were organized in hexagon-shaped areas where boundaries were coterminous with the existence of distinct homogeneous communities;[18] and why the policing of each standard marketing community was provided by private protective agencies in the form of secret societies. That theory may also be used to explain why nation-states tend to be organized along *ethnic* lines.[19]

REFERENCES

Akerlof, George. 1976. "The Economics of Caste and of the Rat Race and Other Woeful Tales." *Quarterly Journal of Economics* 90 (November): 599–617.

Alchian, Armen, and Harold Demsetz. 1972 "Production, Information Costs, and Economic Organization." *American Economic Review* 62 (December): 777–95.

Arrow, Kenneth J. 1963. "Classificatory Notes on the Production and Transmission of Technological Knowledge." *American Economic Review,* Papers and Proceedings, 59 (May): 29–33.

Belshaw, Cyril S. 1965. *Traditional Exchange and Modern Markets.* Englewood Cliffs, N.J.: Prentice-Hall, Inc.

Blau, Peter M., ed. 1975. *Approaches to the Study of Social Structure.* New York: The Free Press.

Boorman, Scott A. 1975. "A Combinatorial Optimization Model for Transmission of Job Information through Contact Networks." *The Bell Journal of Economics* 6 (Spring): 216–49.

Buchanan, James M. 1965. "An Economic Theory of Clubs." *Economica* 32 (February): 1–14.

17. Tiebout (1965) points out that urban areas can be efficiently organized in a system of many small homogeneous communities whose populations have similar tastes for public goods. Tiebout's "voting with the feet" theory relies on the ability of people to move, in fact, to choose one's jurisdiction of residence.

18. See Landa (1978).

19. Singapore provides an excellent example. Although Singapore and West Malaysia form an economic entity, Singapore, with its predominantly Chinese-merchant community pulled out of the Federation of Malaysia on August 9, 1965, to form an independent nation-state (the Republic of Singapore) within the Commonwealth.

———. 1978. "Markets, States, and the Extent of Morals." *American Economic Review* 68 (May): 362–68.

Coase, Ronald. 1937. "The Nature of the Firm." *Economica* 4 (November): 386–405.

Colson, Elizabeth. 1974. *Tradition and Contract: The Problem of Order.* Chicago: Aldine.

Dales, John H. 1972. "Rights and Economics." In *Perspective of Property,* edited by Gene Wunderlich and W. L. Gibson, Jr., 152. State College, Pa.: Institute for Land and Water Resources, Pennsylvania State University.

Dewey, Alice G. 1962. *Peasant Marketing in Java.* New York: Free Press of Glencoe.

Fortes, Myer. 1969. *Kinship and the Social Order: The Legacy of Lewis Henry Morgan.* Chicago: Aldine.

Geertz, Clifford. 1978. "The Bazaar Economy: Information and Search in Peasant Marketing." *American Economic Review,* Papers and Proceedings, 68 (May): 28–32.

**Greif, Avner. 1989. "Reputation and Coalitions in Medieval Trade: Evidence on the Maghribi Traders." *The Journal of Economic History* 49, no. 4 (December): 857–82.

Landa, Janet. 1978. "Central-Place Theory, Social Distance Costs, and Nozickian Minimal States." Paper presented at the Public Choice Society meetings in New Orleans, La., March 3.

Marschak, Jacob. 1968. "Economics of Inquiring, Communicating, Deciding." *American Economic Review,* Papers and Proceedings, 62 (May): 1–18.

Morgan, Lewis H. 1970. "Systems of Consanguinity and Affinity of the Human Family." *Smithsonian Contributions to Knowledge.*

Posner, Richard. 1980. "A Theory of Primitive Society, with Special Reference to Law." *Journal of Law and Economics* 23 (April): 1–53.

Sahlins, Marshall D. 1965. "On the Sociology of Primitive Exchange." In *The Relevance of Models for Social Anthropology,* edited by Michael Banton. London: Tavistock Publications.

Spence, A. Michael. 1974. *Market Signalling.* Cambridge: Harvard University Press.

Tiebout, Charles. 1965. "A Pure Theory of Local Expenditures." *Journal of Political Economy* 64 (October): 416–24.

Tollison, Robert D. 1972. "Consumption Sharing and Non-Exclusion Rules." *Economica* 39 (August): 276–91.

White, Harrison C. 1963. *An Anatomy of Kinship.* Englewood Cliffs, N.J.: Prentice-Hall, Inc.

CHAPTER 6

The Economics of Symbols, Clan Names, and Religion

Jack L. Carr and Janet T. Landa

Standard theories of exchange depict trade as an impersonal exchange between anonymous partners. Jevons's "Law of Indifference," in particular,
emphasizes the impersonality of transactions: it is a matter of indifference to
the buyer or the seller with whom they do business provided that they obtain
the same (homogeneous) commodity at the same price (see Jevons 1871). For
a world of contract certainty, this is an acceptable theory. In a world of
contract uncertainty, however, it is no longer a matter of indifference with
whom one trades.

In underdeveloped economies where the legal framework is underdeveloped, one observes the ubiquity of personalistic trading networks that
manifest themselves in homogeneous trading groups: the East Indians in East
Africa, the Syrians in West Africa, the Lebanese in North Africa, the Chinese
in Southeast Asia, the Jews in medieval Europe, and the Medici merchant
group in fifteenth-century Florence. Even in developed countries with well-
developed legal frameworks, the identity of one's partner in exchange becomes important in a number of transactions. Old boy networks still exist
where individuals prefer to enter into exchange with "old boys" rather than
"new boys"[1] and certain religious groups dominate certain economic activ-

Professor of Economics and Assistant Professor of Economics, Department of Political
Economy, and Research Associates, Institute for Policy Analysis, University of Toronto. Earlier
versions of the chapter were presented at the Southern Economic Association Annual Meetings,
Washington, D.C., November 5–7, 1980; at the Law and Economics Workshop, Faculty of Law,
University of Toronto, November 26, 1980, and at the Western Economic Association Annual
Meeting, San Francisco, July 2–6, 1981. We would like to thank Richard M. Bird, Thomas A.
Borcherding, Harry W. Chappell, members of the Law and Economics Workshop, Faculty of
Law, University of Toronto, and an anonymous referee for helpful comments. This chapter
originally appeared in the *Journal of Legal Studies* 12, no. 1 (January 1983): 135–56. The
authors gratefully acknowledge the permission given by the journal's publisher, The University of
Chicago Press, to reprint the paper. [©1983 by The University of Chicago press. All rights
reserved.]

1. For a discussion of the role of old boy networks as information networks, see Carr,
Mathewson, and McManus 1972.

115

ities; for example, orthodox Jews dominate the diamond trade in New York City and the Mafia dominate criminal activity in a number of North American cities.

In this chapter we propose to analyze the economic functions of certain institutions and customary practices of trading groups. These include kinship and ethnic groups, clan names, symbols of group identity and religious practices such as Chinese ancestor worship, the keeping of genealogical records, and religious dietary restrictions. Sociologists and anthropologists have provided explanations of these institutional practices and customs. We are providing additional or alternative explanations that look to the economic rationales of these phenomena.

In recent years, some economists have turned their attention to the analysis of nonmarket institutions such as marriage, the family, and the law in developed societies.[2] Richard Posner, in his insightful paper,[3] has extended the analysis to certain social and legal institutions of so-called primitive and archaic societies, including kinship groups, gift giving, polygamy, and so on. Posner rationalizes these institutions used by primitive societies as alternative insurance mechanisms for coping with the problems of uncertainty and high information costs. Our theory is a contribution to this new subfield within law and economics. We emphasize that many of the institutions and customs of trading groups in underdeveloped economies are clublike arrangements, which serve as an alternative to explicitly enforceable contracts in an environment characterized by contract uncertainty and high information costs.

In the next section, we shall examine the question of why the identity of one's trading partner may be important and why clubs based on certain shared characteristics of members are formed. In doing so, we will be utilizing the economic theory of clubs.[4] We will develop our theory from a partial equilibrium member's "within-club" point of view and will not address ourselves to general equilibrium analysis of the model.[5]

In the third section, we will extend our theory to include the economics of signaling and screening in order to provide an economic rationale to a number of institutional practices and customs such as Jewish dietary laws,

---

2. See, e.g., Becker 1976b and Posner 1977.

3. See Posner 1980. See also Geertz 1978, who rationalized the customary practice of "clientalization" (the pairing off of buyers and sellers in recurrent transactions) in bazaars in underdeveloped economies as a response to high information costs associated with uncertainty regarding qualities of goods and the reliability of trading partners.

4. For the economic theory of clubs, see Buchanan 1965. For an extension of Buchanan's theory, which incorporates discrimination in the choice of consumption-sharing partners, see Tollison 1972. For a survey of the economic theory of clubs, see Sandler and Tschirhart 1980. *See also Sandler 1992.

5. See Cooter and Landa (1984) for a general equilibrium analysis of the model.

Chinese ancestor worship, and the keeping of written genealogical records.[6] The final section will provide a brief conclusion.

Generalized Theory of Personalistic Exchange

Introduction

Imagine a world in which there are no clubs and in which the state affords no protection of contracts. In such a world of contract uncertainty, any trader can break a contract whenever it is profitable to do so. Breach of contract imposes breach costs or externalities on the victim of breach. In general, five kinds of externalities, which correspond to different kinds of "games of breach," can be identified (see chap. 3).

These different kinds of externalities are a major component of transaction costs in an environment characterized by contract uncertainty. Where these costs bulk large in a world of contract uncertainty, some individuals would refrain from trading altogether. Where these costs do not prohibit trade altogether, trade will take place but at a price that takes contract uncertainty into account.

Personalistic Exchange

Individuals can reduce these kinds of risks by discriminatory choice of a network of trading partners. Individuals can form a clublike arrangement for reduction of contract uncertainty. For our purposes, we will define a club or clublike arrangement as any voluntary group deriving mutual benefit from the reduction of contract uncertainty, a public good for members, because: (a) information about propensity to cheat or breach can be obtained cheaper for club members than non-club members; and (b) sanctions in addition to normal market sanctions exist and are imposed on members who violate the rules of the game set by the club, thereby making it more expensive to breach contracts with club members than contracts with non-club members.

In a Knightian sense, it is assumed that clubs reduce both risk and uncertainty in trading with club members.[7] Clubs may and will have many other purposes other than trading. But in the nature of exchange with club members whether economic or social, one obtains as a by-product valuable trading information about club members (for example, information about the likelihood that any club member will breach a contract). Also since club

---

6. For the economics of signaling and screening in the context of a job market paradigm, see Spence 1974. See also Akerlof 1976.

7. Knight 1921 made a distinction between risk and uncertainty.

members have, in general, both economic and social exchange with one another, social as well as economic sanctions can be imposed on club members who breach contracts (for example, club members who break contracts can be removed from the club and prohibited from having either social or economic contact with all club members). On the other hand, similar social sanctions cannot be imposed on nonmembers breaching contracts with members. For example, if one views a family as a club, many more social sanctions are available in dealing with family members than in dealing with non-family members. If one belonged to a club and breached a contract, the victim of the breach could impose economic sanctions (for example, withdraw credit, exclude him in future transactions) on the offending club member and can forbid all club members from having any contact whatsoever with the offender. In this way clubs increase the costs of breaching contracts with other club members.

Let us set up a simple model that defines in an analytical way the economic advantages that accrue from joining a club. In setting up this model we will investigate the question of the optimal size of a club (from an economic point of view). Let us consider a world where there are $N + 1$ individuals of whom $n + 1$ belong to a club.[8] For simplicity we will assume that each member engages in one trade per period with each member of the market (both club and non club)[9] and further we will assume the existence of one type of breach of contract that if it occurs, imposes a cost of BC on our trader.[10] If our trader enters into exchange with a club member, the probability of breach is Π_1 and, if our trader enters into exchange with a non-club member, the probability of breach is Π_2. Since it is more costly to breach a contract with a club member than with a non-club member we assume Π_2 is greater than Π_1. Hence expected breach costs in exchange with a club member are $\Pi_1 BC$ and with a non-club member $\Pi_2 BC$. It should be noted that our probabilities of breach can be used to define the concept of trustworthiness. In our simple model we assume only two levels of trustworthiness; $\Pi_2 - \Pi_1$ being the

---

8. We will assume the existence of the club already, for whatever purposes, and any economic advantages that accrue from club membership accrue without any additional pecuniary cost to the club or to its individual members.

9. In this economy we can hypothesize the existence of a standardized commodity and hence define a standard trade. It should be noted that in reality costs of trading with club members will be lower and hence one would expect more trade with club members than non–club members.

10. We assume BC is the same in dealing with club or non–club members. In the real world this may not be the case. A number of clubs (for example, local better business bureaus, various religious groups, and so on) have their own mediation systems for solving disputes. If BC includes current costs, then BC may in fact be lower for club than non–club members.

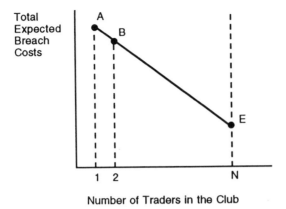

Fig. 6.   Total expected breach costs and size of club

degree of trustworthiness for club members and $\Pi_2 - \Pi_2$ or zero being the degree of trustworthiness for non-club members. At this stage in our model we ignore the complications that could arise where each club member has a different degree of trustworthiness. If the probability of breach from a non-club member was still Π_2 but the expected probability of breach for a club member was Π_{1i}, $i = 1, \ldots, n$ then we would have $n + 1$ degrees of trustworthiness. In this case non-club members would have a degree of trust-worthiness of zero and club members would have degrees of trustworthiness of $\Pi_2 - \Pi_{1i}$ for $i = 1, \ldots, n$. Our definition of trustworthiness measures expected comparative probabilities of breach.

Since our trader is assumed to make one trade per period with all N individuals in the market, then equation (1) measures total expected breach costs (*TEBC*):

$$TEBC = n\Pi_1 BC + (N - n)\Pi_2 BC \qquad (1)$$

To examine the economic aspects of the club, let us see what will happen as we add more members to the club. As the number of trading partners who join the club increases, total expected breach costs will decrease. See figure 6. For example, point A represents the expected breach costs that the trader expects will be imposed on him if only one of the trading partners joins the club. Point B represents the breach costs that the trader expects will be imposed on him if two of his trading partners join the club, where $B < A$. When all of his trading partners join the club, expected breach costs are assumed to be reduced to E. Consider the addition of one more member to the club. Now *TEBC* with $n + 1$ members is

$$TEBC' = (n + 1)\Pi_1 BC + (N - n - 1)\Pi_2 BC \qquad (2)$$

Therefore the change in *TEBC* is

$$\Delta TEBC = TEBC' - TEBC$$

$$= [(n + 1)\Pi_1' BC + (N - n - 1)\Pi_2 BC] -$$

$$[n\Pi_1 BC + (N + n)\Pi_2 BC]$$

$$= (n + 1)(\Pi_1' - \Pi_2)BC\Pi_1 BC - \Pi_2 BC$$

$$= (n + 1)(\Pi_1' - \Pi_1)BC - (\Pi_2' - \Pi_1)BC \qquad (3)$$

Adding new members involves additional costs as well as additional benefits. The term $(n + 1)(\Pi_1' - \Pi_1)BC$ represents the marginal costs (*MC*) of adding one more member. For a club to accrue economic benefits to its members it must be able to impose sanctions on its members who breach contracts. To impose sanctions it must inform all members when breaches occur. A mechanism is needed, therefore, to ensure that individual club members do not trade with boycotted club members. Clearly the cost of informing club members of breaches and enforcing sanctions is a function of the size of the club.

As more members are added to the club, more time and effort is needed to inform the additional members; hence enforcement costs are expected to rise with the increase in club membership.[11] Although it is certainly true that information costs will increase with club membership, the size of this increase is an empirical question. Cutting in the opposite direction, larger clubs can inflict larger damages on breaching members, which will tend to decrease the likelihood of breach. For purposes of analysis we assume that the first factor outweighs the second, with the result that as n increases, Π_1 increases. For simplicity we assume Π_1 is a linear function of n (see fig. 7) where

$$\Pi_1 = (\Pi_2 - c - bN) + bn$$

$$= \Pi_2 - c + b(n - N), \qquad (4)$$

---

11. For an analysis of a different situation involving increased "decision-making costs" as size of group increases, see Buchanan and Tullock 1962, chap. 6.

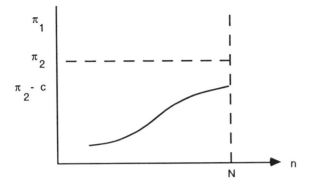

Number of Traders in the Club

Fig. 7. Probability of Breach and Size of Club

that is, when $n = N$, $\Pi_1 = \Pi_2 - c$, where c is the reduction in probability of breach that occurs in going from a world where there are no club members to a world where everybody belongs to the club.[12] With n club members $\Pi_1 = \Pi_2 - c + b(n - N)$; and with $n + 1$ club members $\Pi_1' = \Pi_2 - c + b(n + 1 - N)$. Therefore the change in Π_1 due to the addition of one more member (that is, $\Delta\Pi_1$) equals b. The greater are information costs, the greater is b. Now the increase in total expected breach costs due to the addition of one more club member is given in equation (5).

$$MC = (n + 1)(\Pi_1' - \Pi_1)BC$$

$$= (n + 1)\{[\Pi_2 - c + b(n + 1) - N] -$$

$$[\Pi_2 - c + b(n - N)]\}BC = (n + 1)b.BC \qquad (5)$$

With the addition of one new club member, all $n + 1$ club members' costs increase by $b.BC$. Therefore, we have an upward-sloping marginal cost curve, which is depicted in figure 8.

---

12. It is also true that as club membership increases, it becomes increasingly more difficult to recognize club members. Hence, as n increases, the perceived value of Π_1 also increases. This formulation assumes the homogeneity of traders. Each trader added to the club adds the same amount to breach costs. As stated in the text, as n increases, there are factors that tend to decrease Π_1 as well as factors that tend to increase Π_1. If these factors operate with different intensities for different values of n, then Π_1 may not be strictly increasing in n. For small n, it is possible that increases in n may result in a fall in Π_1. If this is the case, marginal cost may first fall and then rise. In addition, it should noted that equation (4) assumes the homogeneity of traders. Each trader added to the club adds the same amount to breach costs.

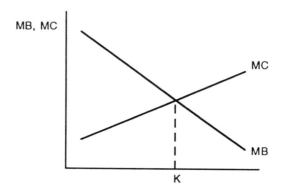

Fig. 8. Optimal club size

The term $(\Pi_2 - \Pi_1)BC$ may be considered the marginal benefit (*MB*) of adding one more member. Adding members to the club clearly reduces expected breach costs. Adding more members to the club brings more of the market under club sanctions to the club members. The marginal benefits of adding one more member to the club are given by equation (6):

$$MB = (\Pi_2 - \Pi_1)BC$$

$$= \{\Pi_2 - [\Pi_2 + b(n - N)]\}BC$$

$$= -b(n - N)BC$$

$$= b(N - n)BC \tag{6}$$

The marginal benefit expression in equation (6) clearly shows the benefit to be had by adding new club members. New club members are more trustworthy (that is, have lower expected probability of breach) and hence they are lower cost traders. Equation (6) also shows that *MB* declines as n increases. Under general conditions, there will be economic limits to the size of a club. Optimum size club is reached where, as depicted geometrically in figure 8, the marginal benefit curve intersects the marginal cost curve at optimal club size, K.

Differences in Degree of Homogeneity and Solidarity of Club Membership in Optimal Club Size

To this point we have assumed that all individuals in the club were homogeneous with respect to contract behaviour and with respect to costs of informing other club members about contract breaches. In terms of the model developed in the previous section this means that: (1) any individual brought into the club will have the same expected probability of breach (that is, will have the same common Π_1) and (2) individuals when brought into the club will have identical effects on the costs of informing club members about breaches (that is, any individual brought into the club will increase Π_1 by b) and hence our *MC* curve will be a straight line.

We have thus far ignored real world complications of differences in the degree of homogeneity and degree of solidarity of club members. Taking these complications into account will alter the shape of the *MC* and *MB* curve and hence effect optimal club size.

We shall take these two complications into account. For some clubs the degree of homogeneity will vary with the proportion of club members who belong to the same clan, ethnic, or religious group. The degree of solidarity may be measured by the proportion of club members who stand in a certain social distance from each other. Thus, a club composed of a group of kinsmen or clansmen, all related by blood ties, exhibits a higher degree of solidarity than a club composed of a group of people from the same ethnic group.

Differences in the degree of homogeneity of club membership is reflected in:

1. A shift in the *MC* curve. For example, the higher the degree of homogeneity of club membership, the lower the costs of transmitting information to members regarding a member's breach; hence the *MC* curve corresponding to a more homogeneous club lies everywhere to the right of the *MC* curve corresponding to a less homogeneous club. This implies that the optimal size club will be larger for a more homogeneous trading club (K_2) than for a less homogeneous club (K_1). See figure 9.

2. A kink or discontinuity of the *MC* curve. When trading members included in the club are also drawn from outside the trader's own ethnic group, the difficulties of communication across ethnic and linguistic boundaries may become so serious that enforcement becomes prohibitively costly and there is a kink or discontinuity in the *MC* curve. We have a case where *MC* rises much faster than group size as club members become heterogeneous. Where an *MB* curve intersects an

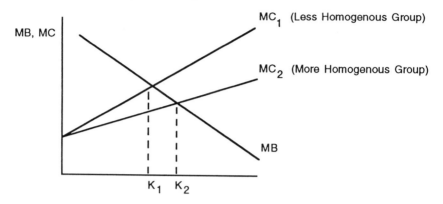

Fig. 9. **Differences in the degree of homogeneity of club members and optimal club size**

MC curve at the kinked portion determines not only the optimal size of the club (*K*) but also the boundary of the club at the level of the ethnic group. (See fig. 10.) The impact of the degree of solidarity of club membership, on the other hand, is reflected in:

3. A shift of the *MB* curve. We may expect that the greater the degree of solidarity of club membership, the greater the sense of shared values and norms—a sense of belonging to a "moral community"—hence

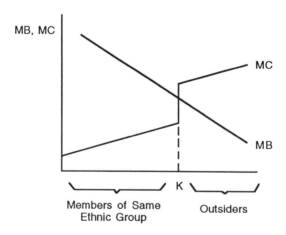

Fig. 10. **Degree of homogeneity of club members and optimal size of ethnic trading club**

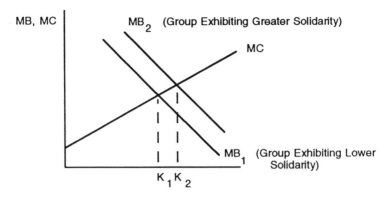

Fig. 11.   **Degree of solidarity of club members and optimal club size**

the *MB* curve for a club that exhibits a high degree of solidarity lies everywhere above the *MB* curve for a club that exhibits a lower degree of solidarity. This implies that the optimal size of a club is larger for a club showing greater group solidarity than one showing lower group solidarity (see fig. 11).

4. The existence of a kink in the *MB* curve (see fig. 12). For a heterogeneous group composed of members of one's own ethnic group and outsiders, we may expect that the *MB* curve exhibits a kink at the

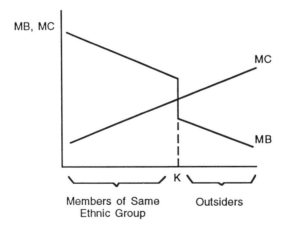

Fig. 12.   **Heterogeneous group and optimal size of ethnic trading club**

boundary of the ethnic group, reflecting the discontinuity in the group norms which do not extend beyond the group. Where the *MC* curve intersects a kinked *MB* curve, we have not only the optimal size club, but also a club whose boundary is marked off by members of one's own ethnic group.

An Economic Interpretation of Symbols, Clan Names, and Religion

In a world of contract uncertainty, we have argued that the identity of the potential trading partner matters. In a world of contract uncertainty, other things being equal, we prefer to trade with fellow club members rather than with non-members. The lower transaction costs are one of the main economic advantages of belonging to a club. In this section we will argue that it is mainly these economic advantages of clubs that explain the continued existence of many clublike arrangements. To be sure, there are costs of belonging to a club. We are assuming that benefits outweigh these costs; otherwise clubs would not be viable. The costs of belonging to a club include: (a) the opportunity costs of keeping contracts with club members when outsiders offer the club member a better contract; (b) the costs of observing club rules (for example, dietary restrictions); and (c) discrimination by outsiders.

So far we have assumed that club members can costlessly identify other club members. The assumption will now be relaxed. We will extend our theory of clubs to include the economics of signaling. In a world where there are positive costs in defining and identifying club members, we will argue that many customs or rituals of various clublike organizations are means to reduce the costs of defining and identifying club members. Various reasons have been advanced by sociologists and anthropologists as to why these institutional arrangements and practices persist. We, however, have given these institutional arrangements and customary practices an additional economic raison d'être as well. Let us consider these various arrangements and practices and see if we can extend the theory developed in the first section to include the economics of signaling to explain their existence.

Names and Clan Names

Two important functions are performed by the institution of naming individuals. First, the named individual is now a uniquely identified individual and thus distinguished from all other anonymous individuals. That is, the named individual is identified as a person with specific physical characteristics and a history and biography that extends back in time to his birth. A person's name may therefore serve as a proxy for reputation. In a society with *n* number of named individuals, there are *n* number of persons with distinct reputations, some better than others. Second, each named individual also bears a surname that serves to identify him as a member of a social group, the nuclear family. The nuclear family is the smallest kinship unit in which kinship status is ascribed by birth and in which mutual aid obligations among kinsmen are severest. In this way kinship groups are a prime example of a clublike arrangement. In kinship-based societies like traditional China, the named individual is also embedded in larger kinship units (the extended family, the lineage,[13] and the clan)[14] so that he is a member of a series of ever-widening mutual aid groupings of kinsmen and clansmen. For the larger kinship groups surnames are a means of identifying club members. Since surnames are inherited and transmitted from generation to generation, great care is taken by rich and powerful families to maintain or preserve the reputation of well-known names since reputation is an invaluable intangible asset. Kinsmen and clansmen of well-known families assert kinship/clanship status to gain preferential access to job and trading opportunities provided by wealthy clan members, who in turn prefer their kinsmen/clansmen as cooperating partners because of their greater trustworthiness and reliability. Kinship status, like reputation, therefore is a valuable intangible asset for those possessing such a status. This may explain the following institutional arrangements and practices:

1. Named Trading Groups. These are ubiquitous in the Middle Ages in Europe and in contemporary underdeveloped economies. Excellent examples are the Medici-merchant bankers in fifteenth-century Florence, the Rothchilds in eighteenth- and nineteenth-century Europe, and the Hokkien-Chinese rubber middleman group in contemporary Singapore and West Malaysia, dominated by a few major clans from Fukien province in China. These named trading groups are clublike arrangements for protection of contracts under conditions of uncertainty. The Chinese middleman group, as a clublike arrangement alternative to contract law, emerged in response to conditions of contract uncertainty prevailing in Singapore and West Malaysia and also in response to a political environment in which the dominant ethnic group in West Malaysia—the Malays—are often hostile to the Chinese (see Rabushka and Shepsle 1972).

---

13. A lineage organization is composed of the agnatic descendants of a single ancestor together with their unmarried sisters and their wives. The lineage organization is a corporate group, i.e., a group that endures over time in which members share common interests and activities. For a discussion of Chinese lineage, see Freedman 1966.

14. The sharing of a surname is itself a fact of agnatic kinship. A clan is one in which lineages of like surname are held together genealogically but are not members of a corporate group. For a discussion of Chinese clans, see Freedman 1966.

2. Change of Surname. Because kinship status is a valuable asset, practices such as change of surname sometimes occur. The following anecdote tells of such change.[15] An immigrant from China, upon arriving in Singapore in the early 1920s, inquired as to which clan in Singapore was the most powerful and wealthiest and, was told the Tan Kah Kee clan (Tan Kah Kee was then the "Rubber King" in Singapore and Malaya). The man thereupon changed his surname to Tan and went to look for a job in Tan Kah Kee's firm. He was given a job by Tan Kah Kee and eventually rose to become a rubber millionaire himself.[16] If one can easily change one's name and get away with it (that is, be taken for a clan member), then clans have to look for other methods of identifying their members (see the next section).

Immigrants to foreign countries often change or shorten their surnames to resemble more closely the common names used in their new country. Generally this is *not* done to claim membership in a clan. The immigrant can be considered to belong to a club, whose members consist of all immigrants from a particular geographical region. Since sometimes club members are discriminated against by non-club members it is sometimes necessary to hide one's membership in a club from outsiders.[17] Foreigners may change their names so they can no longer be recognized as foreigners; if they do they will find other methods to identify themselves to other club members.

3. Ancestor Worship and Genealogy. In kinship-based societies like traditional China, ancestor worship is an important institution.[18] This institution may be explained by our theory of clubs as a way of economizing on the costs of identifying members of the same descent group, numbering into the hundreds and scattered in different localities, who trace back to a common ancestor. Together with ancestor worship goes the practice of keeping genealogical books. These books include all members of the same clan or lineage and are financed by rich members of the clan. Written Chinese genealogies convey many kinds of information, including biographies, place of residence, and records of members of the lineage who have moved elsewhere to form

---

15. Told to Janet Landa by Hsu Yun-Ts'iao, editor of the *Journal of Southeast Asian Research* (Southeast Asian Research Center, Singapore, October 27, 1969).

16. For a case study of the role of kinship and ethnic networks in facilitating the growth and diversification of the Tan Kah Kee firm, see Landa and Salaff 1980.

17. For an alternative discussion of the motives for concealment of personal information in the marketplace, see Posner 1981.

18. For a discussion of Chinese ancestor worship, see Freedman 1966. Ancestor worship and the keeping of genealogical books were also important in Italy in the Middle Ages (see Heers 1977).

new lineage settlements.[19] Keeping genealogical records reduces information costs because: (a) it allows for the precise identification of a group of persons from whom members could expect help and favor (persons will know many more kinsmen clansmen because of standardized genealogies); and (b) it excludes those who would otherwise fraudulently claim kinship or clanship status and hence free-ride the benefits of group membership.[20]

4. Creation of Fictive Kinship. Where two or more unrelated individuals have established relations of mutual trust and would like to maintain their relationship on a longer-term or permanent basis, the individuals may resort to a "legal fiction" via the creation of fictive or artificial ties of kinship on the basis of mutual agreement.[21] Anthropologists have cited many examples of the creation of artificial kinship in primitive societies. For example, in primitive societies, agricultural teams were often composed of kinsmen and fictive kinsmen because kinsmen—real or fictitious—were thought to be reliable people for long-term agricultural cooperation (see Gulliver 1971 and Leach 1961). Again, in relationships requiring a great deal of trust, such as in secret societies, unrelated individuals seal their relationship by becoming "blood-brothers" through the ritual of mixing the blood of two participants and swallowing the mixture.[22] The classic example of ritual brotherhood is the Freemasonry, an institution that first appeared in seventeenth-century England.[23] Another legal fiction treats adopted children as if they are natural children with all the rights and obligations of kin status conferred upon them by their adopting parents.

These various ways of creating artificial kinship imply that the boundaries of the kinship group are not rigidly fixed by genealogical connections but

---

19. For a discussion of the types of information in Chinese genealogies, see Ahern 1976.

20. For the role of genealogical records in excluding outsiders who might fraudulently claim kinship or clanship status, see Freedman 1966. See also Heers 1977. We provide another reason, in addition to Posner's insurance function argument of kinship groups, why certain societies "devote so many of their linguistic, legal, and informational resources to delineating kinship groups much larger than the modern family or, for that matter, the primitive household" (Posner 1980, 12).

21. For a discussion of this topic, see Fuller 1967. The creation of fictive kinship ties itself reveals the importance of real kinship ties. But there is an interesting asymmetrical aspect of kinship to be noted, that is, it is easier to create kin ties than to get rid of real kinsmen that have become burdensome.

22. For a sociological discussion of secret societies, see Simmel [1908] 1950. See also MacKenzie [1967] 1971.

23. For a discussion of Freemasonry, see the chapter by Jones in MacKenzie [1967] 1971.

themselves are endogenous and subject to individual choice.[24] But there is a definite limit to the size of the kinship group. There are limits of kinship morality or "altruism" not extended to everyone in the world.[25] We argued above that there is an optimal size to the club. The optimal size depended on a number of factors. Here we argue that there is an optimal size to kinship clubs and this optimal size depends on economic factors and is not determined exogenously. To a certain extent, who is considered to be your kin is a question of choice.

Ethnic Identity

Since every individual is also a member of an ethnic and linguistic group, another external marking or sign of identity is a person's ethnic identity. In a multiethnic society, where assimilation is low, ethnicity serves to classify people into social categories and, from the decision maker's point of view, implies an "insiders-we" and "outsiders-they" distinction. The significance of ethnic identity in the context of multiethnic society is that very often the "limits of morality" end at the boundary of the ethnic group (see Buchanan 1978). As the anthropologist Fredrik Barth (1969, 15) puts it:

> . . . the ethnic boundary canalizes social life—it entails a frequently quite complex organization of behaviour and social relations. The identi-fication of another person as a fellow member of an ethnic group implies a sharing of criteria for evaluation and judgement. It thus entails the assumption that the two are fundamentally "playing the same game", . . . On the other hand, a dichotomization of others as strangers, as members of another ethnic group, implies a recognition of the limita-tions on shared understandings, differences in criteria for judgement of value and performance and a restriction of interaction to sectors of as-sumed common understanding and mutual interest.

---

24. The sociobiological literature treats kinship in terms of genealogical connections. For a discussion of the sociobiological literature, see Becker 1976a.

25. In the literature on sociobiology, the claim is made that altruistic behavior will vary with kinship distance as a function of similarity of the genetic pool. We, however, emphasize an individualistic-choice calculus that looks at social distance including kinship distance, in terms of reducing transaction costs under conditions of contract uncertainty. Thus, we emphasize the importance of social ties, which may or may not be genetically based. Furthermore, we empha-size the importance of a shared code of conduct, and not shared genes, among members as a basis for mutual trust and mutual aid ("reciprocal altruism" in the sociobiology literature) since shared codes of conduct may exist among individuals who are not genetically linked.

Ethnicity is thus a signaling device that transmits nonprice information regarding the potential performance or behavior of the potential partner.[26] Ethnic identity or status is thus an intangible asset for those who are members of the dominant ethnic group. While a person can change his surname, his religion, very often a person cannot change his ethnic status.[27] Because of this and because there are advantages of in-group cooperation, the boundaries of ethnic groups tend to persist over time. This may explain the following phenomena and practices:

1. Ethnic Trading Groups. Numerous examples of ethnic trading groups can be cited.[28] Thus, for example, we find Chinese middlemen groups in Southeast Asia, the Jews in medieval Europe, the Jews dominating the diamond trade in New York (where transactions involving million-dollar deals are concluded with only a handshake, and the Hebrew, "mazel un b'rachah" ("luck and blessing"), with no cash changing hands, transactions being on credit, and the Mafia engaged in illegal activities in a number of North American cities.

2. Occupational Status Defining Ethnic Status. In Thailand, a high rate of intermarriage has occurred between the Chinese and the Thai in the past. As a consequence, physical characteristics no longer clearly differentiate a Chinese from a Thai since there are "degrees of Chineseness." Because of this, Szanton (1983) found that in certain cases occupational status defines ethnicity; for example, anyone who engages in trade or commerce (a traditional Chinese occupational role) is defined as a Chinese even though the person may be a Sino-Thai or a Thai.

Religious Identity

There may be clublike economic advantages in belonging to a religious organization. In an economic exchange one can place more trust in members

---

26. We are extending Spence's 1974 concept of ethnicity as a signaling device from a job market context to an exchange economy.

27. It should also be noted that surnames highly correlate with ethnicity. Thus from surnames, one may infer an individual's ethnicity with a high degree of accuracy. While it is possible to change one's surname, it is hard to change one's physical (ethnic) characteristics.

28. A number of sociologists have pointed out the ubiquity of foreign ethnic trading groups. They have developed "outgroup" (or "marginal men," "strangers") arguments as to why foreign ethnic minorities are successful in middleman roles. See Hagan's (1962) discussion of these arguments. Our theory differs from theirs in that we emphasize their ability to form clubs that promote mutual trust among members and hence reduce transaction costs.

of one's religious club. This phenomenon explains the existence of religious trading groups such as the Jews in medieval Europe and the Arab merchants in Malaya and the Netherlands East Indies during the nineteenth and twentieth centuries.[29] However, not all religious organizations will yield substantial economic advantages to their members. If a religious organization is very large in relation to the potential trading population, then little economic advantage will be received by belonging to it. As a testable implication, we should not expect the dominant religious organization in an area to form the basis of a trading group. If membership in a religious group is very large, the religious group may be far in excess of the optimal size for economic purposes (see above). Too large a group may imply too small an ability to impose sanctions on those who breach contracts. If this is the case, preferential treatment will not be given to fellow co-religionists. Substantial economic advantages will probably accrue to smaller religious groups. And if a religious organization has its members spread throughout the world, economic advantages will accrue to its members both in local and international trade.

It is these economic advantages to smaller religious groups that may explain why no single religious group has dominated the world scene. Small religious groups that have provided economic advantages to its members (as well as seeing to their spiritual needs) have tended to survive through the ages. Because of economic advantages to smaller groups, there is no natural monopoly in religion.

Religious organizations have many customs and rituals that are difficult to explain. However, a number of these can be explained by applying the theory of clubs. A few religious groups prohibit the lending of funds at interest to fellow co-religionists. On one interpretation this may be one of the costs of belonging to a club. Consider the Jewish religion, where these costs involved the Talmudic prohibition of lending at interest to fellow Jews ("Unto a foreigner thou mayst lend upon usury, but unto thy brother thou shalt not lend upon usury" (Deuteronomy 23:20) (see Poliakov [1965] 1977). The costs of observing the Talmudic prohibition, however, were reduced by several devices. One of the most interesting was to lend money at interest to a fellow Jew via the intermediary of a real or fictitious Christian (see Poliakov [1965] 1977). Moreover, the costs imposed by the Talmudic prohibition were outweighed by papal protection of the Jewish money trade in the Middle Ages. The Holy See helped Jews to get around the usury laws in order to lend money at interest to Christians (Poliakov [1965] 1977).

There is another interpretation of the usury rules of religious groups. To

---

29. See Morley 1949. Our theory of the connection between entrepreneurship and religion differs from that of Max Weber in that we do not invoke the Protestant (Calvinistic) work ethic as a basis for the emergence of entrepreneurship. See Weber 1956.

look at this other interpretation let us examine the Jewish usury laws again. These laws were interpreted so that they applied mainly to "consumption loans" rather than loans for normal commercial transactions. Jews engaged in normal commercial transactions could lend funds to one another at interest. The usury laws did not impede normal commerce; they were applied when an individual had a bad year with low income and had to borrow in order to maintain a minimal consumption pattern. Such a rule imposed costs on lenders and yielded benefits to borrowers. However, since unfavorable events could strike any member of the club, the usury rule could be interpreted as an insurance scheme enforced by the club.[30] With this interpretation an interest-free loan is not a cost of belonging to the club but an insurance premium paid by a club member. The insurance premium buys an insurance policy that protects club members against declines in their income. When these occur, the club provides its members with interest-free loans. The religious club in this instance provides another service: the enforcement of usury rules. These rules are not costs, but benefits of joining clubs, as they provide insurance unavailable to non-members (except possibly at substantially higher costs).[31]

A number of religious groups impose dietary restrictions on their members. Until the last generation Roman Catholics could not eat meat on Fridays, Muslims still may not eat pork, and Jews have a stringent set of dietary laws known as the kashruth. Why do members of these religious organizations restrict their eating behavior when there seem to be no apparent benefits from doing so?[32] We argue that there *are* benefits. Dietary laws give religious members a feeling of shared values. These shared values give members of the religious organizations a sense of a common identity and distinguish them from non-members.[33] It is exactly this difference between members and non-members that is needed to facilitate economic exchange under conditions of contract uncertainty. It is interesting to note that Jewish dietary laws were

---

30. Following Posner, we may interpret a consumption loan without interest as a "gift" from the lender to the borrower. For a thorough examination of the general phenomenon of gift giving in primitive economies, see Posner 1980. Posner develops the idea of gift giving serving as an insurance function in primitive societies, but does not explicitly examine the phenomenon of interest-free consumption loans of Jewish usury laws. For an analysis of the Kula Ring gift-exchange system as a clublike arrangement designed to facilitate barter exchange between different tribal communities living in the region of Massim in Papua New Guinea, see Landa chap. 7.

31. For a more detailed discussion of these issues, see Carr and Landa chap. 6.

32. Some people claim Jewish kashruth laws serve a cleanliness purpose. A thorough examination of these laws would indicate that this is not the case. Orthodox Jews claim these laws are a matter of faith and are not a matter of cleanliness.

33. Anthropologists have also put forth a functionalist interpretation of the role of dietary restrictions or food taboo as a boundary-maintenance device to help members to achieve group identity and solidarity and to exclude outsiders. See especially Douglas 1966.

expanded greatly around the fifth century A.D. just as the Jews were being dispersed over the Middle East and Europe. The dietary laws were artificially created to keep Jews, Jews. Dietary laws help identify club members,[34] an especially important function if club members are geographically dispersed.[35] Dietary laws discourage conversion by increasing the costs of joining the organization and thus serve as a barrier against those seeking to become members in order to receive the economic benefits. (Conversion, from an economic point of view, is a behavior similar to changing one's name to gain access to a club.) This theory predicts that religious organizations that yield clublike economic advantages to their members will not be missionary organizations seeking converts. Judaism does not seek converts; Protestant sects, on the other hand, do. This theory predicts, in addition, that religious organizations yielding club-like economic advantages will have stringent rules of behavior, like dietary restrictions, whereas the other organizations will not. In this respect, dietary laws serve very much like a signal, as education and ethnicity do in Spence's model. For dietary laws to be a signal like education, the marginal product of following them would have to be less for non-members of the religious group than for members. There is some empirical evidence that this is the case with Chinese converts to Islam in West Malaysia. Converts to these small religious groups are generally treated with suspicion. Converts are not trusted to the same extent that bona fide long-standing co-religionists are. Hence, converts adopting dietary laws do not receive the same benefits from following these dietary laws as existing religious members do.

According to Siow (1983), since the "New Economic Policy" was adopted in West Malaysia after the race riots in 1969—a policy that established quotas giving Malays preferential access to job and educational opportunities over non-Malays—there has been a trend toward conversion by Chinese who are economically disadvantaged (the unemployed, laborers, drivers, carpenters, and workers holding menial jobs). The incentive for Chinese to convert to Islam was motivated by short-term monetary benefits provided by PERKIN, an organization formed in 1960 specifically to convert non-Malays to Islam, and long-term benefits of job security for future generations who choose to remain in West Malaysia. The costs to Chinese converts, however, are not zero. Chinese Muslims are met with suspicion by Chinese—even though Chinese Muslims have not been ostracized from their respective clans, dialect associations, or ethnic communities—and by Malays even though Malay officials call the Chinese Muslims "*Saudara, saudara bahru*" ("new brothers"). Furthermore, some Chinese Muslims found it difficult to give up eating pork.

---

34. One of the ways this is achieved is that Jews will buy their food from common locations.

35. As is the case with Jews dispersed throughout the Diaspora.

Insignia and Signs: Symbols of Group Identity

Yet another way of reducing the costs of identifying a potential cooperating partner is to look for insignia—the external markings or symbols of group identity. These include coats-of-arms, blazons, flags, totems, clothing and decorations, and so on. For example, many Jews now wear a *chai* symbol around their necks, which is suppose to bring a long life. The symbol is easily recognized by other Jews; however, to non-Jews, it is meaningless and in no way identifies the wearer. It would seem, because of its technical superiority (unrecognizability by non-club members), that the *chai* has replaced the Star of David as the symbol of Jewish identity.

In Genoa in the Middle Ages, coats-of-arms were flown from every merchant ship in war and in peace. The Medici merchant bankers in fifteenth-century Florence used their famous trademark—a heart surmounted on a cross—for bales of merchandize and for addresses on business letters; for every other aspect of social life they identified themselves to others (apart from revealing their names) by the blazons that characterized their houses and palaces.[36]

In Scotland, clans wore clothing in special colors and patterns, each clan having one or more tartans to distinguish from others. Scottish names, like MacDonald and MacLeod, also identify clans. Because of the need for secrecy, symbols, insignia, and signs play a very important role in the initiation ritual ceremonies of new members of secret societies. Members learn the symbols and signs of group identity of a secret society; and severe penalties are imposed on those who betray the society's secrets. Chinese secret societies were widespread in Singapore and Malaya in the eighteenth and late nineteenth centuries. Wealthy Chinese merchants were invariably also leaders of Chinese secret societies until the societies were suppressed by the British government in 1870. These leaders, among other things, maintained law and order among members of their own community.[37]

Conclusions

In a world with zero transaction costs, clubs or clublike arrangements to define and identify club members and to constrain members' behavior would be redundant. In a world of contract uncertainty, on the other hand, the identity of the potential cooperating partner matters. By forming clubs or clublike arrangements in which members' behaviour is constrained, transaction costs can be reduced.

---

36. For a discussion of the use of insignia by Italian merchants in the Middle Ages, see Heers 1977.

37. For a discussion of Chinese secret societies in Singapore and Malaya, see Blythe 1969.

Our model, constructed in the second section, is a class of models that fall into the economic theory of clubs. We examined the economic benefits of belonging to clubs and abiding by the rules of the game of the club. We argue that the benefits of club membership—lowered transaction costs—explain the continued existence of clubs, whatever their origins.

In the preceding section, utilizing the theory of clubs together with the economics of signaling, we were able to provide economic rationales for a number of social customs and practices discussed by sociologists and anthropologists but ignored by economists. We explain these customs and practices as ways members economize on defining and identifying club members.[38]

REFERENCES

Ahern, Emily M. 1976. "Segmentation in Chinese Lineages: A View through Written Genealogies." *American Ethnologist* 3, no. 1 (February): 1–16.

Akerlof, George A. 1976. "The Economics of Caste and of the Rat Race and Other Woeful Tales." *Quarterly Journal of Economics* 90:599–617.

Barth, Frederik, ed. 1969. *Ethnic Groups and Boundaries*. Boston: Little, Brown & Co.

Becker, Gary S. 1976a. "Altruism, Egoism, and Genetic Fitness: Economics and Sociobiology." *Journal of Economic Literature* 14 (September): 817–26.

———. 1976b. *The Economic Approach to Human Behavior*. Chicago: The University of Chicago Press.

Blythe, Wilfred. 1969. *The Impact of Chinese Secret Societies in Malaya*. Royal Institute of International Affairs. London: Oxford University Press.

Buchanan, James M. 1965. "An Economic Theory of Clubs." *Economica* 32 (February): 1–14.

———. 1978. "Markets, States, and the Extent of Morals." *American Economic Review,* Papers and Proceedings, 65 (May): 225–30.

Buchanan, James M., and Gordon Tullock. 1962. *The Calculus of Consent*. Ann Arbor: The University of Michigan Press.

Carr, Jack L., and Janet T. Landa. 1981. "The Deuteronomy Law of Usury: An Economic Analysis." Institute for Policy Analysis, University of Toronto. Unpublished manuscript.

Carr, Jack L., G. F. Mathewson, and J. McManus. 1972. *Cents and Nonsense: The Economics of Canadian Policy Issues*. Holt, Rinehart and Winston.

Cooter, Robert D., and Janet Landa. 1984. "Personal versus Impersonal Trade: The Size of Trading Groups and the Law of Contracts." *International Review of Law and Economics* 4 (June): 15–22.

---

38. **Iannaccone (1992) has developed a club-theoretic model of religion very similar to ours. He explains that rational church members may benefit from bizarre behavioral restrictions, such as observing dietary restrictions, painful initiations, etc., because such restrictions can overcome free-rider problems associated with collective action.

Douglas, Mary. 1966. *Purity and Danger.* London: Routledge and Kegan Paul.

Freedman, Maurice. 1966. *Chinese Lineage and Society: Fukien and Kwantung.* London: The Athlone Press.

Fuller, Lon L. 1967. *Legal Fictions.* Stanford, Calif.: Stanford University Press.

Geertz, Clifford. 1978. "The Bazaar Economy: Information and Search in Peasant Marketing." *American Economic Review,* Papers and Proceedings, 68 (May): 28–32.

Gulliver, P. H. 1971. *Neighbours and Networks.* Berkeley: University of California Press.

Hagan, Everett. 1962. *On the Theory of Social Change.* Homewood, Ill.: The Dorsey Press, Inc.

Heers, Jacques. 1977. *Family Clans in the Middle Ages.* Amsterdam: North-Holland Publishing Company.

**Iannaccone, Laurence R. 1992. "Sacrifice and Stigma: Reducing Fee-riding in Cults, Communes, and Other Collectives." *Journal of Political Economy* 100 (April): 271–91.

Jevons, William Stanley. [1871] 1957. *Theory of Political Economy.* New York: Kelly and Millman.

Jones, Mervyn. [1967] 1971. "Freemasonry." In *Secret Societies,* edited by N. Mackenzie. New York: Collier Books.

Knight, H. Frank. 1921. *Risk, Uncertainty and Profit.* Boston: Houghton Mifflin Company.

Landa, Janet T. 1983. "The Enigma of the Kula Ring: Gift-Exchanges and Primitive Law and Order." *International Review of Law and Economics* 3 (December): 137–60.

Landa, Janet T., and Janet Salaff. 1980. "The Socio-Economic Functions of Kinship and Ethnic Networks in Promoting Chinese Entrepreneurship in Singapore: A Case Study of Tan Kah Kee's Firm." Paper presented at the Structural Analysis Program Workshop Series, Department of Sociology, University of Toronto.

Leach, E. R. 1961. *Pul Eliya: A Village in Ceylon: A Study of Land Tenure and Kinship.* Cambridge: Cambridge University Press.

MacKenzie, Norman, ed. [1967] 1971. *Secret Societies.* New York: Collier Books.

Morley, J. A. E. 1949. "The Arabs and the Eastern Trade." Part 1. *Journal of Malayan Branch of the Royal Asiatic Society* 22:143–77.

Poliakov, Leon. [1965] 1977. *Jewish Bankers and the Holy See.* Translated by Miriam Kochan.

Posner, Richard A. 1977. *Economic Analysis of Law.* 2d. ed. Boston: Little, Brown.

———. 1980. "A Theory of Primitive Societies: with Special Reference to Primitive Law." *Journal of Law and Economics* 23 (April): 1–53.

———. 1981. "Privacy as Secrecy." In *The Economics of Justice.* 231–67. Cambridge: Harvard University Press.

Rubushka, Alvin, and Kenneth A. Shepsle. 1972. *Politics in Plural Societies: A Theory of Democratic Instability.* Columbus, Ohio: Merrill.

Sandler, Todd. 1992. *Collective Action: Theory and Applications.* Ann Arbor: The University of Michigan Press.

Sandler, Todd, and John T. Tschirthart. 1980. "The Economic Theory of Clubs: An Evaluative Survey." *Journal of Economic Literature* 18 (December): 1481–1521.

Simmel, Georg. [1908] 1950. *The Secret and the Secret Society.* Part 4, *The Sociology of Georg Simmel.* Edited and translated by Kurt H. Wolff. New York: Free Press.

Siow, MoLi. 1983. "The Problems of Ethnic Cohesion among the Chinese in Peninsular Malaysia: Intraethnic Divisions and Interethnic Accommodation." In *The Chinese in Southeast Asia: Identity, Culture, and Politics,* vol. 2, edited by L. A. Peter Gosling and Linda Y. C. Lim. Singapore: Maruzen Asia.

Spence, A. Michael. 1974. *Market Signalling.* Cambridge: Harvard University Press.

Szanton, Cristina B. 1983. "Thai and Sino-Thai in Small Town Thailand: Changing Patterns of Interethnic Relations." In *The Chinese in Southeast Asia: Identity, Culture, and Politics,* vol. 2, edited by L. A. Peter Gosling and Linda Y. C. Lim. Singapore: Maruzen Asia.

Tollison, Robert P. 1972. "Consumption Sharing and Non-Exclusion Rules." *Economica* 39 (August): 276–91.

Weber, Max. 1956. *The Protestant Ethic and the Spirit of Capitalism.* New York: Charles Scribner's Sons.

Part 4
Gift-Exchange

CHAPTER 7

The Enigma of the Kula Ring: Gift-Exchanges and Primitive Law and Order

There is no such thing there as a free gift. (Radin 1971, 133)

Exchanges are peacefully resolved wars and wars are the result of unsuccessful transactions. (Lévi-Strauss 1969, 67)

As long as ceremonial exchanges continued to take place assuring that peace prevailed, the linked groups could continue to carry on other mutually advantageous activities, such as trade in ordinary goods. . . . (Dalton 1978, 160)

The classic economic paradigm of exchange is a *discrete* (one-shot) bilateral exchange of two different goods by isolated pairs of traders.[1] Eighty years of ethnographic description in the anthropological literature on the economies of stateless tribal societies in Papua New Guinea and elsewhere in Melanesia reveal a different reality: the dominance of *recurrent gift-exchanges* of the

I would like to thank the following for very helpful discussions and comments on earlier drafts of this chapter: economists James M. Buchanan, Gary Becker, Jack Carr, Robert W. Clower, Robert D. Cooter, Harold Demsetz, and Gordon Tullock; political scientists Robert H. Bates and Bernard Grofman; sociologist Theodore Caplow; anthropologists Elizabeth Colson, Frederick Damon, and Victor W. Turner; and three anonymous referees. I greatly benefited from my participation at the "1981 Kula Conference" held at the University of Virginia, Charlottesville, May 31–June 9, 1981; I would like to thank Frederick Damon for inviting me to the conference. Earlier versions of the paper were presented at the Public Choice Society annual meetings, San Francisco, March 14–16, 1980, and at the Law and Society annual meetings, Amherst College, Massachusetts, June 12–14, 1981. I also benefited from discussions at invited seminars at the University of Bielefeld (April 21, 1980), University of the Federal Armed Forces (Munich, April 24, 1980), University of Basel (April 25, 1980), University of Zurich (April 28, 1980), and the University of California at Berkeley, Law School (Jurisprudence and Social Policy Program, February 13, 1981). This is a revised version of Institute for Policy Analysis, University of Toronto, Working Paper, No. 8123 (June, 1981), published in *International Review of Law and Economics* 3 (1983): 137–60. I gratefully acknowledge the permission of the journal's publisher, Butterworth-Heinemann, to republish the paper.

1. Macneil (1974) defines a "relational contract" as a long-term contract between seller and buyer involving ongoing contractual relations. Goldberg (1976) points out that the paradigmatic contract of neoclassical economics and of legal analysis is a "discrete" transaction, whereas a large set of contracts are of the "relational contracts" type.

same ceremonial goods or two different kinds of ceremonial goods between pairs of trading partners chain-linked in complex trading networks. Of the many gift-exchange systems in Papua New Guinea—such as the *Hiri* of Central Papua (Seligman 1910), the *Te* of the Central Highlands (Bus 1951), and the *Moka* of Mount Hagen (Strathern 1971) to name a few of the better known systems—the classic is the Kula Ring of the Massim region, which is described in great detail by Malinowski ([1922] 1961). In terms of the *structure* of gift-exchange the Kula Ring is unique among the gift-exchange systems in Papua New Guinea. Unlike other gift-exchange systems such as the *Moka,* in which partners are linked directly and indirectly to form an open-ended chain or a "rope," Kula partners are linked directly and indirectly to form a "ring."

Interpreting this fascinating institution, Malinowski rejected the notion that Kula gift-exchanges were motivated by economic considerations. Rather, Malinowski ([1922] 1961, 173) emphasized that the motives were social and psychological. Thus began a long debate among anthropologists attempting to unravel the puzzle of the Kula Ring. As a result of subsequent work by anthropologists, a view began to crystallize that the instrumental function of the Kula Ring was the creation of political order via the creation of networks of alliances among stateless societies so as to facilitate commercial trade. This view, implicitly or explicitly, attributed an underlying *economic* function to Kula gift-exchanges and did much to explain a major puzzle of the Kula Ring. The anthropological viewpoint—that the Kula gift-exchange system creates primitive law and order in stateless societies—is consistent with modern PR-PC theory,[2] which emphasizes the importance of institutions in facilitating exchange. Richard Posner (1980), in his insightful paper on the economic functions of institutions of primitive societies, explains the Kula Ring as an institution that facilitated trade. Quoting Belshaw (1965), Posner (1980, 25) says:

> The *kula* itself was not oriented to individual trade in its ceremonial activities. But alongside the *kula* persons visiting their partners took advantage of the opportunities to engage in trade. Malinowski makes the point that *kula* partners would exchange gifts of a trade character in addition to *vaygu'a* [the ornamental objects exchanged in the *kula* ring], and that the security afforded by the partnership would make it possible for the visitor to make contact with other persons in the village and trade with them.

---

2. For the literature on PR-PC theory, see Furubotn and Pejovich 1972, Goldberg 1974, and Mueller 1976 and 1989.

An explanation of the Kula Ring in terms of its role in facilitating trade, while explaining one major puzzle of the Kula Ring, leaves unanswered two other major puzzles of the Kula Ring—not explained by anthropologists or anyone else. The two puzzles, which this paper will attempt to explain, are

1. Why is the Kula trade organized in the form of a *ring* of connected partners? and
2. Why in the Kula Ring are there *two different* ceremonial goods circulating in opposite directions perpetually around the Ring?

In this chapter, we draw on PR-PC theory and the economics of signaling (see Spence 1974 and Akerlof 1970) to develop a theory of the Kula Ring that will unravel the Kula puzzles. Fundamental to our theory of the Kula Ring is the assumption that transaction costs are positive. The emphasis on the importance of transaction costs in explaining economic institutions has been at the foundations of modern PR-PC theory and modern monetary theory.[3] Recently, the insight that "institutions matter" in a world with positive transaction costs has been extended to explain certain institutions of primitive societies. Anthropologist Geertz (1978) rationalizes the "institutional peculiarities" of the bazaar economy (i.e., "clientalization," the pairing off of buyers and sellers in recurrent transactions) in terms of the bazaar's function in reducing information costs under contract uncertainty. Posner (1980) explains many of the institutions of "primitive and archaic societies," including kinship groups, gift giving, polygamy, etc., as alternative insurance mechanisms used by these societies for coping with the problems of uncertainty and high information costs. The theory of the Kula Ring presented in this chapter is consistent with the transaction costs approach to institutions in emphasizing that the Kula Ring is an institutional arrangement that emerged primarily in order to economize on transaction costs of intertribal commercial exchange in stateless societies.

This chapter is divided into four parts. The next section describes the essentials of the Kula Ring and the environmental setting within which it operates. The third section unravels the first of the two Kula puzzles, drawing on property rights theory. We shall show that the ring structure of Kula exchange is an efficient institutional arrangement for organization of exchange: each trader needs to visit only *two* adjacent markets in order to acquire traded commodities from all markets within the Kula Ring. The fourth section attempts to unravel the second Kula puzzle, drawing on the economics

---

3. For contributions to modern monetary theory, see for example, Niehans 1969, Brunner and Meltzer 1971, and Ostroy 1973.

of signaling as well as PR-PC theory. We shall show that the Kula Ring, with its double circuit of Kula valuables circulating in opposite directions, is an efficient clublike arrangement for the enforcement of the rules of the game which, in turn, helps to maintain the two adjacent-market system in the Kula Ring. In the fifth section, we shall extend our theory to a world in which costs of identifying Kula Ring members are high. Using the economics of signaling, we shall provide an economic rationale to certain institutional practices and customs that accompany the Kula trade, such as mortuary rituals and magical rites. We argue that these ritual aspects of the Kula exchange are institutional ways of establishing individual and group identity in a world characterized by uncertainty and high information costs.

The Kula Ring and Its Environmental Setting

Kula Islands, Kula Communities, and Tribes

The Kula Ring is a system of gift-exchange carried on between different East Papuo-Melanesian tribal communities.[4] The communities are found scattered on a ring of islands that lie off the southeastern extremity of Papua New Guinea in the region of Massim. Each "Kula community" defined by Malinowski ([1922] 1961, 103) as a community that makes overseas Kula trade expeditions as an independent unit, makes about "two expeditions overseas every year" (Fortune 1932, 22). The ring of "Kula islands," the various "Kula communities" and tribes participating in the Kula Ring are shown in map 1.

The East Papuo-Melanesian or the Massim group, differs from other tribal communities—the Papuans and the West Papuo-Melanesians—living in the interior of Papua New Guinea and the Gulf of Papua. The Massims, however, are by no means a culturally homogeneous group. Malinowski divided the Massims into two broad groups:

1. The Northern Massim group, which can be further subdivided into three culturally homogeneous groups, form a relatively homogeneous group both in terms of language and culture; the dominant language spoken by the North Massim group, is the Kiriwinian language of the Trobrianders; and
2. The Southern Massim group, which is further subdivided into three culturally homogeneous areas or groups (see map 1). The Southern Massims differ quite sharply from the Northern Massims. For example, the Dobuans differ not only in physical appearance from the

---

4. This section is based on the work of Malinowski ([1922] 1961) unless otherwise indicated.

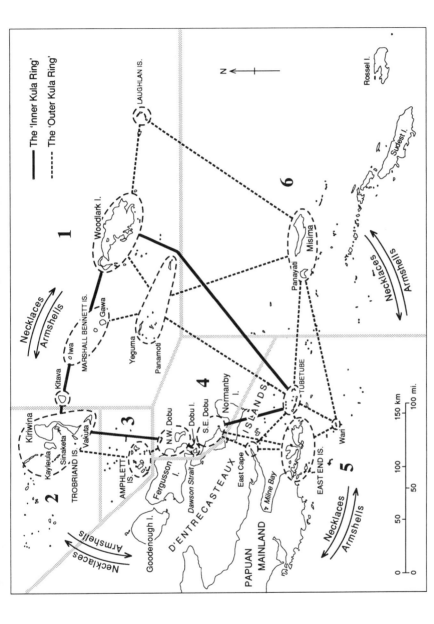

Map 1. Kula islands, Kula communities (circled in the map), and tribes in the Kula Ring. 1: The east branch of the Northern Massim group; 2: Trobrianders; 3: Amphlett Islanders; 4: Dobuans; 5: the west branch of the Southern Massim group; 6: the east branch of the Southern Massim group. (Adapted from Uberoi [1962] 1971.)

Trobrianders but also speak their own Dobuan language, which is used as lingua franca all over the D'Entrecasteaux Islands, the Amphlett Islands, and as far as the Trobriand Islands; on the other hand, the Dobuans do not speak the Kiriwinian language of the Northern Massims. Furthermore, in the pre-Kula days, the Dobuans were cannibals whereas the Trobrianders were not.

Social Structure of the Kula Communities

Kinship structure in these Kula communities is predominately matrilineal, that is, children belong to the mother's lineage or clan. Thus, for example, every Trobriander belongs matrilineally to one of the four named totemic clans. In these matrilineal societies, wealth and status are inherited from maternal uncle to nephew. The family is the basic unit of procreation and economic production. Beyond the family, the basic structural unit for group cooperation, is the "local lineage" or sub-clan, which consists of clansmen living in a particular village. Members of the local lineage or village community "exploit jointly their garden lands, perform ceremonies, wage warfare, undertake trading expeditions, and sail in the same canoes or fleet of canoes as one group" (Malinowski ([1922] 1961, 57).

Each village consists of one or more local lineages. Several neighboring village communities make up a district. The tribe is the widest social group within which members share a common bond. The limits of morality do not extend beyond the tribe: members of a sub-clan consider each other as real kinsmen, members of the same clan as pseudo-kinsmen, and those not belonging to the same tribe as "outsiders" or strangers (Malinowski [1922] 1961, 191–92, 276, 345). Political and economic power in each village is vested in the hands of chiefs, as in the case of the Trobrianders (who have the most complex political system in the Massim area, in that they have a system of ranked chieftainship), or in the hands of village elders, headmen, or "Big-men" elsewhere in the Massim region. Because these Big-men (or chiefs in the Trobriands) do not have any executive or judicial authority that could be called governmental, these tribal societies have been called "stateless societies" by anthropologists.[5]

Structure of Kula Trade and the Rules of the Game

It is among these stateless societies in Massim that the gift-exchange network between different tribes is found in its most developed and novel form as the Kula Ring:

---

5. See Uberoi [1962] 1971. See also Dalton 1978.

The trade consists of a series of . . . periodic overseas expeditions, which link together the various groups, and annually bring back big quantities of *vaygu'a* (valuables) and of subsidiary trade from one district to another. The trade is used and used up, but the vaygu'a—the arm-shells and the necklaces—go round and round the ring. (Malinowski [1922] 1961, 103)

One of the most striking features of the Kula trade is the existence of two different ceremonial goods—necklaces (*soulava*) and armshells (*mwali*)—perpetually circulating around the ring in opposite directions.

A well-defined set of rules of the game exists to regulate the Kula trade. One set of rules governs the geographic direction of the movement of the two ceremonial gift-exchange objects around the Kula Ring. The necklaces must travel in a *clockwise* direction while the armshells must travel in a *counter-clockwise* direction. From map 1, which shows the circular paths along which Kula objects travel, we may distinguish two non-concentric Kula rings: (1) the "Inner Kula Ring," which involves gift-exchanges between Kula communities located on six Kula islands (Trobriand Islands, Marshall Bennett Islands, Woodlark Island, Tubetube, S.E. Dobu, and N.W. Dobu); and (2) the "Outer Kula Ring," which involves gift-exchanges between the Kula communities located on eleven Kula islands (Trobriand Islands, Marshall Bennett Islands, Woodlark Island, Laughlan Islands, Misima and Panayoti Islands, Wari Is-lands, East End Islands, East Cape Islands, S.E. Dobu, N.W. Dobu, and the Amphlett Islands). Tubetube performs the specialist long-distance middleman function of connecting Kula islands in the "Outer Kula Ring" in the Southern Massim region to the "Inner Kula Ring." The "Inner Kula Ring" forms the main circuit of Kula trade and it is only this "Inner Kula Ring" that is described in great detail by Malinowski.[6] All the dates of the overseas Kula expeditions are fixed in advance. Passed on by a series of ceremonial gift-exchanges, the most valuable Kula objects acquire personal names and histo-ries of their own; they are ranked in terms of their reputation and are greatly sought after. In addition, the more valuable Kula objects have genealogies that list all those traders throughout the Kula Ring who have possessed them (Malinowski [1922] 1961, 271).

A second set of rules governs the ethics of gift-exchange. When the

---

6. Thus it is very difficult to understand Malinowski's map of the Kula Ring (which includes what we called the "Outer Kula Ring") and the role Tubetube played in the Ring, because very little is said about the movement of the Kula valuables in the "Outer Kula Ring" and the pattern of movement of Kula valuables when they enter into the hands of Tubetube middlemen. Fortunately, however, the main circuit of the Kula valuables is described in great detail by Malinowski. In 1978, the main circuit of the Kula trade is still this Inner Kula Ring. See Irwin 1981.

visiting Kula partner arrives with a "solicitary gift" (e.g., food) and is given an "opening gift," say a necklace, from his host Kula partner, the gift must be reciprocated with a counter-gift, an armshell, of equivalent value at a *future* date. It should be noted that no Kula valuables are carried on overseas Kula expeditions; the visiting Kula partner visits his host partner in order to *receive* gifts and not to give them. Between any two Kula partners, there is institutionalized *delayed reciprocity* involving two opposite kinds of objects. But at the same time, each of these two objects must be passed on in one direction only so that a chain of unidirectional trading Kula partners is built up in the Kula Ring. The global structure of the Kula exchange is one that is characterized by cyclical, indirect reciprocation between connected pairs of partners.[7] Furthermore, a time limit is also prescribed for a recipient of a gift to pass it on to one of his partners:

> A man who is in the Kula, never keeps any article for longer than, say, a year or two. Even this exposes him to the reproach of being "niggardly" and certain districts have the bad reputation of being "slow" and "hard" in the Kula. . . . (Malinowski [1922] 1961, 93)

In this Kula gift-exchange, the equivalence of the closing gift is left to the giver. What are the mechanisms for ensuring that the partners will honor the obligation to reciprocate? Four mechanisms can be identified:

1. Role of "intermediary gifts": If a Kula partner cannot repay his partner when the latter visits him, he must reciprocate the opening gift with a smaller gift, an "intermediary gift" (*basi*), given in token of good faith, which itself must be reciprocated by his partner. Thus the time interval between receiving the opening gift and reciprocating the closing gift is bridged by a series of smaller gift-exchanges between Kula partners (Malinowski [1922] 1961, 356);
2. Role of reputation: A Kula partner who does not repay a gift will eventually lose his reputation and his Kula partners (see below);
3. Role of "give and take" moral code in which the wealthy man is obligated to share wealth: The higher the rank the greater the obligation (Malinowski [1922] 1961, 97);
4. Role of public magical rites and ceremonial acts: magical rites and

---

7. In Lévi-Strauss's (1969) terminology, the structure of trade in the Kula Ring is composed of "restricted exchange" and "generalized exchange." Restricted exchange refers to isolated pairwise exchange between two parties. On the other hand, for a three person trading network, the generalized exchange operates as follows: A → B → C → A, where "→" indicates "gives to."

public ceremonial acts always accompany an overseas Kula expedition; these rites and ceremonies "act directly on the mind (*nanola*) of one's partner and make him soft, unsteady in mind and eager to give Kula gifts" (Malinowski [1922] 1961, 102). Malinowski ([1922] 1961, 214, 359) also suggested the use of sorcery by a Kula trader against the defaulting partner.

A third set of rules governs membership in the Kula Ring. Kula exchange is not free exchange between anonymous parties whenever the opportunity arises. Strict rules govern who can enter the Kula Ring. To enter the Ring, a man must *inherit* a Kula object and magic from his father or mother's brother. Once he obtains a Kula object, he can initiate a Kula partnership with his father's or mother's brother's partners or other partners in the Kula Ring. Once a Kula partnership is established, it is a *lifelong* partnership and is passed on from generation to generation: "Once in the Kula, always in the Kula."[8] Not all East Papuo-Melanesians in Massim, however, can participate in the Kula Ring. For example, certain "inferior" sub-clans in Kiriwina are excluded.

A man can have few or many partners depending on his rank. A commoner in the Trobriands would have a few partners who lived in nearby islands, whereas a chief would have hundreds of partners distributed over several islands. But there is a geographic limit beyond which no Kula traders, not even the most influential chief, has any partners and the furthest limits of Kula partnership are the same for all the members of the Kula community. Thus, for example, no man in Sinaketa has any partners in Kitava, and no man in S.E. Dobu or Dobu Island has Kula partners in Sinaketa. Beyond the geographic limit, however, a Kula trader still knows the names of his indirect partners, i.e., the partners of his partners. Participants of the Kula Ring regard the Kula trade as a *circular* system (Damon 1983). The pattern of Kula exchange is very complex. The simplest structure of exchange would be one in which:

If we were to imagine that in the Kula Ring, there are many people who have only one partner at each side, then the Ring would consist of a large number of closed circuits, on each of which the same articles would constantly pass. (Malinowski [1922] 1961, 278)

---

8. "Once in the Kula, always in the Kula," (Malinowski [1922] 1961, 85), however, should not be taken to imply that all Kula partnerships are stable overtime. Partnerships do break up when one of the partners defaults on his obligations. And according to Fortune (1932, 214) "partnerships between the most powerful men who exchange the finest valuables are the most stable." See also Campbell 1983.

However, the actual structure of Kula exchange is much more complex since

> . . . every small Kula man, as a rule, has on one side or the other, the big one, that is a chief. And every chief plays the part of a shunting-station for Kula objects. Having so many partners on each side, he constantly transfers an object from one strand to another. (Malinowski [1922] 1961, 278)

When a man has a number of Kula partners, he can manipulate his partnerships so as to increase the supply of ceremonial objects. If he receives four objects from four partners, for example, he will make promises to repay, but he will honor his promise only to *one* of the four partners. Eventually, however, he must honor all promises to repay. But in the short run, an enterprising Kula partner can accumulate a supply of ceremonial objects via delayed reciprocity.

> I have become a great man by enlarging my exchanges at the expense of blocking theirs for a year. I cannot afford to block their exchange for too long, or my exchanges will never be trusted by anyone again. I am honest in the final issue. (Fortune 1932, 217)

Kula expeditions overseas typically involve large groups of men. Thus, for example, five hundred N. W. Dobuans were on a particular trip to Sinaketa in 1918. In these group expeditions, the chief or Big-man assumes the role of the leader of the expedition and he would make Kula exchanges with fellow-chiefs/Big-men. The need for group expeditions under a leader is designed to overcome many dangers, including the need to "conduct their operations with partners living in communities of different culture, not bound by the same rules of overall behavior, nor answerable to a single political authority" (Belshaw 1965, 14). Within the Kula Ring, the consequence of the rules of partnership is one in which

> . . . all around the ring of Kula there is a network of relationships. . . . Men living at hundreds of miles sailing distance from one another are bound together by direct or intermediate partnerships, exchange with each other, know of each other, and on certain occasions meet in a large intertribal gathering. Objects given by one, in time reach some very distant indirect partner or other. . . . It is a vast, intertribal net of relationships, a big institution, consisting of thousands of men all bound together by one common passion for Kula exchange. (Malinowski [1922] 1961, 92)

Structure of Intertribal Commercial Trade and
Middleman Entrepreneurship

What is the functional role of this big institution of Kula exchange? Whereas Malinowski himself minimized the role of Kula trade in facilitating commercial exchange, latter-day anthropologists (see Campbell 1983; Dalton 1978; Mauss [1954] 1979; Sahlins [1965] 1969; Uberoi [1962] 1971) reinterpreting Malinowski's evidence have emphasized its political-economic function in facilitating trade, among its several functions.[9]

Intertribal commercial exchange presupposes specialization and division of labor among various Kula communities, which reflects underlying differences in resource endowment. Trobrianders, primarily agriculturalists, produce large quantities of yams, taro, sweet potatoes, bananas, and coconuts. Some Trobrianders also specialize in fishing and in the manufacturing of wooden bowls, combs, baskets, lime pots, and the like. The foodstuffs and manufactured goods are exported to other Kula communities in which these goods are in short supply, for example, the Amphlett Islands and N. W. Dobu.

The Amphlett islanders specialize in pottery manufacturing; the finest pots in the Massim region are made in the Amphletts. The pots are exported to the Trobriands via the Kula trade in exchange for Trobriand foodstuffs and manufactured goods. Amphlett pots circulate over great portions of the Kula Ring; they are found in the Marshall Bennett Islands, Woodlark Island, and in Dobu.

North West Dobu exports sago to the Trobriands and Amphlett Islands which produce no sago. Dobuan sago, unlike Amphlett pots, circulates over a small portion of the Kula Ring.

Gawa, one of the Marshall Bennett Islands, is a major producer of seagoing canoes and is a major link in the "Inner Kula Ring." It links up with Trobriand Islands in the west via Kitava (another Marshall Bennett island) and with Woodlark Island to the east. Gawan canoes are exchanged directly for armshells as overseas payments, and the canoes move long distances via a chain of middlemen to the southern portion of the Kula Ring (see Munn 1983). In the southern part of the Kula Ring, Tubetube middlemen exchange armshell valuables in payment for Gawan canoes.

---

9. Kula valuables perform a number of functions. Besides their function in creating political alliances between different tribes in the Kula Ring, Kula valuables are used in a wide range of internal exchanges within a community: for dowries, for payment of canoes and pigs, for mortuary debts and homicide payments, and for hiring the services of a sorcerer. The degree to which a Big-man can successfully manipulate his internal exchange networks through the Kula valuables obtained from external trade in the Kula Ring determines his status within his community. See Uberoi 1962. See also Damon 1983.

Woodlark, in the eastern portion of the Kula Ring, is the center of manufacturing of the Kula armshell valuables that are used for circulation all around the Kula Ring. Woodlark links up with the Marshall Bennett Islands in the east and Tubetube in the south. Woodlark also builds large seagoing canoes that are exported to Tubetube.

Tubetube, a tiny volcanic island, which is poor in natural resources, manufactures clay pots and nose ornaments for export; Tubetube pots circulate over a large portion of the Kula Ring, for example, reaching Gawa in the northern portion of the Ring. Except for pots and nose ornaments, there are no manufactures to exchange for the many products imported into Tubetube. Tubetube, however, is centrally located vis-à-vis Kula communities in the Southern Massim region. Its strategic location was recognized by a number of ethnographers (see Irwin 1981; Malinowski [1922] 1961, 495; Seligman 1910, 526). Tubetube islanders exploited its locational advantage to specialize in long-distance middleman trade; they are the sole carriers and organizers of long-distance trade in the Kula Ring. Their positions as long-distance middlemen enable Tubetube islanders to obtain almost every article made and used by the communities with whom they trade. Manufactured goods from the Trobriands are imported into Tubetube via Duau (Normanby); canoes are imported from Gawa, from Panamoti, and from Woodlark. In its role as the specialist long-distance middlemen, Tubetube islanders distribute Kula valuables and manufactured goods obtained from Kula communities in Northern Massim to those in Southern Massim. Because it is linked directly with Woodlark and with Dobu, Tubetube forms one of the most strategic links in the "Inner Kula Ring." In its long-distance middleman role, Tubetube links up communities in the "Outer Kula Ring" with communities in the "Inner Kula Ring." Situated at the southern portion of the Ring, Tubetube is also a point of entry for Kula necklaces which are produced in two sources outside the Kula Ring: Rossel Islands and central Papua.

Kitava, one of the Marshall Bennett Islands, like Tubetube, forms another strategic link in the northern half of the Kula Ring: all goods—ceremonial and commercial—originating in Woodlark Island and in the Trobriand Islands must converge in Kitava. Kitava traders, however, unlike Tubetube traders are not specialist long-distance middlemen. In addition to trading, Kitava islanders are builders of the finest seagoing canoes.

Underlying differences in resource endowment make commercial exchange mutually beneficial because of regional interdependence. And Kula partnerships by offering security to the visiting partner (see the next subsection) make it possible for the latter to engage in barter trade (*gimwali*). The visiting Kula partner

> . . . enters into a threefold relation with the . . . natives. First, there is his partner, with whom he exchanges general gifts. . . . Then there is the

local resident, not his personal Kula partner, with whom he carries on *gimwali*. Finally there is the stranger with whom an indirect exchange is carried on through the intermediation of the local men. (Malinowski [1922] 1961, 363)

In terms of the movement of the goods involved in the *gimwali* trade, non-durable foodstuffs like sago circulate over shorter distances of the Kula Ring than durable manufactured goods like pottery and canoes which circulate over long distances of the Kula Ring. With manufactured goods circulating in the Kula Ring through a chain of intermediaries, opportunities arose for middlemen making profits from buying and reselling the same goods (Malinowski [1922] 1961, 363).

Warfare, Raids, Cannibalism, and Mortuary Rituals

Commercial exchange (*gimwali*) between members of various tribal groups were facilitated by the creation of friendly political alliances via Kula partnerships. In the pre-Kula days, intertribal warfare and raids were common.[10]

The natives of Tubetube were fierce raiders, while the Dobuans were notorious cannibals and sorcerers widely feared in the Massim region. The institution of Kula partnerships formed between foreigners, i.e., members belonging to different tribes (for example, between the Trobrianders and the Dobuans), is a way of turning hostile tribes into friendly allies. Thus for example:

> . . . a Bwaioan [N.W. Dobuan] cannibal definitely exempts from his legitimate menu those foreigners who are his *kula* partners namely, the Sinaketens in the north and the Dobu islanders to the south. (Uberoi [1962] 1971, 96)

The overseas partner is a host, patron, and ally in a foreign district, so that Kula partnerships:

> provide every man within its ring with a few friends near at hand, and with some friendly allies in the far-away, dangerous foreign districts. (Malinowski [1922] 1961, 92)

---

10. Malinowski did not provide many examples of pre-Kula warfare, raids, or cannibalism. It is from many of the papers presented at the 1981 Kula Conference held at the University of Virginia, Charlottesville, May 31–June 9, that I realized the importance and frequency of pre-Kula intertribal warfare, raids, and cannibalism practiced by tribes within the Kula Ring and also outside the Ring.

The ring of Kula partnerships thus integrated the various tribal stateless societies into a wider Kula intertribal polity, which greatly reduced intertribal warfare and cannibalism.[11]

When Malinowski arrived in Papua New Guinea in 1915 to do his fieldwork, the Kula Ring had already developed into its full-blown form. Thus Malinowski provided no ethnographic data on the origins, history, or development of the institution of the Kula Ring. As Uberoi (1962, 67) puts it

> The history of the Kula ring is unknown, or at any rate unpublished. Nor do we know how the islands of the Kula ring came to be inter-linked by this remarkable cycle of ceremonial exchanges.

Thus, while economic specialization and division of labor provided a basis for the existence of commercial trading networks, supported by the Kula alliances, they do not by themselves provide an explanation as to how the complex *ring* structure of Kula trade was evolved.

Magical rites and public ceremonies always accompany overseas Kula expeditions to foreign Kula communities separated by distance and the sea.[12] These magical rites and ceremonial acts surrounding overseas Kula partnerships are a way of extending the limits of morality to foreigners who had previously been enemies.

But how is a friendly Kula partnership maintained when one of the Kula partners dies? The institution of mortuary rituals help to create enduring intergenerational Kula partnerships. When a partner dies, a mortuary or mourning taboo is placed on the dead man's sub-clan; no Kula valuables can be given away, but members expect to receive as many Kula valuables as possible. After a certain time, the mortuary taboo is lifted when a public distribution of valuables—Kula and non-Kula alike—to the heirs of the dead has been held. The heir who inherits most of the valuables organizes a mortuary feast (*so'i*) in which all the Kula partners of the deceased are invited; he then gives Kula valuables to the Kula partners, to cancel out old debts and to create new debts. The functions of mortuary rituals:

> . . . serve, in effect, to pull together the *kula* links of the dead man for the last time in his own name, and establish them afresh for his suc-

---

11. Dalton (1978) emphasized the role of colonial state-imposed law and order in reducing warfare and raiding in Kula societies. Participants of the 1981 Kula Conference also emphasized the important role of missionary activities in abolishing warfare, raiding, and cannibalism in the Southern Massim region.

12. This contrasts with the so-called Inland Kula trade carried out between members of two contiguous communities or members of the same Kula community. In the former, little magic rites are performed since members of two contiguous communities tend to be friendly neighbors; in the latter, no magic and public ceremonial gatherings take place.

cessor, who is presumably the "master of the *so'i*." The "sub-clan" or village community of the deceased reaffirms its unity by keeping the taboos and observances incumbent upon it following his death; and the continuity of its *kula* alliances is applied expressly in the procedure whereby new exchanges are opened with the assembled partners *before* the old ones are closed, the initial gifts (*vaga*) being given before the return gifts (*yotile*) due as debts remaining from earlier transactions. (Uberoi 1962, 107)

The "Big-Man" and His "Kitoums"

A man becomes successful in the Kula by accumulating a large supply of Kula valuables and passing them on to his partners; he becomes a Big-man in the Kula Ring. Thus a Big-man is an entrepreneur who is successful in playing the Kula game and abiding by the rules of the game. But the intriguing question arises: What motivates a man to put a Kula valuable into circulation in the Kula Ring in the first place? Malinowski and his predecessors provided no facts for answering this question. But Uberoi ([1962] 1971, 107) and present-day ethnographers do answer this question. For example, one of the most significant findings by present-day ethnographers, doing fieldwork on the Kula Ring in the Massim region, is the discovery of the significance of Kula valuables in their roles as "kitoums" (see Campbell 1983; Damon 1983; Munn 1983; Weiner 1976). Damon (1983), in particular, emphasized the importance of the "kitoum" in answering the question: "What moves the Kula?" All Kula valuables are initially *produced* by some *specific named persons* so that they are *privately owned:* as such they are "kitoums" to be distinguished from other Kula valuables that are circulating from hand to hand in the Kula Ring. A person puts his "kitoum" into circulation in the Kula Ring in order to "produce a person's name." The institution of Kula thus

> functions to differentiate one person from another. . . . The result of the Kula then is a skyline of differentiated persons, some of whom have "high" names while others have "low" or no names at all. (Damon 1983, 318)

In the Woodlark Island, three persons were identified by Damon as being the most successful Woodlark people participating in the Kula Ring. Their names are the highest because they have circulated around the Kula Ring more than other names by means of exchange of Kula valuables. When a person produces a "kitoum" and puts it into circulation in the Kula Ring, this means that "if and when things do break down then the kitoums may be called in, no matter who is holding them, and where they are" (Damon 1983, 326). Furthermore, a person who owns a "kitoum" can pass it on to his own sons or to his nephew so that all "kitoums" not produced by the present owners are inherited from their original owners. Success in the Kula builds up a person's name, which in turn is a path to leadership positions being contested by persons equally eligible to assume them.

The Enigma of the Kula Ring: Organization of Markets

We shall attempt to unravel the first of the two Kula puzzles: Why is the Kula trade organized in the form of a *ring* structure of trading partners? We shall develop a theory of the Kula Ring as an efficient structural arrangement for economizing on costs of trading. Our theory, drawing on Property-rights theory, is based on the following assumptions:

1. Societies in the Kula Ring are stateless societies that lack institutions for the protection of life, property, and contracts.
2. Societies in the Kula Ring are nonliterate societies.
3. Big-men in the Kula Ring are approximately equal in rank and power.
4. There is specialization and division of labor among the societies in the Kula Ring so that potential gains from foreign trade exist.
5. Trade is an ongoing process so that incentives for further trade are not eliminated.
6. Trading activities are not costless. Trading costs consist of (a) transportation costs; (b) transaction costs[13] such as search, contract-negotiation, and enforcement costs; and (c) setup costs[14] of establishing friendly political alliances with other Big-men. We shall call such setup costs "alliance costs."

N-isolated Markets: The "Kula Tree" Economy

Imagine an abstract "Kula Tree" economy with seven Big-men ($V_1, V_2, \ldots, V_7$) located in a sequence of spatially separated markets[15] arranged in a

---

13. For a survey and discussion of the concept of transaction costs, see Ulph and Ulph 1975.

14. For a discussion of "setup costs" see Heller 1972.

15. Some anthropologists consider the Kula system to belong to a "nonmarket" system (as well as belonging to a nonstate system). Perhaps the correct terminology is the distinction between what Belshaw (1965) calls "traditional markets" as distinct from "modern markets." As Belshaw (1965, 8) himself cautions, "To talk of some exchange systems as market systems and others as non-market systems is bound to raise objections of classificatory accuracy. Paul Bohanan and George Dalton seem closer when they write of the applicability or inapplicability as the case might be, of the 'market principle' to those institutions which are empirically examining as market-places. Market-places are sites, with social, economic, cultural, political, and other

circular pattern. In the absence of institutional arrangements linking markets either directly or indirectly together, each Big-man in such a "Kula Tree" economy will have to incur high costs of trading if he wishes to buy traded commodities from all six foreign markets. Transportation and alliance costs would bulk large in total trading costs. Each Big-man must either take six separate overseas trips to six foreign markets, or he must make one single trip visiting a sequence of N-spatially separated markets. In addition to the usual transaction costs associated with exchanges *within* a particular market, each Big-man must also incur "alliance costs" with six other Big-men prior to exchanges with the natives of each foreign market. The "Kula Tree" economy is inefficient as long as markets remain isolated from one another.

But entrepreneurs will emerge to link up markets, because in spatially separated markets, price differentials can exist for the same (homogeneous) commodity. The existence of price differentials gives rise to a class of entrepreneurs whose very function is to *discover* opportunities for making a profit by arbitrage—buying goods at a lower price in one market and reselling the same goods at a higher price in another market.[16] Their entrepreneurial activities will therefore link up hitherto isolated markets,[17] thus lowering costs of trading. There are alternative institutional arrangements for linking up markets that are superior to the "Kula Tree" economy: a central marketplace (the "Kula Star" economy) and two adjacent markets (the "Kula Ring" economy).

A Central-Place Market: The "Kula Star" Economy

Imagine that V_1 is an entrepreneur who perceives opportunities for making a profit by establishing a central marketplace, a "community fairground" (Clower 1969, 11) to which all other Big-men would come to trade. The specialist middleman who emerges thus functions as a central clearinghouse, buying and reselling goods at a profit to the other nonspecialist Big-men traders. The emergence of a central marketplace, which transforms the "Kula Tree" economy into the "Kula Star" economy, economizes on total trading

---

referents, where buyers and sellers (or perhaps exchanges of other types) meet for the purpose of exchange. The degree to which they use the market principles is highly variable, but it may be that market principles are seldom wholly absent. It is also common to find market principles applied in quite other institutional contexts." In this chapter, the notion of "markets" is used in the sense of Belshaw to mean marketplaces where buyers and sellers meet to trade.

16. Austrian theory of entrepreneurship developed by Kirzner (1973) emphasizes the role of entrepreneurship in discovering opportunities for making profits by intermarket arbitrage.

17. Littlechild and Owen (1980) use an Austrian model of the entrepreneurial market process to show how profit-seeking entrepreneurs discover markets and link them together.

costs. In the first place, alliance costs are reduced, since each Big-man needs to establish only one friendly alliance with the middleman. In the second place, transportation costs are reduced. This is because (a) if previously each Big-man undertook six separate trips, he now undertakes only one trip; and (b) if previously he undertook a long trip all the way around the Ring, visiting a sequence of markets, now he only goes to the center of the Ring, where the central marketplace is located. The "Kula Star" economy is an efficient institutional arrangement for economizing on trading costs in a world where transportation and alliance costs are high.

In order for a "Kula Star" economy to emerge, however, two conditions would have to exist; the Big-man entrepreneur would have to: (1) establish a ready market that is *centrally* located vis-à-vis other markets, so that other Big-men would find it worthwhile to come to the central place to trade; and (2) make profits large enough to cover operating costs and still yield an attractive profit margin. The operating costs involve costs of carrying inventories of all traded goods in the surrounding markets as well as establishing and enforcing rules of the game necessary to ensure law and order in the central marketplace.

Historically, a central place for the Kula communities in the "Inner Kula Ring" did not emerge. This may be explained by the fact that the conditions necessary for the emergence of the Kula Star economy did not exist. In the first place, there is no group of islands within the "Inner Kula Ring" that is centrally located vis-à-vis the Kula islands. The Yeguma group is situated peripherally within the "Inner Kula Ring" (see map 1). Second, societies in Massim are stateless societies in which Big-men are of approximately equal rank and status. As such, no Big-man can emerge to become a "Super Big-man" to dominate other Big-men, thus creating a hierarchy of Big-men of unequal ranks. The costs of establishing such a political dominance would be very high because the central place, of necessity, must be a large-scale market able to accommodate the influx of various visiting Big-men and members of their tribes. Such a large-scale central marketplace would exhibit significant diseconomies of scale especially where certain tribes practice cannibalism and raiding. The Kula Star economy for the societies in the "Inner Kula Ring" could not have emerged given the geography and the institutional context within which these societies operate.

In the "Outer Kula Ring," on the other hand, a "Kula Star" economy did emerge for the Kula communities located in the southern portion of the Ring. Tubetube serves as a "central place" for these communities (see map 1). Why did a "Kula Star" economy emerge in the "Outer Kula Ring" but not for the communities in the "Inner Kula Ring"? Two reasons account for this. First, with the exception of clay pots, Tubetube has no traded goods of any major significance, but it has a locational advantage in that it is centrally located vis-à-vis Kula communities in the Southern Massim region. Taking advantage of its strategic location, Tubetube traders seized the opportunities for making profits from arbitrage by linking up foreign markets in Southern Massim with Tubetube. But Tubetube, a tiny volcanic island, could not establish a central marketplace to which all traders in Southern Massim could come to trade. Instead Tubetube traders emerged as specialist *long-distance* middlemen who traveled to foreign markets and organized foreign trade in Southern Massim. Because of its strategic location,[18] Tubetube monopolizes the specialist long-distance middleman function in the "Outer Kula Ring." The Kula Star economy is an efficient structure for organizing foreign trade since for each Big-man in the Outer Kula Ring—transportation and "alliance costs" are minimized since these costs are borne mainly by Tubetube long-distance traders. The fact that the Yeguma group is not centrally located vis-à-vis the Kula communities within the Inner Kula Ring explains why more foreign trade in the Massim region is not organized by such specialist long-distance middlemen as those from Tubetube. It also explains why, as earlier noted, the Kula Star economy did not emerge in the Inner Kula Ring.

Two Adjacent Markets: The Kula Ring Economy

The existence of a central marketplace is efficient, but its existence requires certain conditions that are not met in the societies in the Inner Kula Ring. The second-best solution would be for each Big-man to visit *two* adjacent markets in order to acquire all traded commodities. This two adjacent-market institutional arrangement is possible only if N-spatially separated markets are linked directly and indirectly together in a ring structure so that each market in the ring is directly linked to the next. In this "Kula Ring" economy (see fig. 13), each Big-man in a market performs the role of middleman for its two adjacent markets passing traded goods sequentially from one market to the adjacent market. In addition, each Big-man needs to execute only a sequence of two pairwise bilateral exchanges with a Big-man on the left- and right-hand side of the ring in order to acquire traded goods from all N markets in the ring. Thus, for example, for V_1 to buy goods from V_5, V_6, V_7, Big-men located in markets on the left segment of the ring, V_1 needs only to buy from V_7. This is because V_7 acquires V_6's goods directly and V_5's goods indirectly via V_6 in the role of middleman (see fig. 13). Similarly, V_1 can acquire goods from V_2, V_3, and V_4 by buying only from V_2. This is because V_2 can buy V_3's goods directly and V_4's goods indirectly via V_3 acting as middleman. If submarkets are not all connected, on the other hand, then each Big-man must visit *more* than two

---

18. Irwin (1981) has shown that Tubetube is the only central place serving the Southern Massim region.

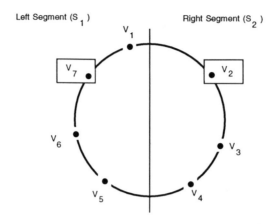

Fig. 13. Two adjacent markets: the Kula Ring economy

markets in order to acquire traded goods from all N markets. Thus, for example, if V_4 is a Big-man whose market is isolated from all the other connected markets in the Ring, then V_1 must visit not only the two adjacent markets but must also make a separate trip to V_4's market in order to obtain traded goods from all N markets. In the absence of a central marketplace, a Kula Ring economy would be superior to a Kula Tree economy because it economizes on transportation and alliance costs. A Kula Ring economy may even be superior to a Kula Star economy as far as *transportation costs* are concerned if traveling distances to the two adjacent markets are *less* than traveling distances to the central marketplace. It can be shown, with the aid of Theorem 1, that for $N \geq 6$ the Kula Ring structure of trade may be superior to a Kula Star trading structure in minimizing total transportation costs.[19]

Conceptually, we may imagine that the Kula Ring emerged by an "invisible hand" process: the structural effects of each Big-man, establishing two pairwise Kula partnerships with neighboring Big-men, located on a ring of islands, will generate a decentralized trading network in the form of a ring of Kula partners.[20] This invisible-hand process is, in effect, an entrepreneurial

---

19. Theorem 1: for $N \geq 6$, for a uniform distribution of traders in a circular pattern, a decentralized pairwise trading structure ("ring") is more efficient in minimizing transportation costs than is a centralized trading structure ("star"). See Grofman and Landa 1983.

20. For a detailed analysis of the conceptual emergence of the decentralized Kula Ring trading network, see Grofman and Landa 1983.

process in which each Big-man entrepreneur $(V_1, V_2, \ldots, V_7)$ perceives opportunities for making a profit by engaging in arbitrage between adjacent markets and seizes the opportunities by linking up a set of all submarkets. In this way, the entrepreneurial process will ensure that all seven markets, arranged in a circular pattern, are eventually connected directly and indirectly in a decentralized ring pattern of trading network. An implication of our theory of the emergence of the Kula Ring is that each Big-man entrepreneur will try to protect his middleman role by taking precautions to prevent Kula traders from short-circulating his market. Our theory may also explain why there is a geographic limit beyond which no Kula traders has any partners and that the furthest limits of Kula partnership are the same for all members of the Kula community.

Barter, Middlemen, and the Ethnically Homogeneous Middleman Group: Institutional Alternatives in Reducing Contract-Enforcement Costs

Just as the evolution of an economy from a barter economy to money economy reduces transactions costs (Clower 1969, introduction), so the evolution of the Kula Tree economy into the Kula Ring economy economizes on total trading costs. Once the Kula Ring economy emerges, total transaction costs could be reduced further by reducing contract-enforcement costs of trading in a particular market. Thus, each Kula trader when visiting an adjacent foreign market, can reduce contract-enforcement costs by resorting to (1) barter trades with the local natives, thus eliminating the problem of contract uncertainty,[21] and (2) barter trades with strangers via the clansmen of the host Kula partner acting as middlemen. The institution of *middleman* eliminates the need for trust between members of different tribes who do not trust each other but trust the local natives who act as the middlemen. This is because local natives, being members of the same ethnic group as the host Kula partner, share the same codes of behavior embedded in an EHMG that function as constraints on their behavior.[22] In stateless societies, barter, middlemen, and the EHMG all help to achieve social order within markets and hence economize on the costs of protecting property and contracts.

---

21. The institution of barter exchange turns out to be an institutional arrangement that overcomes the problem of trust. See Niehans 1969. See also chapter 9.

22. For an economic analysis of the EHMG as a clublike arrangement, alternative to contract law, for the enforcement of contracts, see chapter 5. For a general theory of ethnic trading clubs as institutions for enforcement of contracts, see chapter 6. For a general theory of trading clubs, from a mathematical perspective, see Cooter and Landa 1984. For a further extension of the theory of the EHMG, see LaCroix 1989.

The Enigma of the Kula Ring: Club Enforcement of the Rules of the Game

The Kula Ring, as noted earlier, is an efficient institutional arrangement for organization of markets. That explains the first Kula puzzle: Why is the Kula Ring a ring of trading partners? There remains a second puzzle: Why in the Kula Ring are there *two different* ceremonial objects circulating *perpetually in opposite* directions? In explaining this enigmatic aspect of the Kula Ring, we shall be utilizing the PR-PC approach, as well as the economics of signaling.

In order for the Kula Ring economy (two adjacent-market system) to be viable, all seven Big-men located on islands within the Kula Ring must obey the rules of the Kula game. Each Big-man must continually give, receive, and pass on Kula valuables to his direct partners. But why do two *different* cere-monial objects of equal value circulate perpetually in the Ring? We shall argue that the two different items of value serve as signaling devices of *mutual cooperative* intent on the part of both giver and receiver *who are of equal rank*. Suppose V_1 gives a necklace to V_2 with the intention of establishing a friendship alliance with V_2 but this need is not reciprocated by V_2, then gift-giving will be *unilateral*. But if V_1 and V_2 are of equal rank, and are poten-tially hostile strangers, then the need for establishing friendship alliance is mutual and gift-giving will be *bilateral*. But V_2 cannot reciprocate V_1's gift of a necklace with the same necklace. This is because V_1 may interpret this as a rejection of V_1's friendship. In order to provide unambiguous signaling of V_2's cooperative intent, V_2 must reciprocate with a *different* kind of countergift (e.g., an armshell) of equal value. Thus it is only by the use of *two different* kinds of gifts that the parties concerned signal to each other their mutual intentions of entering into friendship alliances; receiving gifts alone is not enough. Three different kinds of gift-exchange items circulating around the Kula Ring, like only one gift item will again give rise to ambiguous signaling. Thus, a double ring structure of Kula alliances composed of bi-directional flows of two different exchange objects (transmitting distinguishable signals) circulating in opposite directions between *adjacent* Big-men would be an efficient signaling device.

Because only two ceremonial objects, originating from different "nodes" (i.e., Big-men), circulate in opposite directions around the Ring, Kula gift-exchange, by its very nature, cannot be simultaneous but must be charac-terized by *delayed reciprocity*. Delayed reciprocity, however, implies credit transactions, which in turn requires *trust* that the recipient will reciprocate the gift. How is such trust created and maintained? Malinowski, we recall, identi-fied four mechanisms for the enforcement of gift-exchanges. But none of the mechanisms provide *effective* sanctions. Take the role of the intermediary gifts and the role of reputation for example. The role of the intermediary gifts is to reduce the size of the loss associated with gift default, but by themselves do not eliminate contract uncertainty. Loss of reputation by itself also does not provide an effective sanction against default unless the Big-man also loses the underlying economic advantages of middlemen-entrepreneurship that accompanies the Kula trade. It is this potential threat of loss of commercial trade that we identify as the effective sanction against breach. We shall show that this effective mechanism for contract enforcement is built into the ring structure of Kula exchange with its two objects circulating in opposite directions.

Assume that V_1 always receives the armshell one year before the arrival of the necklace. In the event that the necklace arrives *before* the armshell, this triggers off a signal to V_1 that one of the Kula partners has either violated the norms of the group by not passing on the necklace or being too tardy in holding it for too long. Thus the use of two different Kula gift items, circulating in opposite directions, also serves the additional function of disseminating information about possible violations of the rules of the game by some Kula members.

So V_1 needs to find out who the deviant party is and to bring pressure on the offending party. Because the necklace always travels in a clockwise direction, V_1 can reasonably assume that since the necklace has already arrived, the armshell must have already passed half way around the Ring. Thus he can economize on search costs by decomposing the network of partners into a subset of partners, located on the left half of the Ring, and confines his search activity within the subset. And because V_1 himself is directly connected to his Kula partner, V_2, and indirectly to others in the Ring, he must disseminate information to his partners directly and indirectly that he is not the deviant party. As a consequence of information flowing in two opposite directions— an information-search flow and an information-dissemination flow—eventually everyone in the Ring will know who the deviant party is (for example, V_7).

Because everybody is connected directly and indirectly together in a ring, V_7's deviant behavior caused a chain of victims of default. A process of implicit coalition formation of "six against one"[23] to put pressure on V_7 will be predicted to emerge. From V_7's point of view, the pressure on him is exerted directly by V_1 and V_6 so that it appears as if a coalition "of the extremes against the intermediary" (Lorrain and White 1979) has been formed. In actual fact, the direct pressure exerted by V_1 and V_6, reflects the collective wrath of the whole coalition of six partners against V_7, the person

---

23. This is analogous to Caplow's (1968) concept of "two against one" coalition formation process. Caplow argued that "dyads" have no mechanism of conflict resolution built into it, whereas "triads" have such mechanisms because of the possibility of "two against one" coalition formation.

violating the norms of the group. The coalition can attempt to alter V_7's behavior by imposing sanctions, either by choosing (a) to declare war on the defaulting party, a costly sanction, or (b) to exclude V_7 from future Kula transactions by bypassing V_7.

It is the threat of excluding V_7 from the Kula Ring that provides the incentive for V_7 to honor his obligations. If V_7 is excluded from the Kula Ring, not only his direct partners will refuse to trade with him, but *all* the partners of his partners as well; in short, all the other Big-men in the Kula Ring, acting as members of the "Kula Ring Club" will not trade directly with him.[24] Mutual trust, established through particularistic Kula partnerships, is thus reinforced by the sanctions built into the very structure of the *ring* of Kula partnerships. The Kula Ring, with its double circuit of two different objects, turns out to be a clublike arrangement in which everyone is watching everyone else, gossiping about each other, and monitoring each others' behavior.[25] And because Kula partnerships are passed on from generation to generation, hence excluding outsiders, an unbroken chain of Kula partners exist. A man in the Kula Ring knows that mutual trust exists between any two overlapping future generations of Kula partners. Thus he can predict with a high degree of accuracy the trustworthiness of current and future generations of Kula partners. The Kula Ring, with its double circuit of two different objects perpetually circulating in opposite directions, is thus an efficient institutional arrangement for the enforcement of gift transactions between present and future generations of Kula partners. The Kula Ring provides the functional equivalent of law and order which in well-developed societies is provided by the state.

Property rights–public choice theory emphasizes the importance of the legal structure, a public good, in facilitating the emergence of markets. Without constraints on behavior, individuals will have the incentive to choose the dominant strategy to steal and to break contracts. The result is market failure. To get out of this PD, individuals will get together to enter into a social contract to create the state for the protection of private property and contracts. The state thus emerges out of Hobbesian anarchy by public choice.

Like Hobbes, modern public choice theorists, in particular Buchanan, emphasized the role of the state in achieving social/political order. This is because public choice theory is the study of the economics of politics of *highly developed societies*. But if we extend PR-PC theory to the analysis of primitive stateless societies, we find that alternative institutional arrangements exist to achieve ordered anarchy. It is here that PR-PC theorists must turn to Marcel Mauss's ([1954], 1974) famous work, *The Gift*, for inspiration.

---

24. Because everybody in the club will exclude the breaching party from future transactions, the costs of breach are very high.

25. Primitive societies thus lack privacy, a point that is emphasized by Posner (1980).

Mauss's major contribution to anthropology was to point out that the gift is the primitive way of achieving social order that in developed societies is secured by the state. The role of gift giving is to create friendship alliances between potentially hostile groups. This is because the "extent of morality"[26] of primitive man does not extend beyond the boundaries of his own clan/lineage or tribal group. One trusts one's own kinsmen or members of one's own tribal group and distrusts outsiders, for as Mauss ([1954], 1974, 79) says, " . . . there is no middle path: There is either complete trust or complete mistrust." The gift, or in Mauss's terminology "prestation," is an institution of primitive societies for extending the limits of morality beyond one's own clan or tribe, and hence making it possible to trade with one another.

Because Kula partnerships are passed on from one generation to the next, the Kula gift-exchange is played as a "supergame" in which enduring mutual trust and mutual cooperation occurs between present and future generations of Kula partners.[27] Once we analyze the Kula Ring from a PR-PC perspective, the second Kula puzzle disappears: The Kula Ring may be interpreted as the outcome of primitive public choice of the rules of the game for facilitating intertribal commercial exchange in stateless societies.

An Economic Interpretation of Kula Valuables, Magical Rites, and Mortuary Rituals: Symbols of Individual and Group Identity

In a society that lacks institutions for protecting life, property, and contracts, an institution like the Kula Ring may be interpreted as a clublike arrangement for economizing on costs of transacting across tribal boundaries. So far we have assumed implicitly that it is costless to identify club members. This assumption will now be relaxed. Using the economics of signaling we are able

---

26. See Buchanan's (1978) discussion of the limits of morality. See also Sahlin's ([1965] 1969) discussion of the narrow social horizon of primitive peoples and the possibility of "negative reciprocity" when members transact across tribal boundaries.

27. For a survey of economists' contributions to game theory literature, including PD model, see Schotter and Schwodiauer (1980). **See also Kreps 1990.

In his pure consumption loan model, Samuelson (1958) pointed out that the market in pure loans fails to solve problems of intertemporal transfers efficiently, in the absence of a general asset. The way out of such market failure is a social compact whereby present and future generations implicitly agree not to break the chain of giving and receiving. In the Kula game, present and future generations explicitly enter into a social compact via mortuary rituals not to break the intergenerations vertical chain of Kula partnerships. It is the existence of this social compact between *vertical* chains of Kula partners that makes it possible for the *horizontal* chain of Kula partners in the Ring to mutually trust each other and hence play the Kula game as a "supergame." With respect to the discussion of vertical and horizontal chains of trust, this is discussed in the anthropological literature by Lévi-Strauss (1969) in terms of marriage alliances that are perpetuated over the generations.

to explain some of the customary practices and institutions associated with the Kula trade—such as the circulation of Kula valuable ("kitoums"), totemic clan names, magical rites, and mortuary rituals—as institutional responses to the high information costs of identifying members of the "Kula Ring Club."

Magical Rites and Circulation of Kitoums: Symbols of Individual and Club Identity

Recall that the aim of putting a "kitoum" into circulation in the Kula Ring, according to Damon, is to build up a person's name.[28] But Damon did not provide an answer as to why individuals wish to build up their names in the Kula Ring because he is not concerned with the problem of contract uncertainty.

In a world characterized by contract uncertainty, it is important to build up a person's name because a person's name serves as a proxy for reputation. In a society with n named individuals, there are n persons with distinct reputations, some betters than others, because some invest in building up their names. Reputation is an intangible asset in a world of contract uncertainty[29] because a person's reputation for reliability and honesty in transactions assures him of, among other things, maintaining a network of trading partnerships. The Kula gift-exchange system is a means of establishing and maintaining reputations among a network of Kula partnerships. With a network of Kula partnerships, a man thus assures himself of the economic benefits of a network of commercial trading partners, as well as a supply of Kula valuables to be used in internal exchange. These, in turn, have important local effects, for example, it is Big-men with reputations who organize certain productive activities.

A man's reputation thus signals his degree of reliability in Kula transactions. Because famous Kula objects, such as "kitoums," are named and attached to individual named and ranked Kula traders, the named Kula objects become symbols of the individual Kula trader's identity and his reputation. In a preliterate society, Kula valuables thus transmit information or signals to

---

28. Damon (1983), without realizing it, has provided a solution to what public finance theorists call the "free-rider" problem in public goods supply; the public good in question in the Kula Ring is law and order. Since no one can be excluded from the benefits of law and order once provided, no one has the incentive to contribute to the cost of the public good. They would, instead, free-ride on the benefits of law and order without incurring the costs. In the Kula Ring, on the other hand, individuals can derive private benefits from the provision of a public good, i.e., build up their name, and thus there is no incentive to free-ride.

29. For a discussion of names serving as a proxy for reputation, see chapter 6. See also chapter 5.

other Kula traders of the identity and reputation of members of the Kula Ring Club. Each "Big Man" in the Kula Ring is also an entrepreneur with superior reputation for honesty in Kula transactions. Each successful Kula trader is also the trader who is careful in his choice of Kula partners whom he can trust.

Kula valuables are passports to entry into the Kula Ring: no Kula valuables, no Kula trade.[30] Possession of a Kula valuable therefore identifies a person as a member of the intertribal Kula Ring Club. No outsider can become a member unless he has acquired a Kula valuable; in this way Kula valuables function as screening devices that sort out members who belong to the Kula Ring Club and those who do not. The magical rites that accompany Kula exchanges further screen members from non-members. A member of the Kula Ring Club not only must possess a Kula valuable, he also must know the magical rites that accompany gift-exchange. Since magical rites take many years to learn, learning the magical rites is like learning to speak the language of the trading group.[31] For those who learn the magic rites at a young age, they can decode at low cost the shared symbolic meanings embodied in the Kula valuables. The costs of entering the club by outsiders, on the other hand, are high because of the difficulty of learning the magic rites.

In preliterate societies like the Kula societies, there must be ways of documenting membership in the Kula Ring Club beyond oral communication. There must be efficient ways of helping improve the memory so as to retain information. Just as Spence (1974) treats ethnicity as a low cost signaling device, so we may treat *physical material objects* like Kula valuables as low-cost *mnemonic* devices which help to screen out members from non-members of the club. Furthermore, Kula valuables (necklaces and armshells) by their very *durability,* are passed on from generation to generation (e.g., at mortuary rituals), so that the person inheriting the Kula object may be considered to be the symbolic equivalent of the Kula partner who has died. In this way, embodied in each named Kula valuable is a "condensed genealogy"[32] of all those members of the sub-clan/clans who are and who have been Kula traders belonging to the "Kula Club." In a preliterate society, the use of Kula valuables thus economizes on information costs of keeping genealogical records of clan members who are members of the Kula Ring Club.

---

30. Kula valuables are thus like money in a monetary economy; possession of money is "so to speak, a passport for entry into the organized market sector of a money economy" (Clower 1969, 14).

31. For a discussion of the difficulties of communication across national boundaries, see Arrow 1963.

32. This is a term that anthropologist Victor Turner invented on the spot while discussing my paper with me (personal conversation, University of Virginia, Charlottesville, June 5, 1981).

Totemic Clan Names and Mortuary Rituals: Symbols of Clan Identity

Each "Big Man" in the Kula Ring is embedded within a family which, in turn, is embedded in a clan. Societies in Massim, like many primitive societies, consist of groups that are divided into named totemic-clans, i.e., clan members identify each other by the use of a totem (typically an animal or bird); the totem becomes the symbol of clan membership and clan solidarity. A man who builds up his name thereby also builds up the name/reputation of his clan. Thus the institution of the Kula not only establishes a rank order of Kula traders with different reputations, but also a rank order of different *clans* with different reputations of clan members for reliability in Kula transactions. Those totemic clans that have established superior reputations for themselves can overcome the reluctance of Kula traders belonging to other clans to trade across clan boundaries.

The institution of mortuary rituals may be interpreted as an arrangement for transmitting information to Kula Ring Club members belonging to *different clans* so that the reputation of the decreased Kula partner and his clan does not die with him, but is passed on to his heirs, who are members of the decreased Kula trader's clan.

REFERENCES

Akerlof, George. 1970. "The Market for 'Lemons': Quality Uncertainty and the Market Mechanism." *Quarterly Journal of Economics* 84 (August): 488–500.

Arrow, Kenneth J. 1963. "Classificatory Notes on the Production and Transmission of Technological Knowledge." *American Economic Review* 59:29–33.

Belshaw, Cyril S. 1965. *Traditional Exchange and Modern Markets.* Englewood Cliffs, N.J.: Prentice-Hall, Inc.

Brunner, Karl, and Allen H. Meltzer. 1971. "The Uses of Money: Money in the Theory of an Exchange Economy." *American Economic Review* 61 (December): 784–805.

Buchanan, James M. 1978. "Markets, States, and the Extent of Morals." *American Economic Review* 68:364–68.

Bus, G. A. M. 1951. "The *Te* Festival of Gift Exchange in Enga (Central Highlands of New Guinea)." *Anthropos* 46:813–24.

Campbell, Shirley F. 1983. "Kula in Vakuta: The Mechanics of Keda." In *The Kula: New Perspectives on Massim Exchange,* edited by Jerry W. Leach and Edmund Leach. Cambridge: Cambridge University Press.

Caplow, Theodore. 1968. *Two against One. Coalitions in Triads.* Englewood Cliffs, N.J.: Prentice-Hall, Inc.

Clower, R. W., ed. 1969. *Monetary Theory: Selected Readings.* Harmondsworth, Middlesex, England: Penguin Books Ltd.

Cooter, Robert, and Janet T. Landa. 1984. "Personal vs. Impersonal Trade: The Size of Trading Groups and Contract Law." *International Review of Law and Economics* 4 (June): 15–22.

Dalton, George. 1978. "The Impact on Colonization on Aboriginal Economies in Stateless Societies." In *Research in Economic Anthropology,* vol. 1, edited by G. Dalton.

Damon, Frederick H. 1983. "What Moves the Kula: Opening and Closing Gifts on Woodlark Island." In *The Kula: New Perspectives on Massim Exchange,* edited by Jerry W. Leach and Edmund Leach. Cambridge: Cambridge University Press.

Fortune, R. F. 1932. *Socerers of Dobu.* London: Routledge and Kegan Paul.

Furubotn, Eirik G., and Svetozar Pejovich. 1972. "Property Rights and Economic Theory: A Survey of Recent Literature." *Journal of Economic Literature* 10 December: 1137–62.

Geertz, Clifford. 1978. "The Bazaar Economy: Information and Search in Peasant Marketing." *American Economic Review,* Papers and Proceedings, 68 (May): 28–32.

Goldberg, Victor P. 1974. "Public Choice-Property Rights." *Journal of Economic Issues* 8:45–61.

———. 1976. "Toward an Expanded Economic Theory of Contract." *Journal of Economic Issues* 10:45–61.

Grofman, Bernard, and Janet Landa. 1983. "The Development of Trading Networks among Spatially Separated Traders as a Process of Proto-Coalition Formation." *Social Networks* 5:347–65.

Heller, Walter. 1972. "Transaction with Set-up Costs." *Journal of Economic Theory* 4:465–78.

Irwin, Geoffrey J. 1981. "Archeology in the Kula Area." Paper presented at the Kula Conference, the University of Virginia, Charlottesville, May 31–June 9.

Kirzner, Israel. 1973. *Competition and Entrepreneurship.* Chicago: The University of Chicago Press.

**Kreps, David H. 1990. *Game Theory and Economic Modelling.* Oxford: Oxford University Press.

**LaCroix, Sumner J. 1989. "Homogeneous Middleman Groups: What Determines the Homogeneity?" *Journal of Law, Economics, and Organization* 5:211–22.

Lévi-Strauss, Claude. 1969. *The Elementary Structures of Kinship.* Trans. James Harle Bell, John Richard von Sturmer, and Rodney Needham. Boston: Beacon Press.

Littlechild, S. C., and G. Owen. 1980. "An Austrian Model of the Entrepreneurial Market Process." *Journal of Economic Theory* 23:361–79.

Lorrain, F., and Harrison White. 1979. "Structural Equivalence of Individuals in Social Networks." *Journal of Mathematical Sociology* 1:49–80.

Macneil, Ian. 1974. "The Many Futures of Contracts." *Southern California Law Review* 47 (May): 691–816.

Malinowski, Bronislaw. [1922] 1961. *Argonauts of the Western Pacific.* E. P. Dutton and Co.

Mauss, Marcel [1954] 1979. *The Gift: Forms and Functions of Exchange in Archaic Societies.* London: Routledge and Kegan Paul.

Mueller, Dennis C. 1976. "Public Choice: A Survey." *Journal of Economic Literature* 14:395–433.

————. 1989. *Public Choice II. A Revised Edition of Public Choice.* Cambridge: Cambridge University Press.

Munn, Nancy D. 1983. "Gawan Kula: Spatiotemporal Control and the Symbolism of Influence." In *The Kula: New Perspectives on Massim Exchange,* edited by Jerry W. Leach and Edmund Leach. Cambridge: Cambridge University Press.

Niehans, J. 1969. "Money in a Static Theory of Optimal Payments Arrangements." *Journal of Money, Credit and Banking* 1:706–26.

Ostroy, Joseph. 1973. "The Informational Efficiency of Monetary Exchange." *American Economic Review* 63:597–610.

Posner, Richard A. 1980. "A Theory of Primitive Societies." *Journal of Law and Economics* 23:1–53.

Radin, Paul. 1971. *The World of Primitive Man.* New York E. P. Dutton and Co., Inc.

Sahlins, Marshall D. [1965] 1969. "On the Sociology of Primitive Exchange." In *The Relevance of Models for Social Anthropology,* edited by Michael Banton. London: Tavistock Publications.

Samuelson, Paul. 1958. "An Exact Consumption-Loan Model of Interest with or without the Social Contrivance of Money." *Journal of Political Economy* 66: 467–82.

Schotter, A., and G. Schwoediauer. 1980. "Economics and the Theory of Games: A Survey." *Journal of Economic Literature* 18:479–527.

Seligman, C. G. 1910. *The Melanesians of British New Guinea.* Cambridge: Cambridge University Press.

Spence, A. Michael. 1974. *Market Signalling.* Cambridge: Harvard University Press.

Strathern, Andrew J. 1971. *The Rope of Moka: Big-Man and Ceremonial Exchange in Mount Hagen, New Guinea.* Cambridge: Cambridge University Press.

Uberoi, J. P. Singh. [1962] 1971. *Politics of the Kula Ring: An Analysis of the Findings of Bronislaw Malinowski.* Manchester: Manchester University Press.

Ulph, A. M., and D. T. Ulph. 1975. "Transaction Costs in General Equilibrium Theory—A Survey." *Economica* 42:355–72.

Weiner, Annette B. 1976. *Women of Value, Men of Renown.* Austin: University of Texas Press.

Part 5
Altruism and Cooperation in Honeybee Colonies

CHAPTER 8

Socioeconomic Organization
of Honeybee Colonies

Janet T. Landa and Anthony Wallis

And the Amorites, which dwelt in that mountain, came out against you, and
chased you, as bees do, and destroyed you in Seir, even unto Hormah.
—Deuteronomy 1:44 (King James Version)

The behavior and organization of social insects has been extensively investigated and documented (Wilson 1971 and 1978). The highest degree of social-
ity, known as *eusociality,* is found in termites and in many species of the order
Hymenoptera (ants, bees, and wasps). In the latter, the superfamily *Apoidea*
(bees) and one particular species, *Apis mellifera* (the honeybee), has been the
subject of special attention (Michener 1974). This is largely due to its domes-
tication, consequent widespread distribution, the past importance of its agricultural products (honey and beeswax) and the current economic significance
of its pollination function (*The Hive and the Honeybee* 1975). Because the
honeybee has been by far the most intensively studied of all social insects, it is
available as a baseline for comparative sociobiological studies (Wilson 1971).
In this chapter the word "bee" will, unless otherwise indicated, mean the
honeybee.

This chapter was originally published as an article in the *Journal of Social and Biological
Structures* 2 (1988): 353–63. We gratefully acknowledge the permission of the journal's publisher, the Academic Press Limited, for reprinting the article.

Earlier versions of this paper were presented at the Public Choice Society Annual Meeting,
New Orleans, La., February 21–23, 1985, and at the Canadian Law and Society Association
Conference, Montreal, May 31, 1985. We would like to thank Professors Anatol Rapoport,
Nicolaus Tideman, Gordon Tullock, Reuven Brenner, Christopher Bruce, and two anonymous
referees for helpful comments. An earlier version appears as Hoover Institution Working Paper
E-86-50, September 1986.

Anthony Wallis is at the Department of Computer Science, York University, Toronto.

A *colony* of bees normally consists of one fertilized and egg-laying mother (queen) and her offspring, which are divided into a few hundred males (drones) and tens of thousands of infertile females (workers). This population, except when swarming or migrating, occupies a *nest* constructed of wax in which young bees are reared and the colony's food reserves (honey and pollen) are stored.

An analysis of bee behavior must recognize that honey is stored energy, and that a colony is operating an economy that is dominated by energy. In the natural state, this economy yields little or no honey surplus—the economy can be said to be in an almost permanent energy crisis (Heinrich 1979). In the temperate zones, colonies must store enough honey to survive the winter. In the tropics, this is not necessary and colonies frequently migrate, abandoning an empty nest and its investment of wax, presumably in search of better forage, i.e., floral food sources. In either case, any potential for surplus is diverted into an increase in population. When it is large enough, and depending upon a number of other factors (Free 1977), the colony rears additional queens and prepares for reproduction by swarming.

Bee genotypes evolve by competition between colonies. Those colonies that fission and survive more frequently will contribute more to the gene pool. Since the local forage is a dominant factor in determining the potential for a food surplus and hence a population increase, it follows that there is an advantage in evolving behavior that utilizes the local forage more productively.

The range of foraging is constrained by the necessity of making an energy "profit" and by the optimal use of time. Clearly, a bee should not fly any further than the distance at which the energy consumed in the round-trip balances the energy collected (in the form of nectar). The energy profit per trip varies inversely with the trip distance, being maximal near the nest and falling to zero at the energetic range limit. A more significant variable is the energy profit per unit time—this falls off even more strongly with the distance flown. Assuming a more-or-less uniform and constant forage supply, the bees are better employed foraging near the nest than further afield. However, the nearer sources will be depleted faster. Thus, in practice the optimal foraging distance will, depending on local and current conditions, be somewhere between zero and the energetic range limit. The range limit due to economy of time is that distance at which the profit per unit time begins to fall off. The above argument could be made more quantitative by reformulating it as a maximization problem subject to two constraints, but our qualitative aspects given are sufficient for our purposes.

It is important to note that the bee forages for, and transports, energy in the form of a fairly dilute solution of sugars, i.e., nectar. In the nest this is concentrated (by a factor of about 10) to maximum strength into honey to minimize storage costs (and also to prevent fermentation). A mechanism that could extend the economic foraging range would confer an evolutionary advantage on the colonies possessing it. One such mechanism would be the concentration of nectar into honey at a distant site and the transport of the honey rather than nectar to the nest. This would involve the construction of one or more satellite nests in addition to the main or primary nest. This primary-satellite nest organization may be interpreted as an example of an "extended phenotype" (Dawkins 1982) which extends the foraging range of bees, just as the "lake may be regarded as a huge extended phenotype, extending the foraging range of the beaver in a way which is somewhat analogous to the web of the spider" (Dawkins 1982, 200). A possible sequence of events leading to the construction and use of satellite nests is described below.

Assume that the familiar honeybee, denoted A.m., has evolved into a (hypothetical) new subspecies, A.m.*, which has the following additions to its behavioral repertoire:

1. The colony casts queenless "foraging swarms" loaded with honey that alight at sites near the economic boundary of the nest foraging range.
2. Scouts from the swarm investigate the foraging beyond the economic boundary. If it is promising, the swarm begins the construction of a satellite nest in the same way that an A.m. reproductive swarm constructs a new colony nest, converting the honey stored in their bodies irreversibly to wax combs. Alternatively, if the foraging does not look promising the swarm returns home. In this way the colony constructs satellite nests only in the direction of promising forage.
3. Workers based at the satellite nest forage outward beyond the original economic boundary of the primary nest, returning their nectar loads to the satellite to be concentrated into honey. Other workers must stand on guard duty to prevent robbery of the honey.
4. As the honey stores at the satellite build up, it is ferried back to the primary nest. This requires two-way traffic between the primary and satellite nests, the returning bees coming back with essentially empty stomachs to the satellite.[1]
5. (Optional) If the productivity of the extended foraging range de-

---

1. A possible objection to the speculative primary-satellite organization is that the population at the satellite will, since there is no queen present, begin to behave like a queenless colony. However, from beekeeping experience with colonies partitioned vertically by queen-excluding grills into queen-including and queen-excluding regions, it is known that the physical presence of the queen is not necessary. It is enough for there to be sufficient traffic from the queen-present area to the queen-absent area to distribute the "queen substance."

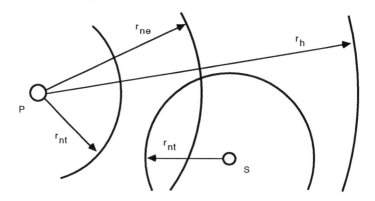

Fig. 14. *P,* primary nest; *S,* satellite nest; r_n, nectar foraging range; r_{nt}, time limit; r_{ne}, energy; r_h, honey collection range

clines, e.g., due to the onset of winter, the bees abandon the satellite and retreat to the primary nest, conveying with them any remaining honey stores. The abandoned wax would be a lost investment, unless fortuitously it was free to be reoccupied the following summer.

The extra behavior of the speculative A.m.* above does not constitute an excessive extension to the known behavioral repertoire of the observed A.m. With respect to the economics of extending the foraging range, it should be noted that a crucial step in the above sequence is the transport of the honey concentrated at the satellite to the primary nest. Since honey is more concentrated than nectar by a factor of about 10, a single round-trip by a ferrying bee is equivalent to about 10 field trips by foraging bees for the same trip distance. The economic limit for fetching honey is thus much further than the economic foraging limit. Thus, the satellite nest could be constructed beyond the economic boundary of the primary nest. See figure 14. Because the transport of honey is so much more efficient than the transport of nectar, and because bees are observed, all other things being equal, to prefer robbing freely available honey to foraging for nectar, we do not consider the energetics of transport of the honey from the satellite to the primary nest to be a critical factor.

The above speculation raises the question as to why A.m.* behavior, and hence the extended phenotype of a primary-satellite nest organization, is not observed in bees. There may be a number of different approaches to an answer to this question, including empirical and simulation studies of the energy flows and their associated costs. In this chapter we emphasize *information* flows, the costs of processing and communicating information, and the costs of *defense*.

Our theory contributes to economics and sociobiology in two ways: First, it extends existing knowledge of the evolution of cooperation among social insects to include a transaction costs approach to the study of insect organizations. Second, it extends the work of Dawkins (1982), and Axelrod and Hamilton (1984), on the evolution of cooperation in biological systems by explicitly incorporating the economics of information. This approach leads to some speculations that enable us to account for the phenomenon of swarming by bees as an efficient solution alternative to the construction of satellite nests. Our approach also yields deeper insights into the role of laws and institutions in achieving cooperation in human societies.

In the next section, we describe the socioeconomic organization of bee colonies. The third section provides an explanation, using a transaction costs approach, as to why bees do not construct satellite nests. The fourth section discusses cooperation in biological and human societies and the importance of laws and institutions for identifying individuals and hence for extending the range of human cooperation. The fifth section provides a conclusion and also suggests a topic for empirical research.

The Socioeconomic Organization of Bee Colonies

Wilson (1978, 26) has described a colony of social insects as

> operating somewhat like a factory inside a fortress. Entrenched in the nest site, harassed by enemies and uncertain changes in the physical environment, the colony must send foragers out to gather food while converting the secured food inside the nest into virgin queens and males as rapidly and as efficiently as possible.

A bee colony can be compared to a factory or firm whose output is more bees. Analogous to the specialization and division of labor, and the co-ordination of interdependent workers within a firm, there is, in a bee colony, caste specialization, division of labor and coordination of activities amongst the castes and workers.

The primary and most obvious division of activities is between the sexes. The functions of males (drones) is sexual reproduction and they constitute a tiny minority of the population of a colony. Essentially, a colony consists of one queen and a very large number of her infertile sisters and daughters. The ratio between sisters and daughters depends on the age of the colony's queen. Initially, it is mainly sisters—eventually all will be daughters. Pursuing the analogy of a bee colony to a firm, we can state that a bee colony is a "family firm."

The definition of caste in the literature on social insects varies somewhat (Michener 1974; Wilson 1971). For our purposes, it is sufficient to consider the two bee castes, queen and worker. These two castes are morphologically different, the differentiation occurring as a result of nutrition in the early larval stages. The behavioral repertoire of a queen is smaller than that of a worker. It includes the following: as a newly developed virgin, fighting with other virgin queens; mating in flight; egg-laying, which is the queen's major specialized function; and secreting "queen substance," a pheromone that maintains colony cohesion and identity. It is a mistake to assume that the queen is the "owner" or "manager" of the colony "firm." In this regard it is interesting to note that the queen has a smaller brain than a worker. While the queen specialized in egg-laying, all other functions are performed by the worker caste consisting of morphologically identical individuals.

There is significant division of labor in the worker caste, the three major categories being "nurse" bees, "house" bees, and "field" bees. Nurse bees clean nursery cells and feed the larvae with secretions from their hypopharyngeal glands. House bees maintain and build combs, receive and process food from the foragers, and stand on guard duty. The field bees are the foragers. Experienced foragers become scout bees when bees swarm to find a new home. Bees progress through these labor divisions as they age. Young bees perform nursery duties and the older bees forage, often working themselves to death in summer. These divisions are known to be very flexible. Field bees will revert to house duties, e.g., guarding, if conditions warrant. They will even redevelop their nurse-bee hypopharyngeal glands if necessary. The proportions of the various divisions of workers tend to be appropriate to the needs of the colony (Free 1977).

Communication and coordination of activities within the nest are largely through the chemical senses (smell and taste) and by movement (dance). A number of chemical transmitters or pheromones are known to be important. These include the "queen substance" mentioned before which, in addition to maintaining colony cohesion and identity, has an inhibitory effect on the development of workers' ovaries, an "alarm" pheromone released by a guard to rally others to defense, and a pheromone released by scout bees to mark a new nest site and to guide a swarm to it.

The "dance language" of bees has been extensively documented in a study by von Frisch (1967), for which he shared a Nobel Prize in 1973. Foraging scouts perform a complex dance to convey distance and direction to a food source in order to recruit other foragers. A similar communication system is used during swarming.

The activity of guarding is not directly productive but is essential. Bees must provide defense against "robbers" from other colonies who, especially in times of scarcity, attempt to steal the colony's honey store. The "fortress" aspect of the insect factory points to the crucial role of defense against robbers. Michener (1974) believes that the evolution of cooperation among bees

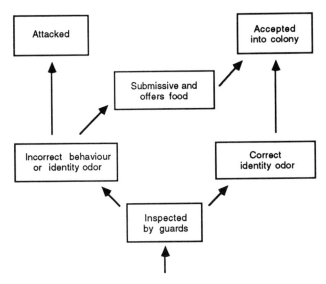

Fig. 15.   Fate of intruders to honeybee colonies. (Adapted from Free 1977.)

has been primarily motivated by the need for defense. So important is the function of defense that all workers are able to defend the nest against intruders in that they can switch to guard duties in response to an increase in the number of robbers.

In order to defend a colony, guard bees must distinguish or discriminate "insiders," their own nestmates, from "outsiders," potential robbers from other colonies. As noted before, all bees in the same colony are morphologically identical and are, in all probability, morphologically identical to bees from neighboring colonies. However, bees from a given colony will share an odor that is specific to that colony. Guard bees can identify insiders partly by the odor of the incoming bee and partly by its behavior. Potential robbers have a jerky, swaying "hesitant" flight approach. An incoming bee approaching as if it knows its way home will be quickly inspected, for no more than two or three seconds (Free 1977) and, if it smells correct, will be allowed to pass into the nest. An aggressive intruder that smells wrong will be repelled or stung to death. See figure 15.

If an intruder is submissive and offers food to the guards it will be escorted into the nest, where after a few hours it will have acquired the nest smell and hence will be recruited into the colony's population. In times of plentiful food supply and forage, intruders are more readily accepted than in times of scarcity, when robbing increases.

Finally, there is the mechanism of reproduction at the colony level. This is known as "swarming," and refers to the process by which a colony fissions into two approximately equal halves, one half leaving the nest with the old queen to establish a new colony nearby (typically a few kilometers away), the other half remaining in the nest with a new queen (Landa 1986, Lindauer 1961; Seeley 1982).

Why Honeybees Do Not Construct Satellite Nests: A Transaction Cost Approach

The transaction cost approach (Furubotn and Pejovich 1972; Williamson 1975 and 1985) emphasizes the importance of "laws and institutions" in economizing on transaction costs and hence promoting cooperation. Transaction costs include the costs of information (searching and identifying cooperating partners), of contract negotiation and enforcement, and the setup costs of engaging in trade (Dahlman 1979). Positive transaction costs account for the choice of modes of economic organization or "governance structure," the institutional matrix within which transactions are negotiated and executed. Markets, firms/hierarchies, and relational contracting are the main modes of economic organization (Williamson 1975 and 1985). Using the transaction cost approach, we shall explain why bees do not construct satellite nests.

Assume that the foraging swarm, loaded with honey, has found a suitable site for the construction of a satellite nest. The costs of establishing and maintaining the nest include: the setup costs of the satellite nest (which would be the same as the primary nest, but on a smaller scale), the costs of defense, and transportation costs from the satellite nest to the primary nest. Once the setup costs have been incurred, the main costs of maintaining the satellite nests are the information costs of identifying colony-mates from outsiders and defense costs.

As noted earlier, the identification of nestmates from outsiders is mainly be a chemical signature that is nest-specific. Although initially members of the primary and the satellite nests share the same odor, eventually each nest will develop its own odor. In theory, if there were a continuous and heavy two-way traffic of bees between the primary and satellite nests, one could argue that this would be sufficient to thoroughly homogenize the odor of the distributed colony. Thus, there would be no problem in identifying returning ferry bees at the satellite nest. The mechanism would be similar to that involved when foraging bees return empty-handed.

In practice, however, the traffic will not be continuous and heavy. There will be a light traffic at the onset of the ferrying-back phase. Also, as night approaches the traffic will decline. Some of the ferry bees will make the satellite-to-primary trip the last leg of the day. From an anthropomorphic point of view, we could consider this as a satellite bee "bivouacking" at the primary nest. However, from the bee's point of view, after staying overnight and acquiring the primary nest odor, it will tend to act as if it were a recruit. Thus, there will be a tendency for ferry bees, nominally resident at the satellite nest, to drift back to the primary nest. As the two nest odor-signatures drift apart, there will be an increasing tendency for returning ferry bees plus any new recruits from the primary nest to appear to the satellite nest guards as potential robbers and to be repelled or killed. The information costs of discriminating colony-mates from robbers will increase.

There is an interesting asymmetry between the treatment of ferry bees, loaded with honey, arriving at the primary nest and the treatment of the same ferry bees, with empty honey stomachs, returning to the satellite nest. Even though their odors are different, guard bees at the parent nest will treat them as "gift-bearing" intruders who will be allowed to enter and not be attacked. However, this is not true of ferry bees returning with empty stomachs to the satellite nest. To the guard bees at the satellite nest the ferry bees may appear as potential robbers.

As a further complication to the above scenario, assume that there is another independent bee colony nearby whose members engage in attempted robbery of honey from the primary and the satellite nests. The guard bees at both the primary and satellite nests will have to incur the costs of screening genuine robbers from apparent robbers. Interesting enough, there is also the possible scenario of a robbing impulse developing in the primary-plus-satellite colony itself. Bees intent on robbing will scout from the primary nest, and to them, the satellite nest will appear as just another independent colony, a good target for robbing. Of course, for bees from the primary nest to "rob" the satellite nest of its stores of honey does not constitute robbing as such, because "property rights" in the honey are vested with the members of the parent and satellite nests as a whole—the honey is communal property. Similarly, bees from the satellite nest, developing an impulse to rob, will also attempt to "rob" the primary nest of honey. In this case, however, the whole purpose of having ferry bees transport honey to the parent nest is defeated, since the "robbers" are "carrying coals to Newcastle" as it were. Given the above scenarios, the costs of defense will rise because more workers will have to switch from productive activities to the activity of defense. It might be necessary to recruit more workers from the primary nest to defend the satellite nest, which raises the interesting possibility of the satellite guards attacking the new recruits.

An efficient bee organization is one that economizes on the sum of setup costs, information costs, and defense costs. In the case of the primary-satellite nest arrangement, the costs of maintaining the arrangement may be so high as to outweigh the benefits. A straightforward, "ingenious" solution to economize on information and defense costs would be for the foraging swarms to carry a queen with them to the new site and begin its existence as an independent new colony. This is exactly what is observed in the behavior of bees in the phenomenon of colony reproduction by swarming.

This new independent colony would still incur the setup costs of establishing a colony, but the costs of identifying ferry bees commuting between the primary and satellite nests would be eliminated. Defense costs would also be greatly reduced. The establishment of an independent new colony as opposed to a satellite nest also, of course, eliminates the cost of transporting the honey from the satellite to the primary. However, this is not a particularly significant factor. As noted earlier, because honey is many times more concentrated than nectar, bees are energetically better employed at transporting honey than nectar if it in any small way gives the colony a competitive advantage. The transport of honey from a satellite essentially doubles the foraging area of a colony. We consider this to be a significant competitive advantage.

Setting up an independent new colony via swarming is an efficient arrangement because it enables bees to channel their time to productive activities of producing more bees rather than to the activities of detecting robbers and defense. The creation of a new colony may be viewed as the bees' solution to the costs of maintaining a satellite nest in a world where activities cannot be costlessly coordinated across nests. The phenomenon of fission and separation of the group by swarming is analogous to the vertical disintegration accompanying the growth of large firms which make it profitable for new tasks to be hived off to new firms (Stigler 1951).

Altruism and Cooperation in Biological and Human Societies: The Role of Identity

Sociobiologists have emphasized the importance of genetic kinship (Dawkins 1976) and reciprocity (Trivers 1971) as the basis for altruism and cooperation in biological systems.[2] Axelrod and Hamilton (1981) have made further contributions to this body of literature. They emphasized the importance of individuals to be able to recognize each other in order to be able to cooperate at all, an elementary but important factor which is overlooked in iterated PD models of the evolution of cooperation:

> The basic idea is that an individual must not be able to get away with defecting without the other individuals being able to retaliate effectively.

---

2. Economists like Becker (1976), Tullock (1978), and Hirshleifer (1978 and 1982) are interested in sociobiology for insights that may shed light on patterns of conflict and co-operation, and the evolution of altruism in human society.

The response requires that the defecting individual not be lost in a sea of anonymous others. Higher organisms avoid this problem by their well-developed ability to recognize many different individuals of their species, *but lower organisms must rely on mechanisms that drastically limit the number of different individuals or colonies with which they can interact effectively.* (Axelrod and Hamilton 1981, 1395, emphasis added)

Axelrod and Hamilton have pointed out that those organisms or species with no ability or limited ability to recognize the other cooperating partner have developed mechanisms to compensate for this by (1) maintaining continuous contact with the other member, (2) choosing a fixed place of meeting, and (3) establishing "stable territories" (which involves two quite different kinds of interaction: with those in neighboring territories where the probability of interaction is high, and with strangers where the probability of future interaction is low). For example, male territorial birds recognize each other via songs.

In contrast with biological systems, Axelrod and Hamilton point out that human beings are able to extend their range of cooperation because the ability to recognize one another is well developed. For example, a person can "name someone from facial features alone" (Axelrod and Hamilton 1981, 1395). In addition, human beings' ability to "monitor cues for the likelihood of continued interaction is helpful as an indication of when reciprocal co-operation is not stable" (Axelrod and Hamilton 1981, 1395). Illness or aging in the partner are such detectable cues. In short, for Axelrod and Hamilton (1981, 1392):

The discrimination of others may be among the most important of abilities because it allows one to handle interactions with many individuals without having to treat them all the same, thus making possible the rewarding of co-operation from one individual and the punishing of defection from another.

An important implication of the Axelrod-Hamilton theory is that if individuals cannot recognize each other, then they cannot cooperate even though they are closely related. Thus, the limits of cooperation are determined by the individual's capacity to identify its cooperating partner, and not necessarily by kinship-relatedness or reciprocity. Their theory throws light on the central question of this chapter—why bees do not establish satellite nests. As noted earlier, bees have very primitive means of identifying each other: primarily though chemical signatures which are the main cues of identity. Since chemical signatures tend to be specific to individual nests, bees cannot easily discriminate between their members spread across two or more nests.

Extending the work of Axelrod and Hamilton, as well as Dawkins, can yield deeper insights into the role of laws and institutions in human societies. Human beings have a well-developed ability to identify each other based on recognition of faces, as noted by Axelrod and Hamilton, but have developed institutions such as names (see chap. 6) and the ethnically homogenous trading group as a "club" which facilitates cooperation among insiders (see chap. 5). Furthermore, they have also evolved institutions, which facilitate cooperation between insiders and outsiders, such as money (Landa 1979), middlemen, gift-exchange,[3] and contract law.[4] Implicitly assumed in this area of research on laws and institutions is a well-developed and finely-tuned system for creating identities and performing identification, i.e., the ability to recognize, discriminate, and remember.[5] It needs to be explicitly stated, even if we take it for granted, that human beings have this ability extensively and that it is a *sine qua non* for socioeconomic cooperation on the scale of human societies. A study of biological societies (including hypothetical models such as the honeybee satellite-nest system of this chapter, in which this extensive identification ability cannot be assumed and in which only limited cooperation is observed) throws light on the identification function as being a crucial component of the substratum of human socioeconomic organization.

Conclusions and a Suggestion for Further Research

We have provided a theoretical explanation of why bees do not construct satellite nests for the purpose of extending their foraging range. The existing biological and sociobiological literature on the evolution of social behavior in bees has not addressed this problem. Using a transaction costs approach, we argued that the costs of identification of "insiders" (workers commuting between the primary and satellite nests) from "outsiders" (potential robbers from other colonies) are too high relative to the benefits of maintaining the satellite nests. Our theory throws light on the issue of limits to cooperation in insect

---

3. In primitive, stateless societies, gift-exchange is an institutional arrangement whereby exchange is made possible between otherwise hostile tribes. The classic gift-exchange system is the Kula Ring of the Trobriand Islands of Papua New Guinea. For the economics of the *Kula* exchange system, see chapter 7.

4. In modern societies with well-developed legal systems, contract law, which protects a plaintiff's "expectation interest" by assigning liability for damages to a breaching party, facilitates the impersonal process of exchange by encouraging insiders to trade with outsiders (see Landa 1976).

5. With respect to the relevance to humans of research on bees, we quote from a comment (*Scientific American* 252, no. 6 [June 1985]: 72) on a recent discovery by James L. Gould (1985) that bees have an ability, albeit limited, to store visual images: "The enhanced status of bees raises an interesting possibility: the investigating of their relatively simple memory mechanism may produce insights applicable to the study of learning in higher animals, including human beings."

societies by emphasizing economic aspects, and provides some additional arguments to the currently popular genetic-based kinship-relatedness theories of altruism and cooperation. The theory has implications for understanding the role of laws and institutions in promoting cooperation in human societies.

As a suggestion for further research, we envisage a continuum of spatial configurations ranging from two bee nests being adjacent and in contact (and thus essentially one large nest), through intermediate stages where they are linked by short air-bridges, to the full and distant separation discussed in this chapter. The intermediate configurations could be investigated experimentally to determine at what point colony-identity instability sets in.[6]

REFERENCES

Axelrod, R., and W. D. Hamilton. 1981. "The Evolution of Cooperation." *Science* 211:1390–96.
Becker, G. S. 1976. "Altruism, Egoism, and Genetic Fitness: Economics and Sociobiology." *Journal of Economic Literature* 14:817–28.
Dahlman, C. J. 1979. "The Problem of Externality." *Journal of Law and Economics* 22 (1): 141–62.
Dawkins, R. 1976. *The Selfish Gene.* Oxford: Oxford University Press.
———. 1982. *The Extended Phenotype: The Gene as a Unit of Selection.* New York: Oxford University Press.
Free, J. B. 1977. *The Social Organization of Honeybees.* London: Edward Arnold.
Furubotn, E. G., and S. Pejovich. 1972. "Property Rights and Economic Theory: A Survey of Recent Literature." *Journal of Economic Literature* 10:1137–62.
Gould, J. L. 1985. "How Bees Remember Flower Shapes." *Science* 227, no. 4693 (March): 1492–94.
Hamilton, W. D. 1964. "The Genetic Evolution of Social Behavior." Parts 1 and 2. *Journal of Theoretical Biology* 7 (1): 1–16, 17–32.
Heinrich, B. 1979. *Bumblebee Economics.* Cambridge: Harvard University Press.
Hirshleifer, J. 1978. "Natural Economy versus Political Economy." *Journal of Social and Biological Structures* 1:319–37.
———. 1982. "Evolutionary Models in Economics and Law: Cooperation versus Conflict Strategies." *Research in Law and Economics* 4:1–60.
The Hive and the Honeybee. 1975. Hamilton: Dadant and Sons.
Landa, J. T. 1976. "An Exchange Economy with Legally-Binding Contract: A Public Choice Approach." *Journal of Economic Issues* 10:905–22.
———. 1979. "Money and Alternative Institutional Arrangements for Achieving Ordered Anarchy." *Munich Social Science Review* 2:5–27.
———. 1986. "The Political Economy of Swarming in Honeybees: Voting-with-the-

6. Experiments of this type could be performed by hobbyist beekeepers as well as by professional ethologists. One of the authors (A. W.) is a beekeeper.

Wings, Decision-Making Costs, and the Unanimity Rule." *Public Choice* 51:25–38.

Lindauer, M. 1961. *Communication among Social Bees.* Cambridge: Harvard University Press.

Michener, C. D. 1974. *The Social Behavior of the Bees.* Cambridge: Harvard University Press.

Seeley, T. D. 1982. "How Honeybees Find a Home." *Scientific American* 247:158–68.

Stigler, G. J. 1951. "The Division of Labour is Limited by the Extent of the Market." *Journal of Political Economy* 59:185–93.

Trivers, R. L. 1971. "The Evolution of Reciprocal Altruism." *Quarterly Review of Biology* 46 (4): 35–57.

Tullock, G. 1978. "Altruism, Malice and Public Goods." *Journal of Social and Biological Structure* 1:3–10.

von Frisch, K. 1967. *The Dance Language and Orientation of Bees.* London: Oxford University Press.

Williamson, O. E. 1975. *Markets and Hierarchies: Analysis and Antitrust Implications.* New York: The Free Press.

———. 1985. *The Economic Institutions of Capitalism: Firms, Markets, Relational Contracting.* New York: The Free Press.

Wilson, E. O. 1971. *The Insect Societies.* Cambridge: Harvard University Press.

———. 1978. "The Ergonomics of Caste in the Social Insects." *American Economic Review* 68 (2): 25–35.

Part 6
Exchange Institutions: Their Emergence, Evolution, and Functions

Toward a Theory of the Emergence, Evolution, and Functions of Exchange Institutions in Achieving Ordered Anarchy

Chapters 2 through 7 have developed separate theories of the emergence and functions of contract law, ethnic trading networks, and gift-exchange in facilitating exchange. In this chapter, a general theory of the emergence, evolution, and functions of exchange institutions will be developed within a unifying NIE framework. We shall examine a whole spectrum of nonprice institutions, including money, which facilitate the coordination of plans and expectations of many traders in the economy. We shall show that in an economy without a law of contracts, traders will have the incentive to create institutions of private ordering for enforcing contracts. This chapter arrives at some rather unorthodox views about barter and the role of money in an exchange economy.

The next section will show that it is the institution of middleman, not money, that must be considered to be the "medium of exchange" in a barter economy. The third section will show that money emerges in a middleman economy because monetary exchange economizes on the middleman's transaction costs. The fourth section will examine the conceptual evolution of the abstract "Ostroy middleman" into the historical profit-seeking merchant. The fifth section will examine the dual functions of money in the merchant's M-C-M' trading circuit: money as medium of exchange and money as capital. The sixth section will examine the EHMG as a clublike arrangement for the mobilization of money-capital and the collective trust that helps achieve a stable and efficient Chinese middleman credit economy. The seventh section will show that the institutions of money, middleman, gift-exchange—even barter—take on new functions under conditions of contract uncertainty: they are exchange institutions that achieve trust or sublimate the need for trust and hence facilitate transactions across ethnic boundaries. The eighth section, the concluding section, will discuss how the theory developed in this chapter establishes links with monetary theory and marketing theory.

Material in this chapter was originally published in the *Munich Social Science Review* 2 (1979): 5–27. I gratefully acknowledge permission by the journal's publisher, Dr. Manfred Holler, to reprint the article. I have made some revisions from the original published version.

TABLE 2.   A Barter Economy with Three Traders

Trader	Initial Endowment	Preferred Endowment
v_1	x_1	x_2
v_2	x_2	x_3
v_3	x_3	x_1

The Role of Middleman as "Medium of Exchange" in a Barter Economy

Existing qualitative theories of money (see, for example, Niehans 1969; Brunner and Meltzer 1971; and Ostroy 1973) have emphasized the role of money in the exchange process as a medium of exchange. These theories have assumed that the inconveniences of barter—the lack of double coincidence of wants—cannot be overcome without the intermediate use of money. But this is incorrect. Consider a simple barter economy with three individuals, v_1, v_2, and v_3, with a set of initial endowments who wish to end with a preferred and different set of endowments via exchange. See table 2. If trading is restricted to simultaneous pairwise barter exchange between traders, then no trade can occur because of the lack of double coincidence of wants between any pair of traders and because $n = 3$. If, however, a trading arrangement is instituted that permits *a sequence of barter exchanges via a middleman*, then full execution of all trades is possible. All that is required is for one of the traders, e.g., v_2, to emerge in the role of middleman by engaging in a sequence of two barter exchanges: v_1Ev_2 (read: v_1 exchange with v_2) at t and v_2Ev_3 at $t + 1$, using good x_1 as a medium of exchange (see fig. 16). As soon as v_2 emerges in the role of middleman connecting the other traders together, the problem of the lack of double coincidence of wants disappears for the other traders: for v_1

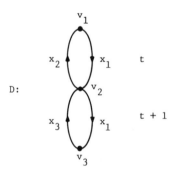

Fig. 16.   A sequence of two barter exchanges with v_2 as the middleman

TABLE 3. Four Traders Located in Two Spatially Separated Markets

Market	Trader	Initial Endowment	Preferred Endowment
I	v_1	x_1	x_4
	v_2	x_2	x_1
	v_3	x_3	x_2
II	v_4	x_4	x_3

and v_3 only one barter exchange via a middleman is necessary to effect ultimate exchange. This is because the middleman's function is precisely that of "*N*-entrepreneurship" (Leibenstein 1968): searching out the right pairs of trading partners and coordinating their activities (by linking them together in just the right sequences) so as to clear markets.

To dramatize the efficiency of indirect middleman exchange in a barter economy, consider a slightly more complicated trading situation depicted in table 3, with four traders located in two spatially separated markets. In this situation, middleman v_2 must now conduct a longer and more complex sequence of three bilateral barter exchanges: v_2Ev_3 at t, v_2Ev_4 at $t + 1$, and v_2Ev_1 at $t + 2$ (see fig. 17). For the other traders in the barter economy, only one indirect middleman exchange is necessary to effect ultimate exchange. Clearly, then, it is the *institution of middleman, not money, that eliminates the necessity for double coincidence of wants in a barter economy.* By shortening producers' and consumers' transaction chain to only one indirect barter exchange via a middleman, the middleman economizes on search costs of all the other traders.

Marketing theorists, of course, have always emphasized the central role of middleman in economizing on the number of transactions to effect ultimate exchange. Wroe Alderson (1967), for example, shows that with five households, each producing a different article, it would need ten direct exchanges among them to effect ultimate exchanges, but only five exchanges if the

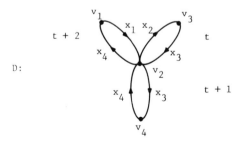

Fig. 17. A sequence of three bilateral transactions with v_2 as the middleman

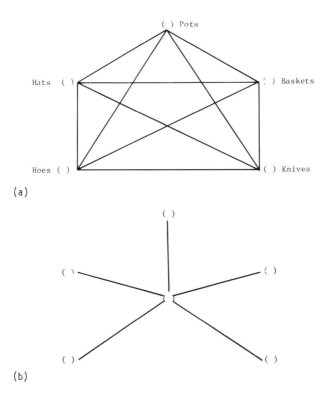

Fig. 18.   The efficiency of middleman exchange. *a*) Direct exchange. *b*) Indirect exchange via a middleman.

exchanges are conducted through a middleman. (See fig. 18.) In general, the number of transactions necessary to carry out direct exchanges is $\dfrac{n(n-1)}{2}$ where n is the number of producers and each makes only one article; the number of transactions necessary to carry out indirect exchanges via a middleman is n. Thus, the "ratio of advantage" of using middleman exchange is $\dfrac{(n-1)}{2}$ (Alderson 1954, 37). From the viewpoint of spatially separated producers and consumers, the middleman is the historical institutional equivalent of the Walrasian auctioneer through which they can improve the efficiency of their transactions via the reduction of search costs. The middleman thus contributes to the trading process by expanding and creating new markets that might remain limited in size or "missing." This neglect of the role of the middleman in a decentralized exchange economy accounts for some of the anomalies in current theories of exchange that consider money as the unique medium of exchange. Beyond a barter economy, both money and middleman must be seen as members of a more extensive family of "media of exchange" which facilitates the exchange process.

The Conceptual Emergence of Money
in a Middleman Economy

So long as the institution of money exists to clear markets, it does not matter to other traders whether money exists or not. But to the middleman, "money matters" because without money the middleman is forced to go through longer and more complicated sequences of exchanges as the number of goods and traders increase. In a three-trader, three-good economy, as noted, the middleman must go through a sequence of *two* bilateral transactions; in a four-trader, four-good economy, the middleman must go through a sequence of *three* transactions. The extra sequence of bilateral transaction arises from the lack of double coincidence of wants associated with barter exchange. More precisely, v_2 cannot clear markets in market I even by engaging in a sequence of barter exchanges because no trader in market I has the good that v_1 wants (i.e., good x_4). Suppose v_2 locates v_4 in market II, with the good that v_1 wants and assuming that v_4 also wants v_2's good, then v_2 needs to engage in a sequence of two bilateral barter exchanges: $v_2 E v_4$ at t and then $v_2 E v_1$ at $t + 1$ in order to effect his ultimate exchange. Assuming the more realistic situation of lack of double coincidence of wants between v_2 and v_4, then v_2 will have to find the right trading partner for v_4, i.e., v_3 located in market I. Under barter exchange, v_2 has to include *all* other traders in order to affect his ultimate exchange. Barter requires centralized coordination of the activities of traders via the middleman. See figure 19a. The existence of money, however, makes it possible to *shorten* the middleman's transaction chain by making some sequence of transactions redundant. In the four-trader, four-good economy, the existence of money (M) makes the exchange, $v_2 v_3$ redundant; v_3 becomes an "isolate" (Harary, Norman, and Cartwright 1965, 17) in the disconnected digraph. See figure 19b. In general, once the middleman has found a consumer who wants the goods (C) of the producer, the middleman can collapse n − 1 sequences of barter transactions into only two monetary transactions: M-C, a purchase with money, and C-M', a sale for a larger sum of money, (M'), in order to realize his profits. The role of money, as medium of exchange in the merchant's trading circuit is to economize on transactions costs by shortening the *middleman's* transaction chain.[1] Money turns out to be a public

---

1. ** Put in another way, traders need trading posts to organize trade before any efficient trade is possible, with or without money. With more complicated cases involving a large number of goods, it seems that both money and middlemen would be needed. Clower [1969] 1971 had emphasized this point.

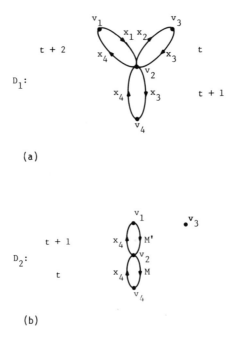

(a)

(b)

Fig. 19. The efficiency of monetary exchange in a middleman economy.
a) **Inefficient centralized coordination in a barter economy, with v_2 as a coordinator.** *b)* **Efficiency of monetary exchange allows decentralization of the exchange process by making v_2Ev_3 redundant: v_3 becomes an isolate.**

good for middlemen because it allows each middleman to decompose or decentralize the exchange process into networks of two person "orthogonal coalition games" (Shubik 1971) without the need to include everybody in the transaction chain.

Because current theories of money do not explicitly incorporate the class of profit-seeking middleman,[2] this explains one of the leading unresolved issues in current monetary theory. As Jack Hirshleifer (1973, 145–46) puts it, "But we do not yet have a model explaining why and how it pays particular economic agents to invent the institution in the first place. . . . "

Once the middleman is incorporated into a theory of money, however, money as an institution may be predicted to emerge in a middleman economy precisely because of the efficiency of monetary exchange which facilitates middleman-entrepreneurship.

---

2. With the exception of Niehans 1969.

The Conceptual Evolution of the "Ostroy Middleman"
into the Historical Merchant

Imagine the emergence of the middleman in the barter economy. The middleman participates in trade on a sporadic basis, because he has "unorthodox" ultimate wants that he must satisfy; call such a *middleman qua consumer* the abstract middleman or the "Ostroy middleman."[3] Consequently, the Ostroy middleman is prepared to go through a sequence of bilateral barter transactions, even to clear markets, in order to effect his ultimate exchange. When the size of the trading group is small, for example, in the situation depicted in table 2, the Ostroy middleman can be viable so long as the benefits of effecting an ultimate exchange outweigh the costs of performing the market-clearing function.

But precisely because exchange is a costly process, the middleman must incur unavoidable out-of-pocket transaction costs such as transportation, search, and contract-negotiation costs. Transaction costs outweigh the benefits of effecting an ultimate exchange when the size of the trading group is large. The Ostroy middleman who performs the market-clearing function free of charge is as abstract and fictitious as the Walrasian auctioneer. Through the implicit assumption that the Ostroy middleman does not charge for performing this market-clearing function, current theories of exchange eliminate any role for the *historical* profit-seeking merchant.

To explain the emergence of the historical middleman or merchant, one must assume that the Ostroy middleman is forced to exit from markets because of high transaction costs, or he must transform himself into the historical merchant if he is to remain viable. The process of transformation into the profit-seeking middleman is hastened by another consideration. The provision of a market-clearing function is, in a fundamental sense, the provision of a public good. The market-clearing function may be considered to be a public good because no trader who wishes to participate in trade can be excluded if all markets are to be cleared.[4] But why should a class of self-interested middleman operating in a private property economy, provide a public good to other traders who benefit from them without charging for their services? Why should other traders "free-ride" on the benefits of the provision of a public good while the middlemen collectively bear the full costs? In a private property economy, the market-clearing function will be provided by a class of middlemen only if they charge for their services, i.e., become *profit-*

---

3. The "Ostroy middleman" is the middleman in Ostroy's theory of money. See Ostroy 1973. See also Ostroy and Starr 1974.

4. Note that the definition of a pure public good used here is in terms of the nonexclusion property rather than the jointness property of a pure public good.

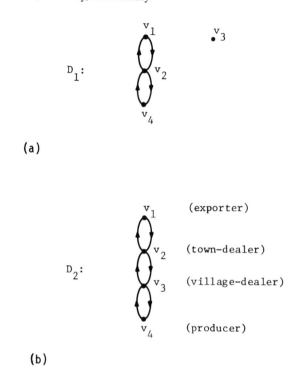

(a)

(b)

Fig. 20. Pareto-superior move occurring with specialization among middlemen. *a*) **Exclusion of free-rider,** v_3**, from** v_2**'s transaction chain.** *b*) **Pareto-superior move with specialization among middlemen.**

seeking middlemen. It is in the process of performing abstract middleman-entrepreneurship that the middleman discovers the costliness of his endeavors. But at the same time, the middleman perceives new opportunities for making a profit from his market-clearing function. Transaction costs involved in the provision of a public good, together with the perception of new opportunities for making recurrent profits from intermarket arbitrage can provide the explanation for the evolution of the abstract middleman into the professional profit-seeking middlemen. Conceptually, one may imagine the process of transformation of the abstract middleman into the historical merchant to be accompanied by the invention of money by the merchant class.[5]

---

5. ** My argument helps solve Hirshleifer's problem about how money might evolve. It seems unlikely that money would readily evolve among isolated individuals. Rather, thinking of money as solving the transaction problem of specialized traders seems much more likely to answer Hirshleifer's question.

Once a profit-seeking middleman emerges, he can *exclude* those who do not pay for his services; for example, in figure 20a trader v_3 is excluded from v_2's transaction chain. The middleman can also further reduce transaction costs of linking ultimate consumers together via specialization of roles so that a marketing network of different levels of middlemen emerges. For example, in the marketing of smallholders' rubber in Singapore and West Malaysia, producers are linked to ultimate consumers via a network of village dealers, town dealers, and packer-exporters. The simplest marketing network for smallholders' rubber may be represented in figure 20b.

Dual Functions of Money in the Merchant's *M-C-M'*
Trading Circuit: Medium of Exchange
and Money Capital

The recurrent process of profit-making through intermarket arbitrage is the key distinguishing characteristic of the entrepreneur as depicted in Kirzner's theory of competition. The formula for middleman arbitrage can however be conveniently represented by Marx's formula of the M-C-M' trading circuit.[6] The middleman begins the process of exchange by using a sum of money, e.g., \$100 to buy goods (C) and resells the same goods for a larger sum of money, M' (\$110), $M' - M$ being the middleman's profit margin. It is in the process of *circulation* in the M-C-M' trading circuit that money has, in addition to its medium-of-exchange function, acquired an additional function: money-as-capital. Current qualitative theories of money, however, have ignored the role of money functioning as capital and have restricted money's role in the exchange process, to its medium-of-exchange function, as well as its function as numeraire. This anomaly can again be explained by the fact that current theories have abstracted from the class of profit-seeking middleman. The trading process appropriate for such direct exchange economies may be represented by Marx's formula of a C-M-C' trading circuit (Marx 1967, chap. 3).

The role of money in such a circuit is simply to facilitate exchange by overcoming the inconvenience of barter exchange. If traders possess money (M), all they need to do when they find their right trading partners is to engage in only *one monetary* transaction, M-C'. If traders start off with no money but with initial endowments (C) then the existence of money allows any trader to

---

6. Economists may find Marx's theory of exchange useful. As Roberts and Stephenson (1973, ix) put it, " . . . Marx was an organizational theorist who saw different economic systems as different forms of social organization. The reader may be startled to discover that economists such as Frank Knight, James M. Buchanan, and Kenneth Boulding, who see economics as the study of how people organize themselves by means of exchange have more in common with Marx than many of those who consider themselves Marxists. Professed Marxists who employ a vocabulary of humanism may be disappointed to find that they are not Marxists at all."

engage in at most only *two* monetary transactions, C-M (sale) and M-C' (purchase) of the final good, C'. Thus, money's function in the C-M-C' trading circuit is restricted only to its medium-of-exchange function.

But what exactly is "money" in its role as medium of exchange? Clower (1967) provides one definition: money is a good that enters into every transaction. Hirshleifer (1973, 144) provides another definition: "Like a catalyst, money facilitates a flow process (exchange) while remaining itself exactly the same at the end of the trading cycle as it was in the beginning."

If a combined Clower-Hirshleifer definition of money in its role as medium of exchange is used, then money in the M-C-M' trading circuit does not function merely as medium of exchange because money at the end of the trading cycle has become *quantitatively* larger in magnitude, M'. As Marx (1967 vol. 1, chap. 3, 150) puts it:

> One sum of money is distinguishable from another only by its amount. This character and tendency of the process M-C-M' is therefore not due to any qualitative difference between its extremes, both being money, but solely to their quantitative difference.

It is in the process of circulation of money in the M-C-M' trading circuit that money has become a quantitatively larger amount thereby transmuting money into a *qualitatively* different thing: "Merchant Capital," (Marx 1967, chap. 4, vol. 1). Once a M-C-M' trading circuit, in the exchange associated with a class of profit-seeking middlemen in the exchange economy exists, it is not possible to restrict the function of money only to its medium of exchange function. Money in a middleman economy is a good that: (a) enters into every transaction; and (b) grows quantitatively larger at the end of the middleman's trading circuit.

The Emergence of the Ethnically Homogeneous Middleman Group: A Clublike Arrangement for Mobilization of Money-Capital and Collective Trust

Profound consequences flow from middleman-entrepreneurship in a money economy. The recurrent process of profitmaking and capital accumulation provides the dynamic element for middlemen to invent Pareto-superior institutional arrangements. In a dual economy, like West Malaysia, characterized by capital scarcity, the requirement that all transactions be conducted on a cash basis acts as a constraint that prevents an individual possessing no money-capital from emerging as a middleman. Money is an essential input in the middleman's transaction technology where the cash constraint is binding.

The inefficiency resulting from the constraint of prior possession in money can be overcome if middlemen resort to trade credit. If v_1, the exporter, for example, extends trade credit in the form of a cash advance to v_2, then v_2 can emerge as a middleman buying commodities from v_3 in order to resell to v_1. The use of trade credit among the Chinese middlemen in West Malaysia and Singapore economizes on the use of a scarce resource, money capital, and is Pareto superior, provided that Chinese middlemen can provide themselves with an institution that can generate networks of collective trust among themselves with sanctions against those who breach that collective trust (by defaulting). The *Confucian code of ethics,* embedded in the EHMG, is precisely such an institution which provides the mechanisms and the sanctions for reducing the risks of loan-contract uncertainty. The creditor-debtor relationship is one of mutual dependence; hence the functional role of mutual aid ethics. From the trade-creditor's point of view, he is extending "aid" by supplying v_2 with cash loans on a continuous basis, loans that the debtor himself cannot obtain from banks. From the debtor's point of view, he is extending "aid" to the creditor because, by repaying debt with goods (rubber), the debtor is assuring the creditor of reliability of supply. By combining the middleman function with the money-lending function, the trade-creditor provides himself with a greater margin of security, hence, *insurance,* against supply-breach of contract. The creditor has a high degree of trust in his debtor in honoring commitments to deliver goods as repayment for the loans. If the debtor violates the trust, the debtor faces the threat of: (a) withdrawal of credit; (b) exclusion from trade by the creditor or possibly by other members of the trading group as word spreads of the debtor's antisocial behavior; and (c) expulsion from the group as punishment to the debtor for violating the collective trust of the Chinese middleman group. These economic sanctions against deliberate breach of the loan-contract make the costs of "exit" (Hirschmann 1970) from an existing exchange relationship very high and provide further mechanisms for constraining traders' contractual behavior. The Confucian ethics embodied in the group and the economic sanctions used against those who breach that collective trust make it possible to develop long chains of credit networks within the Chinese middleman economy, creating an efficient Chinese credit economy.

Across the Chinese ethnic boundary where there is a discontinuity in the Confucian ethics, Chinese middlemen resort to cash transactions to reduce risks of breach of contract to zero under conditions of high contract uncertainty. The limits of Confucian ethics are manifested in the creation of a "dual money economy"—the coexistence of a Chinese credit economy side by side with an indigenous cash economy—within the political boundaries of a plural society (see fig. 21).

D:

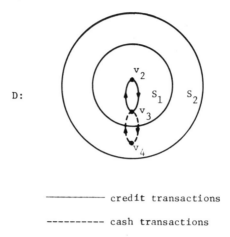

——————— credit transactions

---------- cash transactions

Fig. 21.   The existence of a "dual money economy," reflecting the limits of the Confucian ethics embedded in the EHMG (S_1), and the use of money for impersonal transactions with "outsiders" (S_2)

Money, Middleman, Barter, Gift-Exchange, and Contract Law: Institutional Arrangements Facilitating Transactions with Strangers

The existence of a dual money economy in a plural society brings into sharp focus another function of money, not emphasized in current theories of money: money is an institution that replaces the need for trust in intertribal transactions. Consider an ethnically heterogeneous trading situation depicted in table 4. Given a situation of contract uncertainty, v_3 prefers to trade with v_2 who pays for good C with money. The existence of money makes possible simultaneous quid pro quo exchange of C for money and hence neutralizes a potential conflict-creating situation arising from the risk of default among trading partners. In this setting, the use of money has allowed v_2 and v_3 to achieve pairwise optimality, but the economy is not Pareto optimal because v_1 is blocked from trade by the coalition of traders, v_2, v_3. See figure 22a.

A Pareto-superior move may occur if v_2 is willing to take on the middle-

TABLE 4.   An Ethnically Heterogeneous Trading Situation

Trader	Initial Endowment	Preferred Endowment
v_1 (European, S_1)	"Promise to pay M"	C (rubber)
v_2 (Chinese, S_2)	Money/reputation	Money
v_3 (indigenous, S_3)	C (rubber)	Money

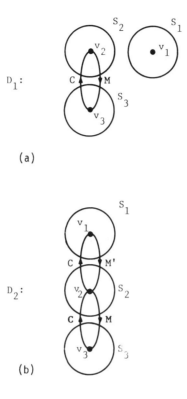

(a)

(b)

Fig. 22.   Money and middleman as Pareto-superior institutions in intertribal transactions. *a*) Money allows Pareto-superior move for v_2 and v_3. *b*) Middleman (v_2) allows for Pareto-superior move.

man risk-bearing function of reselling v_3's goods to v_1 in return for the latter's "promise to pay M" and if v_1 in turn, chooses to trade with v_2 because of v_2's reputation of reliability in honoring "promises to deliver goods." The institution of money *and* middlemen then allows all potential gains from trade to be exploited. See figure 22b. While money allows certain market games to be played as OCGs, not all potentially conflicting contractual situations can be mediated by money alone. Where time-binding contracts are involved between different traders belonging to different ethnic groups, the role of middleman becomes crucial: the middleman plays the role of a "buffer," "mediator," "contract-enforcer," a "cultural broker" who mediates between traders belonging to different tribes, who do not trust each other but mutually trust the middleman because the latter has money/reputation. Seen in this light, the middleman is an institutional arrangement that emerges in response to eth-

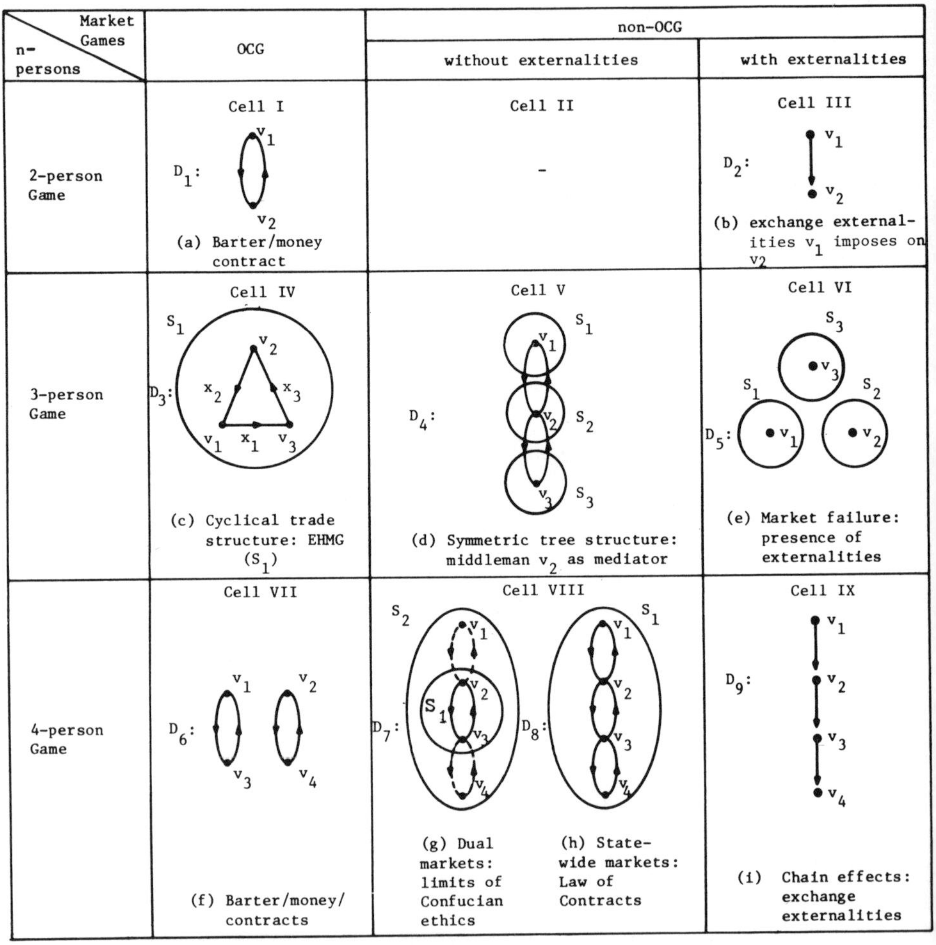

Market Games / n-persons	OCG	non-OCG	
		without externalities	with externalities
2-person Game	Cell I D_1: (a) Barter/money contract	Cell II —	Cell III D_2: (b) exchange externalities v_1 imposes on v_2
3-person Game	Cell IV D_3: (c) Cyclical trade structure: EHMG (S_1)	Cell V D_4: (d) Symmetric tree structure: middleman v_2 as mediator	Cell VI D_5: (e) Market failure: presence of externalities
4-person Game	Cell VII D_6: (f) Barter/money/ contracts	Cell VIII D_7: D_8: (g) Dual markets: limits of Confucian ethics (h) State-wide markets: Law of Contracts	Cell IX D_9: (i) Chain effects: exchange externalities

Fig. 23. The role of "laws and institutions" in creating Pareto-optimal OCG/non-OCG without externalities

nically heterogeneous traders' private choices of an *outsider* or *third party* for the protection of contracts.[7] The "outsider-middleman," in such a setting, is a public good because his existence allows a market game among different ethnic groups to be played as a Pareto-optimal non-OCG without externalities. The institutional setting is that depicted in cell V of figure 23.

But the institutions of money and middlemen do not exhaust traders'

---

7. So that the legal state is not the unique contract-protector.

ingenuity for inventing different institutional forms for the protection of property rights. Consider barter and gift-exchange to belong to this larger family of "laws and institutions" for protection of property/contractual rights.

To dramatize the argument that barter is an institutional arrangement that is a substitute for trust in interethnic transactions, consider the situation depicted in figure 23. In a situation characterized by complete trust among three trading partners, as for example in an ethnically homogeneous trading group (S_1), traders can affect ultimate exchanges by a *cyclical* pattern of trade in which v_1 agrees to transfer title to goods to v_3 at t, v_3 agrees to transfer good x_3 to v_2 at $t + 1$, and v_2 agrees to transfer good x_2 to v_1 at $t + 2$. See cell IV in figure 23. In such a setting, all contracts will be honored as the economy passes through a sequential series of "temporary" equilibrium; no bilateral barter exchanges are necessary to effect ultimate exchanges. However, in a world without perfect trust, for example, between different ethnic groups, this kind of cyclical pattern of trade cannot occur because v_1 has no assurance that after he has transferred goods to v_3 that v_2 will honor his contract to deliver goods to v_1 at $t + 2$; since v_2 and v_3 also have no assurance that the trading partners are going to honor contracts, no trade will occur. The situation is that depicted in cell VI of figure 23. Where potential gains from trade cannot be exploited because of the lack of trust, a Pareto-superior move can be made if exchanges are conducted as a sequence of bilateral barter exchanges via a middleman, v_2. The institutional setting shifts from that depicted in cell VI to cell V. See figure 23. This is because barter exchanges via the middleman involves a quid pro quo exchange of goods against goods simultaneously so that no breaches of contract are possible. Barter exchanges, like monetary exchanges, allow a complex *n*-person exchange network to be decomposed into two-person OCGs; the institutional setting shifts from that depicted in cell V to that depicted in cell I. See figure 23. It is in this context that the barter models of Edgeworth and Walras are not a natural mode of transacting; rather, barter is seen to be an institutional arrangement that is chosen by traders themselves as a least cost method for the policing of property rights in intertribal transactions under conditions of contract uncertainty.

** Consider, next, the institution of gift-exchange, which is prevalent in primitive or acephalous societies. The classic example of a gift-exchange system is the Kula Ring of the Trobriand Islands of Papua New Guinea. A distinctive characteristic of the Kula system, as noted in chapter 7, is its double circuit of two different gift-exchange objects circulating in opposite directions perpetually around the ring of Kula partners. This exchange structure is like the cyclical structure depicted in cell IV in figure 23, but with the addition of a return flow of another gift-exchange object circulating in the opposite direction. This kind of double circuit requires a high degree of mutual trust for the exchange system to function. Such trust is achieved by the ring structure of the Kula system: the ring structure is a closed system in which information about a defaulting partner reaches everybody in the Kula Ring, making it possible for the traders to ostracize the offending party by excluding the offending party from future barter transactions. The Kula Ring turns out to be a clublike arrangement in which everyone is watching everyone else, gossiping about each other, and monitoring each other's behavior. The Kula Ring thus provides the functional equivalent of law and order that in well developed societies is provided by the state. The institution of Kula gift-exchange allows otherwise hostile tribes to engage in trade with strangers across tribal boundaries. Here, the institutional arrangements of barter, middleman, and the EHMG also contribute to intertribal exchange. Malinowski [1922] 1961, describing the transactions between tribes around the Kula Ring, describes how each Kula trader, when visiting a foreign market, conducts barter trades with the local natives via clansmen of the host Kula partner acting as middlemen. The institution of a middleman eliminates the need for trust between members of different tribes around the Kula Ring who do not trust each other but trust the local natives who act as middlemen. That is because local natives, being members of the same ethnic group as the host Kula partner, share the same codes of behavior embedded in an EHMG, which, as noted in chapter 5, has built-in constraints against breach of contract. In stateless, primitive societies, barter, middlemen, EHMG, and gift-exchange all help to achieve social order within markets and across ethnic boundaries, hence economizing on the costs of protecting property and contracts.

Under conditions of contract uncertainty, the identity of trading partners matters, as noted above. The Kula trading system is no exception. The Kula gift-exchange objects are themselves symbols of identity, allowing members of the Kula Ring Club to screen outsiders from those within the club—the possession of a Kula gift object signals his identity as a member of the club.**

One way of looking at the evolution of various exchange institutions is to focus on the incentive of profit-seeking middlemen to invent or create Pareto-superior institutions for achieving greater trust among trading partners so as to reduce transaction costs. Barter exchanges require no trust; but barter is an inefficient mode of exchange as noted. Monetary exchange is Pareto superior to barter; but the use of money requires a minimum degree of trust in the money-creating entity—be it the merchant group or the state—for regulating the supply of money so as to achieve predictability in the value.[8] Credit

---

8. ** Sociologist Georg Simmel ([1907] 1978, 179) explicitly made this point: that the value of money is based on "confidence on the socio-political organization and order," in other words based on the "trust" members of society have in its institutions. See Laidler and Rowe's (1980) review of Simmel's work on money.

transactions among trading partners may be efficient; but credit transactions, in the absence of a legal state, require the existence of a code of ethics embedded in the EHMG. The situation depicted is that in cell VIII (g) in figure 23. Finally, the creation of statewide credit economy as well as state-wide forward market in goods may be even more efficient; but this requires the existence of a statewide law of contracts to achieve "perfect trust" among strangers across ethnic boundaries. The situation shifts from that depicted in cell VIII(g) to that depicted in cell VIII(h). See figure 23. By creating perfect trust among traders, the effect of the law of contracts is to decompose a complex n-person non-OCG into two-person OCGs as noted. The situation shifts from cell VIII(h) to cell I, cell VII. Historically, as noted in chapter 4, the emergence of statewide contract law is via a process involving "double institutionalization of norms." Like contract law, gift-exchange in primitive stateless societies achieves "perfect trust" between strangers across tribal boundaries.

Conclusions

The analysis in this chapter reveals that there are various institutional devices, lying between anarchy and the state, for achieving "ordered anarchy" (Buchanan 1975, 6) for conducting transactions. Barter, money, middleman, and the EHMG must be identified as members of a more inclusive set of "laws and institutions" for the protection of property and contractual rights.

   Because current theories of money have abstracted from the role of the middleman and from the problem of contract uncertainty, it is not surprising that money's role is restricted to the medium of exchange function in facilitating exchange. Once contract uncertainty is introduced, however, the problem of the organization of the relations of mutual trust cannot be ignored; certain laws and institutions, not accounted for in the Walrasian theory of exchange, become possible. As Shubik (1973, 36–37) puts it:

> As the general equilibrium model of the economy is nonstrategic, it is natural for a modeler to implicitly ignore the problem of how strangers in a market economy can trade together efficiently and more or less impersonally with a minimal need for trust. When the economy is modelled as a noncooperative game, this problem must be faced.
>
> If individuals trust only cash and there is no banking system, then although it is highly likely that optimality in trade cannot be attained without credit, at least all trades that are made for immediate value are received by both parties. Hence, as all claims are discharged in the exchange, not only do the individuals not need to trust each other, they do not even need to consider the motivation or rationality of their trading partners.

When a banking system issues credit so that strangers can trade with virtual anonymity, the bank must either trust the individuals to whom it grants credit, or it must have rules which can be enforced that make it unprofitable for individuals to fail to pay their debts. This calls for bankruptcy laws. The economic system that has institutions which grant credit and has bankruptcy laws to police the borrowers can function efficiently only if the creditors are able to assume that the debtors are rationally motivated. If the debtors do not understand that failure to repay is unprofitable, they could destroy the credit system.[9]

While Shubik emphasizes the importance of the institutions of money and bankruptcy laws for policing behavior of traders, the emphasis in this chapter is on a more extended set of institutional arrangements for constraining traders' behavior. Furthermore, the development of a theory of how strangers in a market economy can convert a noncooperative game into a cooperative game necessitates the introduction of the middleman of marketing theory. By emphasizing the crucial interrelationship between markets, middlemen, and money, further insights are obtained in this chapter of the origins, evolution, and functions of some of the "laws and institutions" such as money, credit, code of ethics, and the law of contracts in a middleman economy.

REFERENCES

Alderson, W. 1967. "Factors Governing the Development of Marketing Channels." In *The Marketing Channel: A Conceptual Viewpoint*, edited by B. E. Mallen. New York: John Wiley and Sons.
Arrow, Kenneth. 1970. "Political and Economic Evaluation of Social Effects and Externalities." In *The Analysis of Public Output*, edited by Julius Margolis. New York: National Bureau of Economic Research.
Boulding, Kenneth. 1970. *Economics as a Science*. New York: McGraw-Hill.
Brunner, Karl, and Allan Meltzer. 1971. "The Uses of Money: Money in the Theory of an Exchange Economy." *American Economic Review* 61 (December): 784–805.
Buchanan, James M. 1975. *The Limits of Liberty: Between Anarchy and Leviathan*. Chicago: The University of Chicago Press.
Clower, R. 1967. "A Reconsideration of the Microfoundations of Monetary Theory." *Western Economic Journal* 6:1–9.
Clower, R., [1969] 1971 "Introduction." In *Monetary Theory: Selected Readings*,

9. ** In modern societies, credit bureaus also make it possible for bankers to trust debtors (see Klein 1993). See also Shubik 1975. For a discussion of the important role trust plays in the functioning of a market economy, see Arrow 1970; Boulding 1970, 12–13; and McKean 1975. See also Simmel ([1907] 1978).

edited by R. W. Clower. Middlesex, England: Penguin Books Ltd., Harmondsworth.

Harary, Frank, Robert Z. Norman, and Dorwin Cartwright. 1965. *Structural Models: An Introduction to the Theory of Directed Graphs*. New York: John Wiley and Sons.

Hirschman, Albert. 1970. *Exit, Voice, and Loyalty*. Cambridge: Harvard University Press.

Hirshleifer, J. 1973. "Exchange Theory: The Missing Chapter." *Western Economic Journal* 11 (June): 144–46.

** Klein, Daniel B. 1993. "Promise Keeping in the Great Society: A Model of Credit Information Sharing." *Economics & Politics* 4 (July): 117–36.

** Laidler, David, and Nicholas Rowe. 1980 "Georg Simmel's Philosophy of Money: A Review Article for Economists." *Journal of Economic Literature* 18 (March): 97–105.

Leibenstein, Harvey. 1968. "Entrepreneurship and Development." *American Economic Review* 58 (May): 72–83.

Malinowski, Bronislaw. [1922] 1961. *Argonauts of the Western Pacific*. E. P. Dutton and Co.

Marx, Karl. [1967] 1975. *Capital*. Vol. I. *The Process of Capitalist Production*, edited by Frederick Engels. New York: International Publishers.

McKean, Roland N. 1975. "Economics of Trust, Altruism, and Corporate Responsibility." In *Altruism, Morality, and Economic Theory*, edited by Edmund S. Phelps. New York: Russell Sage Foundation.

Niehans, J. 1969. "Money in a Static Theory of Optimal Payments Arrangements." *Journal of Money, Credit and Banking* 1 (November): 706–26.

Ostroy, J. 1973. "The Informational Efficiency of Monetary Exchange." *American Economic Review* 63:597–610.

Ostroy, J., and R. M. Starr. 1974. "Money and the Decentralization of Exchange." *Econometrica* 42 (November): 1093–1114.

Roberts, P. C., and M. A. Stephenson. 1973. *Marx's Theory of Exchange, Alienation and Crisis*. Stanford, Calif.: Hoover Institution Press.

Shubik, Martin. 1971. "Pecuniary Externalities: A Game Theoretic Analysis." *American Economic Review* 61 (September): 713–18.

———. 1973. "Commodity Money, Oligopoly, Credit and Bankruptcy in a General Equilibrium Model." *Western Economic Journal* 10 (March): 24–38.

———. 1975. "The General Equilibrium Model is Incomplete and Not Adequate for the Reconciliation of Micro and Macroeconomic Theory." *Kyklos* 28:545–73.

** Simmel, Georg. [1907] 1978. *The Philosophy of Money*. Translated by T. Bottomore and D. Frisby. London and Boston: Routledge and Kegan Paul.

Author Index

Subject Index

Action
  collective. *See* Collective action
  decoupling as an, 36
Altruism, ix, 182
  and cooperation among bees, 183–84
  and individual rationality, 19
  and kinship morality, 130
  reciprocal, 6, 17–18, 130n
  varying with kin relatedness, 18, 130n
  See also Bioeconomics (Economics of Biology); Sociobiology
Anarchy, 55n
  Hobbesian state of nature or, 10, 55, 62, 71
  ordered, 164, 205
  See also Breach of contract; Contract uncertainty; Opportunism
Ancestor worship, economic rationale of, 128, 128n
Anthropology, ix, 4–6, 37–38
  the problem of order in, 15–18
Arbitrage, 25, 52–53, 90, 153, 157, 157n, 161, 196–97
Asset
  information as, 53
  reputation as, 59
  See also Intangible asset
Asset specificity, 26
Austrian theory of institutions and entrepreneurship, 24–25

Bankruptcy laws, 206
Barriers to entry
  dietary laws as, 134
  ethnicity as, 108

language/dialect as, 111–12
  magical rites as, 167
  status rights as, 107
Barter, 17, 23
  decouples/decomposes complex exchange networks, 203
  inefficiency of exchange via, 190, 193
  substitutes for trust in intertribal trade, 153, 161, 161n, 203
  See also Exchange; Kula Ring gift-exchange; Middleman; Money
Bazaar, the, 102
Bees
  altruism and cooperation among, 183–84
  biological societies of, xii–xiii
  caste specialization among, 177–79
  colony of, 174–75, 177
  defense important for cooperation among, 178–79
  eusociality of, 173
  identity important for defense of, 178–82
  socioeconomic organization of, 177–80
  swarms and swarming of, 175, 180, 182
  why satellite nests not built by, 180–84
Bioeconomics (Economics of Biology), 6
  Hirshleifer's evolutionary concept of efficiency in, 20
  views altruism shaped by individual rationality, 19
Breach of contract, 27, 50
  as coerced exchange, 7, 57, 75
  and contract uncertainty, 55–56, 71
  "efficient," 77, 77n, 87, 89–90, 92, 94

Janet Tai Landa is Associate Professor of Economics, York University, Toronto, Canada.